Dharamsala Diaries

SWATI CHOPRA

D0062248

PENGUIN BOOKS

PENGUIN BOOKS
Published by the Penguin Group
Penguin Books India Pvt. Ltd, 11 Community Centre, Panchsheel Park, New Delhi 110 017, India
Penguin Group (USA) Inc., 375 Hudson Street, New York, New York 10014, USA
Penguin Group (Canada), 90 Eglinton Avenue East, Suite 700, Toronto, Ontario, M4P 2Y3, Canada (a division of Pearson Penguin Canada Inc.)
Penguin Books Ltd, 80 Strand, London WC2R 0RL, England
Penguin Ireland, 25 St Stephen's Green, Dublin 2, Ireland (a division of Penguin Books Ltd)
Penguin Group (Australia), 250 Camberwell Road, Camberwell, Victoria 3124, Australia (a division of Pearson Australia Group Pty Ltd)
Penguin Group (NZ), 67 Apollo Drive, Rosedale, North Shore 0632, New Zealand (a division of Pearson New Zealand Ltd)
Penguin Group (South Africa) (Pty) Ltd, 24 Sturdee Avenue, Rosebank, Johannesburg 2196, South Africa

Penguin Books Ltd, Registered Offices: 80 Strand, London WC2R 0RL, England

First published by Penguin Books India 2007

Copyright © Swati Chopra 2007

All rights reserved

10 9 8 7 6 5 4 3 2 1

ISBN-13: 978-0-14310-306-6   ISBN-10: 0-14310-306-7

Typeset in Bembo by Mantra Virtual Services, New Delhi
Printed at Chaman Offset Printers, New Delhi

PENGUIN BOOKS
DHARAMSALA DIARIES

Swati Chopra is a writer who focuses on spirituality and religion in her work, with special emphasis on exploring ancient wisdom in a modern context. She is the author of a contemporary guide to Buddhism, *Buddhism: On the Path to Nirvana* (Brijbasi Art Press, 2005). She has worked as editor of a quarterly journal, *Life Positive Plus*, as contributing editor of *Life Positive* magazine and as spirituality correspondent of the *Times of India*.

Her writing has appeared in journals and newspapers in India and abroad, including *Resurgence*, *Tricycle: The Buddhist Review*, *Hindustan Times* and *Daily News and Analysis*. Her essay on the Dalai Lama's dialogue with modern science appeared in the anthology *Understanding the Dalai Lama* (edited by Rajiv Mehrotra, Penguin India, 2004).

Swati is currently working on her next book, which documents contemporary women's spirituality.

Her website is www. swatichopra.com

Praise for the Book

'An evocative, inspiring book that incisively captures the spirit and textures of Dharamsala with sensitivity and passion . . . if you haven't been to Dharamsala this is next best. If you are planning a visit, have been or are there, it will be your perfect guide. The book offers you insights that will deeply enrich your experience and understanding not just about Dharamsala but about Buddhism. A must-read.'—Rajiv Mehrotra, author and honorary secretary/trustee, the Foundation for Universal Responsibility of His Holiness the Dalai Lama

'*Dharamsala Diaries* is an accurate presentation of Dharamsala through personal experience and observation. It gives a flavour not only of the place, but also of the spiritual path. Most importantly, it is an engrossing read.'—Geshe Lhakdor, director, Library of Tibetan Works and Archives, Dharamsala

Contents

Acknowledgements

I owe the greatest debt of gratitude to His Holiness the Dalai Lama, to whose wisdom I often turn for guidance, and whose presence is as central to this book as it is to the place it is about—Dharamsala.

To all those who shared their stories with me, who opened their hearts and answered my questions, I extend my warmest gratitude. Though they are too many to be named here, I thank each one of them, especially little Tenzin.

A special thanks to Shakti Maira for his invaluable advice and encouragement at every stage. I warmly thank Geshe Lhakdor and Rajiv Mehrotra for reading the manuscript and providing helpful comments.

This book would not have happened without V.K. Karthika's instigation and Jaishree Ram Mohan's editing, for which I am very grateful.

I would also like to acknowledge Samchung, the artist whose painting appears on the cover. Born and educated in Tibet, he fled to Dharamsala in 2002. His courage and irrepressible spirit echo the core qualities of Dharamsala. I am honoured to have his work on the cover.

And for her nurture and unwavering support, my heartfelt thanks to my mother.

Introduction

I have known Dharamsala all my life. In the way one knows the taste of strange fruit eaten once years ago—vaguely, at the back of one's mouth, there yet not there. Dharamsala has existed in my consciousness for the longest time because of a grand-uncle who spent part of his life as a wandering yogi here. Dharamsala was for me a luminous presence that gathered around it layers of mystery and secrecy until I had to go to it, touch it, feel it, place it in the real world for myself.

My first visit to Dharamsala happened after years of thinking of it as a special place. To the yogi's mystique was added His Holiness the Dalai Lama's presence. I had become interested in spirituality and my writing was focusing on it, and I was deeply affected by the Dalai Lama's use of spiritual insights in social, political and economic situations. I became inspired to try and interpret ancient knowledge in modern contexts, to communicate an engagement of inner awareness with problems we face today as individuals and as societies.

I came to Dharamsala with a sense of personal pilgrimage. This must be how tirthas develop, with people's instinctive faith in the power of a place. I arrived with a bit of this blind idealization, eager to make holy what I had long carried as a dream in my heart.

That visit turned out to be quite the homecoming! I was

soon wandering the streets, picking up conversations with fellow travellers, rushing into a Buddhist philosophy class every morning, breathless from climbing steep inclines that my citygirl legs and lungs were unused to. It felt as if one had arrived in a temple laden with pooja things that the mad deity knocked away as insignificant—and proceeded to give one the run of the hallowed precincts.

The very air sparkled a diaphanous gold with warm energy as I walked by old Tibetans swirling prayer wheels, monks happy to be on 'summer holidays' from being monks, Himachali women bent double under grass-loads, and people of all hues from all corners of the world clacking rosaries and meditating by the wayside. There was tremendous freedom in the ready access to profound philosophy taught by good-humoured geshes (teachers), and the spirit of earnest inquiry and seeking that wafted through Dharamsala like heady pine incense.

On this first visit, it became apparent that much of the excitement and new energy in Dharamsala was due to the Dalai Lama's presence. Its old Devi temples, ashrams and sadhus had always marked it as somewhat different from its surrounding areas. With the Dalai Lama's growing stature as world guru, this town was acquiring an identity few sleepy hamlets dream about—that of a world spiritual capital.

Dharamsala is today emerging as the centre point in the global upsurge of interest in Buddhism. In times when many spiritual places and institutions are falling into decline, Dharamsala's star is on the ascendant. On days when the Dalai Lama gives public teachings, there is no place in the entire town to set down your backpack, and classes at the Library of Tibetan Works and Archives quickly fill up, mostly with foreign students. Many among these seekers have taken time out of their lives to live in Dharamsala, drawn by the opportunity to study Buddhism and learn something about living and letting go of the familiar.

These seekers-in-residence have turned Dharamsala into a cosmopolitan hub where crazy-exciting ideas and conversations zing about in street corners and cafes, and swapping molten nirvana thoughts keeps you warm in the worst snowstorms. One can close one's eyes and visualize this as a latter-day Nalanda, with the same revolutionary questioning and electric knowledge exchanges that characterized that Buddhist university of old, and from where so many scholars went out to other parts of the world, including Tibet.

It is a case of the chela (disciple) having brought back the gift of knowledge to his amnesiac guru—an analogy the Dalai Lama is fond of citing—that Tibet, the student, has preserved knowledge it received from India, the guru, in the form of the Buddha's dharma and has brought it back to its land of origin, from where it had disappeared centuries ago. What Nalanda and its sister universities were then—holders and disseminators of knowledge—Dharamsala seems to be now.

Access to knowledge secreted away in remote monasteries on the Tibetan plateau until recently draws students from around the world to Dharamsala. What this also signifies is a widespread emergence of Buddhism as *the* consciousness path for our times, a way to live ethically, naturally, peacefully, in awareness without the baggage of compulsory belief in a divine hierarchy. Many of us are slowly coming to a realization that the world is as we create it, and we haven't done such a good job of it. Our inner lives are jumbled up in unruly emotions, and our world enmeshed in violence, war, inequality and repression.

Buddhism is turning up with profound and intriguing

answers to the perplexing problems of our times. It encourages us to watch our reactive mind and allow it to quieten. We are asked to not hold on to anything, for everything is in the process of change. Each moment exists anew and each strand of life is interconnected with the rest of creation. In observing it we change the field of consciousness, enable it to widen and deepen.

This dynamic view of reality, and the acknowledgement of Buddhism as an ancient science of the mind, has led to recognition of points of similarity between Buddhism and modern science—something the Dalai Lama has been exploring with western scientists in yearly conferences. Some of these have been held in Dharamsala, and I attended them in 2002 and 2004.

It has become part of the stage upon which the intense quest of humankind for meaning and depth is unfolding. Dharamsala is where reality and consciousness are being watched, studied and, who knows, even subtly altered, and its impact will be felt far away from the epicentre. At other times there have been other theatres of inner revolution—Kurukshetra, Gethsemane, Mecca, Assisi, Arunachala, Pondicherry. In our times, the potential of nurturing a spiritual renaissance lies in Dharamsala.

Dharamsala could well be a mandala—a map of the world of spiritual journeying. In Sanskrit 'mandala' also refers to a circle, a group or an association. The mandala of Dharamsala represents a unique encirclement of several worlds—of the dharma, of wanderers, of refugees of the spirit. A weaving together is taking place on this mandala that is bringing the seeker in conjunction with the knowledge she seeks, the teacher with the taught, and the pilgrim with the path that will lead her to the objective of her pilgrimage. If there is thirst, Dharamsala presents the possibility of slaking it.

Dharamsala is no Shangri-La. There are no dakinis swirling in the twilight, no elixir-spouting fountains, no supermen or women. It is not a mountain retreat frozen in time and pin-drop quiet. Dharamsala is a hill town with acute water shortages and inefficient sewerage. It is crowded with tourists who pop in to get a darshan (glimpse) of Vishnu's tenth avatar (the Hindu way of appropriating the Buddha) at the Dalai Lama's temple. Greedy builders out to exploit its sudden fame are building indiscriminately, endangering the health of the mountains. The number of vehicles is increasing exponentially so that the air smells of exhaust fumes as often as it does of pine, and it is becoming difficult to walk through the main streets without being constantly honked at.

Dharamsala is not immune to the acquisitional thirst of consumerism or to inefficiency and carelessness. Its spiritual energy and activity are in no way an adamantine shield against the pervasive winds of globalization, greed and the politics of power. The very materialism that people may seek refuge from in Dharamsala stares them in the face here. Money is as important here as it is anywhere in the world. It buys goodies and services and it hurts to have none. In all this, Dharamsala is a mirror of the world. It reflects in micro what already exists in our macro-visions.

What the dirt and weakened hillsides and discarded plastic bags also show is the need for a spirituality that is engaged in matters of daily living, where caring for the environment is interwoven with our contemplative practice. Physically fragile, Dharamsala encourages us to take care of it by becoming careful with our lifestyles. It offers the opportunity for mindful living on and off the meditation cushion, to pluck the fireflies of insight and use them to illuminate our way as we walk, speak, cook, consume, in our everyday world.

Dharamsala has an old body, as old as the Himalayas, and a new mind and spirit that are being shaped by its new adventures. To minds full of questioning, Dharamsala offers to point a way to understanding. If we come to it with pain in our hearts, it will soothe and relieve. It can be mother, teacher, friend, irritant, radical, subversive, depending on what we search for. For Dharamsala is the harbour our spirits seek on rough nights and the guiding light we require to move ahead.

Arrival

Dark, moody clouds are fast filling up the afternoon sky. Will it rain or snow, I wonder aloud, squinting up against the faltering sunlight. I am standing in the wide balcony of a guesthouse, the Dhauladhars to my left, the untidy expanse of McLeodganj below. A voice answers from behind me, 'Anything's possible now.' I look around to find Thondup, the caretaker's beautiful wife, who was drying her long hair in the sun when I checked in earlier that day.

'Anything? You mean it can even snow in October?' I ask her, alarmed at not being told of this possibility by any Dharamsala veteran I had spoken to before setting out from Delhi.

'Well, it hasn't until now,' she concedes. 'But who knows what might happen?' she says mysteriously, adding to the brooding quality of the afternoon.

It was a sunnier Dharamsala, and Thondup, that I found when I got here in the morning. I had taken an overnight bus from Majnu ka Tilla, the Tibetan neighbourhood in north Delhi that owes its name to the legendary lover of many folk songs and fables. Majnu is the Indian Romeo, Laila his forbidden Juliet. The colony's romantic name, a medieval christening most probably, sits oddly with its current identity as a refugee settlement. Prayer flags greet one from afar, and the narrow lanes are crowded with tiny shops selling 'Tibetan' curios, made in Nepal. Young Tibetans hang out in front of the shops and carom games are in progress by the wayside. Babies crawl out of shops, where their mothers are busy sewing or knitting or chatting with friends. There is a warm feeling of community despite the shabbiness of cramped quarters, and the stench that rises from the Yamuna that flows by carrying Delhi's waste.

Overwhelming congestion notwithstanding, the number of guesthouses and small hotels in Majnu ka Tilla has risen phenomenally over the past few years. This is because Majnu ka Tilla is base camp for all travellers headed towards Dharamsala. It is the beginning of the Tibetan trail in India, where you get information about and access to transport, accommodation and dharma courses in Dharamsala and its Tibetan suburb, McLeodganj. Majnu ka Tilla is where you land for a night's rest after your flight has deposited you at Delhi's international airport or, when having 'done' the Taj and Rajasthan, you turn Dharamsala-ward.

In terms of sounds and smells, identity and spirit, Majnu ka Tilla occupies the same continuum as Dharamsala. Geographically, they couldn't be further apart—one in the lush hills of the Himalayan state of Himachal Pradesh, the other a dusty colony perched on the sandy bank of the polluted Yamuna. Yet Majnu ka Tilla exists almost as an island in the heaving waters of Delhi, its heart beating in tune with the pulse of the distant hill town.

The moment you walk into Majnu ka Tilla, you find yourself holding one end of the string that will lead you to Dharamsala.

Dharamsala is the mother of all the 'little Lhasas' that have sprung up around the world and in India where Tibetans have begun putting down new roots—small satellite settlements that revolve around the still centre that is the home of the man who is the thread that links the scattered beads together. His Holiness the Dalai Lama. His image is everywhere in Majnu ka Tilla, and he smiles down at me as I buy a bus ticket at the travel agency named after his lost palace in Lhasa—Potala.

It is dusk when the bus trundles out of Majnu ka Tilla. Cold mist from the Yamuna chases us like a hungry ghost escaped from the hell realms of Buddhist cosmology. One way of making a night journey in a boxed 'luxury coach' tolerable is to keep the window curtains open and allow the darkness to seep into your little wandering island of light. Light busies the mind with chatter and excitement and anxiety. Gazing deep into the dark loosens the grasp of noise, and I gradually slip into its inviting silence.

The journey to Dharamsala is arduous, depending on where you are coming from. As all journeys, it begins in the seed of wanting. How your journey goes, what you ultimately get out of it, depends on the seed you sowed before you set out. Dharamsala draws many over continents, thousands of miles in an aeroplane, and then these last few hundred in a bus whose wide seats are of little use when it hits the severely bumpy bits on an uneven road.

However long or short your physical journey to Dharamsala might be, getting there requires of you a journey of the heart. It begins when you sense a reality more rooted than the material, undercurrents that flow through you and connect you to everything else. You look for what you intuitively feel to be the intangible yet very real point of connection, under all the debris of wanting and needing and loving and hating you have collected over your self, the point where you see through the magic mirror and find the real you.

And so you get yourself into a bumpy, back-breaking bus ride to a Himalayan town that is not even that picturesque.

It is close to midnight. The bus stops for a much-delayed dinner at Prince's Dhaba, whose signboard announces 'the best food in north India'. As we gather around the 'Princely' buffet of rajma-chawal, curried potatoes and thick rotis, I realize what a motley group this busload of travellers is. There are no two groups of people here that speak the same language! There are Germans, Americans, a Slavic group and another of Scandinavian strain, and of course the Tibetans. There is definitely an energy around them that is different from the average tourist's, and I wonder why each of them is heading towards Dharamsala.

The German women in their smart leather jackets and bright red lipstick are definitely on a spiritual quest—they carry sandalwood rosaries and chant silently and intermittently through the night. 'I want to study Buddhist philosophy at the library,' one of them tells me, referring to the Library of Tibetan Works and Archives in Dharamsala. Her eyes are bright and her voice musical with the unfamiliar timbre of English. 'I've finally taken six months out of my life. This is something I just had to do for myself,' she says firmly, almost to herself. I sense a sadness, of someone or something given up to make this journey. But she doesn't tell and I don't ask.

The American girls are also on a spiritual quest, hippie style. They are fascinated with the 'Hindu' tattoos they've got in Rishikesh, and their hair is matted into dreadlocks 'just like sadhoos'. They are free spirits they explain, and want to roam through India and Nepal and maybe even Tibet, provided they get the visa. Dharamsala is the next stop on their trail for a spiritual high. Over dinner they chat with other travellers about cheap accommodation and the possibility of learning yoga. 'Do you think we could meet the Dally Lama?' they want to know. It is a question, and a pronunciation of the Dalai Lama's name, that I will hear often in the days to come.

The Tibetan group sticks together. The girls are in jeans and softly hum tunes from popular Bollywood films. The older women wear traditional chubas, long dresses that embrace the wearer in their warm folds, with a striped apron tied at the waist. The grown-ups keep an eye on their many big bundles wrapped in cloth, possibly goods bought in Delhi for a family-run business in Dharamsala.

The bus takes us through Haryana, Punjab and then into Himachal, parting the dense darkness with its white nose. Shadows loom by the wayside in the dark, thrown by trees, houses, scarecrows in fields, chimneys of factories, and who knows what else. I open the window a crack. A cold wind whispers through. I sense the sleeping forms around me shiver, and quickly close it again.

Around seven in the morning, the bus rolls into what is known as 'lower Dharamsala'. This part of Dharamsala houses government offices and courts, and people from surrounding suburbs and towns head here when they need to get permission from the municipality to build, or hire lawyers to settle legal disputes. Those that work here in offices and small businesses make the daily commute in overcrowded Tata Sumo taxis that lurch drunkenly over bad roads to deposit them at Kotwali Bazaar, literally 'police station market', which runs through the heart of lower Dharamsala.

The early morning cold lifts to reveal school-bound children, tight-faced in anticipation of a long day ahead. Most shops in Kotwali Bazaar have old-style wooden shutters that are closed at this early hour. Only tea shacks are doing business, with steam pouring out of spouts of aluminium kettles and parathas sizzling on heavy griddles, their warm aroma mingling with the putrefied stench of rotting garbage and stagnant water in drains.

This could be any hill town in north India, I think as I peer out of the bus, which is moving very carefully now along the narrow bazaar lanes. The picture before me brings to mind the towns of Kumaon in the western neck of the Himalayas in India, the place of my mother's ancestry. A rush of familiarity comes with finding high mountains in whichever direction you look, in the lined, sunburnt faces of mountain women, and in the evidence of the struggle of a tiny hill community under the onslaught of 'tourist traffic'.

That the local population has made good with appreciating land prices, shops, hotels and restaurants, draws an insidious veil over the larger destruction caused by the ever-increasing hordes that descend upon hill towns looking for cool weather in summer and the unfamiliar thrill of snowfall in winter. Forests have been cleared to make way for hotels and apartment buildings. Unlike the old dwellings that nestle gently along hillsides, the new constructions dominate the landscape and are conspicuously dissonant with their surroundings. They are built not in the old sustainable way with local materials but with concrete and cement and in a harsh architectural style that damages and weakens the mountains.

As the bus begins its steep ascent towards McLeodganj, there is a perceptible shift in the weather. The sun is on the other side of the mountain, and we are in the midst of cold green woods. The trees are increasingly pine, arising out of a sunless ground of dense foliage. The stillness of the forest seems held in place by the unbroken, ceaseless chirping of crickets. Tips of tall trees catch some sun. Filtered by their thick leaves, the light that falls on the ground is dark and green.

I have heard there are rhododendrons in these forests. I strain my eyes looking for the bright crimson flowers but can't see any. I find later that rhododendrons flower in summer, when many hills in these parts are bathed in pink and red.

We pass Dharamsala Cantonment on the way. The first time McLeodganj appeared on the map of British India was as a cantonment town, named after David McLeod, a lieutenant-governor of Punjab in the mid-nineteenth century.

The bus winds up the mountain, drawing steady curves around it. It does that scary thing that buses and mules in the hills often do—moving along the edge of the road until it feels as if one is held up against gravity by sheer will power. The periphery of the road disappears under the wheel of the bus. I taste pure fear as my teeth cut into my lower lip in a moment of panic—the salt of blood mixed with the primal terror of death. Another moment and we have turned the bend. How close to our skin we carry our fear of death. Perhaps we do have to meditate upon corpses in cremation grounds to get it out for good, like so many Tantrics and some Tibetan Buddhists.

As if on cue, an old graveyard appears to the right. It surrounds a church that looks at least a century old. Most of the graves are ancient and the concrete slabs covering them are disintegrating. The thick forest that surrounds the church throws a dark shade around it, and I later discover that the church is quite appropriately named 'Church of St. John in the Wilderness'. Services are still held every Sunday, though its congregation has dwindled much since the days when it was the meeting point of local British residents and officials. The church has that quality that only very old buildings have— of having seen much, of having many stories to tell but no one to tell them to, of the clamour having finally passed out of their confines.

We ascend 550 metres in a mere nine kilometres between Kotwali Bazaar and McLeodganj. In this short distance, the world moults and emerges anew. From a mofussil hill town, we have come to a place of many colours, many streams, many identities. For McLeodganj is the special part of Dharamsala, like the kernel in the fruit or the germ of a new idea. Barely spread over a couple of acres geographically or visually over one ridge of one hill in the Dhauladhar Himalayas, McLeodganj is the suburb to which Dharamsala owes its international popularity. Dharamsala itself is a generous district, its spread taking into its embrace little suburbs like McLeodganj, Naddi and Forsythganj, the first and the last taking their names from obscure British officials who took pride in creating new townships where only deodar forests or a few villagers' shacks existed before.

In a bend in the road, we pass some trees that are dying. Their leaves are long gone, and their bark has turned an ashen grey. Their wooden limbs point stiffly, like corpses' fingers, upwards—towards hope, towards McLeodganj.

The bus rolls under a large green sign that spans the road: The Municipality of McLeodganj welcomes you.

2

Refuge

A pair of dark eyes follows me from outside the window as I stretch my body into surya namaskar, the yogasana that pays homage to the sun. A face pushes into the netting that keeps night insects out. Lips press against the net, find it cold, and a tongue shoots out to warm the spot. I climb on to the mountain asana as if nothing has happened. Then, a finger taps on the pane. Softly at first, and then more insistently, demanding my attention. I whirl around, thrust my face into the window and pull my mouth into a grimace. A loud 'wahhhh . . .' fills the guesthouse, as my little peeping Tom runs into his mother's arms.

Tenzin is six years old and has quickly become my pal. He lives in the guesthouse with his parents, Pema and Thondup, who earn free boarding in return for running this place that is owned by the monastery next door. The guesthouse is pretty basic. I have the best room, with wooden floors and an attached bathroom that has a temperamental geyser that sulks every other day, which is when I bathe with cold water, ascetic style. There is a common kitchen on the roof where you are welcome to cook provided you bring your own pots and pans and stuff to cook in them. Since I have none of these, I end up scrounging the bazaar for healthful places to eat.

The young family struggles to scratch a living. Pema is often away during the day working odd jobs and leaves the guesthouse in his wife's care. 'Living in Dharamsala is so expensive,' Thondup confides in me one day when unseasonal rain drums against the metal awning over the windows. 'We are lucky that we have a decent place to live.' (They have one room and share a bathroom with other tenants.) 'It is very difficult to find a place on rent here. It is hard for us,' says Thondup, a faraway look in her eyes, her hands slowly plaiting her fine hair.

Over the days, I get to know more. Not all Tibetans now in exile in Dharamsala and elsewhere left Tibet with the first wave that accompanied the Dalai Lama in 1959. Many followed in his footsteps over the decades. Pema and Thondup made the journey eight years ago, risking their lives and the well-being of those they left behind. 'We didn't want our children to grow up in Tibet, not like it is now,' whispers Thondup, memories moistening her eyes. 'We walked in the snow for days until we reached the Nepal border. When we came here to Dharamsala, we got to meet the Dalai Lama. That made it all worthwhile in a way.'

Little Tenzin is Pema and Thondup's child of hope. He was born in Dharamsala, in freedom, to parents who chose exile over oppression even if it meant economic hardship and uncertainty. He was named after the other Tenzin—Tenzin Gyatso, the Dalai Lama, whose presence in Dharamsala was the beacon two ragged travellers followed over mountains and snows.

In becoming the principal place of refuge for displaced Tibetans, is Dharamsala fulfilling the destiny encoded within its name? According to Tantra, words and the syllables and accents they are made of are tiny reservoirs of energy. They can be used to create particular energy patterns, as in mantras, so that a vibrational force-field is formed which then attracts experiences according to its nature.

'Dharamsala', a combination of two Sanskrit words—dharma and shala (home)—can be literally translated as 'the home of dharma'. Dharma is frequently translated as 'religion', which is not wholly accurate. The word comes from the root 'dhri', which means to bear or support. Incidentally, dhri also gave birth to the word for earth, 'dharti', symbolic in Sanskrit texts of stability and centredness. Literally, dharma may be said to stand for 'that which is established'. In its range of meanings, dharma enfolds righteousness or duty, natural law, as well as personal ethics.

Dharma is a word of ancient importance for the streams of spirituality that bubbled up in the Indian subcontinent and flowed beyond from thence. This is true for Buddhism as well, in which the notion of dharma is central and multilayered. Dharma is the Buddha's teachings that are about truth, reality—the way things actually are (which is dharma too) and not what the conditioned mind shows us. Dharma is the raft of awareness, insight and balance, which carries one through the turbulent waters of samsara, the world of suffering. Without the anchor of dharma, we are tossed and turned by waves of emotions and circumstances, blinded by unknowing, condemned to suffer. Dharma is thus one of the three 'jewels' in which the novitiate takes refuge, the other two being the Buddha and the sangha (community of seekers).

What quirk of destiny, or perhaps the energy latent in its name, has made Dharamsala the protector of the Buddha's dharma in these times? It is where the sangha of Tibetan refugees took shelter, bringing with them the dharma in the form of teachers, scriptures, institutions and practitioners.

Dharamsala became their refuge, their anchor in a cesspool of political intrigue and dispossession. Dharamsala gives émigrés the opportunity to recoup their energies and their selves, resettle, and perhaps even find new skies to stretch out their wings.

One such adolescent who was eager to fly made the long journey to Dharamsala in January 2000. He walked over snowbound mountainous plains and passes in the dead of winter, his face set southward from where came the winds that had found him in his monastery in Tibet and whispered to him of freedom. He and his companions travelled mostly at night, when the Chinese border patrol guards would be huddled around fires to escape the bitter cold. They picked their way by moonlight, torches holding too great a risk of giveaway. Whenever they stopped for a moment's rest, the young man would look towards the stars that shone cold and hard. He would close his eyes and shove out of the way all inner noise that clamoured about losing toes to frostbite, and the certainty of lifelong imprisonment or even execution in the event of capture.

Quietened, he would formulate and hold this thought—I am going to the land of the Buddha. My feet will soon kiss the soil made holy by his footsteps. We have walked on his spiritual footsteps for centuries. As a holder of his legacy, this is my pilgrimage.

In these moments, he would try not to focus on the politics that had forced him to flee the gilded cage that was his monastery in China-occupied Tibet. He had been born in a poor nomadic family. Life was rough, but it held the comfort of a rhythm that had been set centuries before. His elder sisters loved the ever-smiling baby and nicknamed him Apo Gaga, happy brother. Those uncomplicated childhood days came to an abrupt end in 1992 with his recognition as an incarnation of one of the most important lamas in Tibetan Buddhism— the Gyalwa Karmapa, head of the Karma Kagyu sect.

In the old days in Tibet, recognition of an important reincarnate child would have meant rejoicing in the child's family and village, a tearful parting, followed by years of gruelling study in the lineage's special, and secret, teachings. Years of quietening and watching the mind, controlling and honing vital energies into precise instruments of self-evolution. Until one was deemed qualified by one's tutors and asked to assume official and religious duties.

Things no longer happen that way. Whenever an important lama dies, it gives the People's Republic of China a fresh opportunity to play another round of politics in Tibet. A few years after the young Karmapa was recognized, the party bosses handpicked the Panchen Lama's reincarnation and placed the Dalai Lama's candidate under arrest. No one knows where the imprisoned Panchen Lama is today and he may well be dead, as the spurious lama holds his place and fulfils his religious duties.

Something similar though not as disastrous happened with the young Karmapa, Ugyen Trinley Dorje. Fratricidal feuds followed his recognition, with him being labelled a 'Chinese implant' and rejected by a section of the Kagyu ministry. A rival candidate was recognized by those that suspected his legitimacy, the one proof of which was a letter said to be handwritten by the previous Karmapa giving details of his next birth. These details matched the circumstances of the adolescent Karmapa's early life. That the Dalai Lama had accepted his authenticity gave him all the approval he needed in the eyes of Tibetans, though a cabal of Kagyu Rinpoches continued to uphold his rival. As he fled Tibet, young Ugyen Trinley Dorje hoped to visit the impressive monastery his predecessor had built in Rumtek in Sikkim, which his rival had been unable to lay claim to.

Although he was enthroned at the traditional seat of the Karmapas in Tsurphu in Tibet, and had been lord and master of the monastery there, it had become increasingly obvious that he would forever be forced to live under a microscope, his every action questioned and every word peeled for hidden meanings. For religion is an instrument of the state in communist China, which is determined to snap the close ties that had bound together religion and governance in old Tibet. 'The Tibetans are free to practise their religion,' the Chinese government would say. 'Provided they do it our way,' was the aside no one heard, except those jailed for honouring the 'splittist' Dalai Lama, and the monks and nuns who couldn't complete their monastic studies because there were no teachers left in Tibet.

This was a practical problem the teenaged Karmapa also faced. Those who would have traditionally taken on the role of his teachers and transmitted teachings of the Kagyu lineage to him lived in exile in India and elsewhere. What was the use of being just a figurehead with little actual learning, a puppet living in perpetual fear?

Recent events had borne out his instincts. The Chinese authorities had 'recognized' him as the rightful reincarnation of the Karmapa in a bid to keep him indebted to them. They expected favours in return. For instance, he had been forced to appear with the then Chinese premier Jiang Zemin in Tiananmen Square in Beijing on the occasion of Workers' Day in 1994. Since the Dalai Lama had recognized him as the true reincarnation of the sixteenth Karmapa, he realized how important his words and actions were, how much they would influence his fellow Tibetans. When asked to support the official Chinese position on the Panchen Lama, he had refused, but he knew he couldn't keep doing so. And they wouldn't stop asking, not ever.

It was a sticky web in which he was becoming entangled. It was clear to him that there was only one thing to do—flee to India and from there . . . who knows what jewels the world held and he might too, in the palm of his hand?

His feet heavy with fatigue, the young man barely made it into Nepal. From there, word was sent on to Dharamsala to the Dalai Lama about the newest escapee out of Tibet. The teenager's identity was kept secret until he set foot in Dharamsala one cold January day at the dawn of the new millennium. Then, nothing could be kept hush-hush any more and the news of the Karmapa's daring escape spread all over the town. It didn't take long for the world to hear of it. The Tibetan diaspora was ecstatic on hearing this news, as was another group—the sixteenth Karmapa's extensive following in the west, who felt they could now continue their discipleship with their guru.

If Ugyen Trinley Dorje had expected to be greeted with open arms by the Buddha's land and pressed into her warm, abundant bosom that had mothered so many travellers, pilgrims, even conquerors since time immemorial, he was severely disappointed. Right from the start, suspicion and controversy sprang up around the teenager like a rash of monsoon weeds. His escape seemed too easy, and the Indian government suspected it to be a masterstroke of Chinese espionage. The Chinese government, perhaps embarrassed by having been caught with its pants down, allowed the spy story to perpetuate. The result was near imprisonment for the Karmapa in a makeshift monastery in Sidhbari, a suburb of Dharamsala, with his movement restricted within a ten-kilometre radius. In the following years he was allowed to travel all over India but not abroad, much to the dismay of the overseas sangha that had looked forward to hosting their teacher's reincarnation. The embargo on the Karmapa's foreign travel holds at the time of writing.

The harshest blow for the young man was the restriction, despite repeated requests to successive Indian governments, on entering his predecessor's seat in exile—the monastery in Rumtek. Built by the sixteenth Karmapa with permission from the then prime minister of India Jawaharlal Nehru, Rumtek monastery holds some of the most precious of the lineage's relics, including the famed 'black hat' supposedly created out of the hair of dakinis, feminine celestial beings. Perhaps the Indian government's paranoia stemmed from its discomfort over the disputed status of Sikkim vis-à-vis China, which had longed claimed it and another north-eastern state, Arunachal Pradesh, as its own. If the Karmapa was a Chinese agent, as they were almost certain he was, wasn't it possible that his presence in Rumtek could be used by the Chinese to undermine India's claim to Sikkim?

So the seventeenth Karmapa found himself a denizen of Dharamsala like thousands of other Tibetans. Which is where I met him twice, first in 2001 about nineteen months into his exile, and then in 2004, when he had begun to give teachings and was slowly coming into his own. In between, I had opportunity to speak with him in 2002 in Delhi, when I was working as spirituality correspondent with a national newspaper and he was eager to air his frustration about the restrictions that had circumscribed his world since his arrival in India.

In 2001 Ugyen Trinley Dorje was seventeen years old, and already radiated wisdom and depth far beyond his years. Was it because of his experiences with the nature of life and human beings, or was it because he truly was an old soul now into his seventeenth voluntary appearance on earth as a bodhisattva, bound in compassion to help other beings in their earthly and spiritual journeys?

The Gyuto Ramoche Monastery, where he lives, was at the time an odd, depressing concrete structure ringed by unkempt, overgrown grass. It had none of the beauty one would expect to find in a sacred space. It actually felt like a jail, with omnipresent security, the demand for police permits and checks at various points in the long journey from the entrance to the topmost floor, where the Karmapa lived like a medieval princess held captive in an ivory tower.

Sidhbari, where the Gyuto Ramoche Monastery stands, is downhill from McLeodganj. The land changes from mountain to valley, rolling in gentle curves, and there are meadows and grasslands and rice fields all around. There is a warm perfume in the air from the millions of mountain flowers along the roadside and in hedges surrounding little cottages with lime-washed walls and slate roofs that glint when they catch the sun. A mountain stream burbles through the valley, with a sunny village settled at its every turn.

The Karmapa is composed and remarkably still throughout our first meeting, for which I have had to follow several security requirements, including a promise to refrain from asking any question that might even vaguely smell of politics, and acquiring a permission document from Dharamsala's chief of police authorizing the interview and some photography. Even so, we are interrupted several times by his security, and I am forced to switch off my dictaphone because I don't have a separate permit to use it. I am thrown off balance, but not the calm young man before me. He witnesses the commotion quietly and watchfully, his mind never seeming to ripple after disconcerting thoughts.

At last we begin to talk through an interpreter—a middle-aged monk whose dated English vocabulary fortunately does nothing to obscure the young man's wisdom. My first question is about his relationship with birds, an odd question for those who don't know of the sixteenth Karmapa's great fondness for birds. I want to establish a link between the two, the sixteenth and the seventeenth, to explore the fascinating realm of reincarnating bodhisattvas.

He says, 'His Holiness the sixteenth Karmapa was a Mahabodhisattva and each of his actions was for the benefit of all sentient beings. He did have a collection of birds, which he probably kept to liberate them from suffering. We cannot compare with what the great masters do. As far as I am concerned, I think that birds are essentially free and you and I cannot possibly know what they need. So it is best to let them be as they are, naturally.' A passionate plea for freedom, and the recognition of the sacredness of all life, perhaps stemming from his own life experiences?

The young man's spirit shines through. He seems quite his own person with his own views, even at this precarious and uncertain point in his life. His response also makes me think that perhaps what reincarnates in the case of realized beings is their wisdom and not personal characteristics of a particular birth.

We have met a short time after 9/11, and the world is torn apart by conflict and a violent, divisive rhetoric that pits one slice of humankind against another. What is the Buddhist solution to this crisis? The Karmapa takes a moment before responding: 'To try and bring peace in the world, I believe that whether one is a Buddhist or not is immaterial. Irrespective of religion and nationality, every individual in the world must practise the dharma. And dharma practice not for your own self, but for the benefit of every sentient being in the universe. For as long as we can, each one of us must do this, for lasting harmony and peace in the world.

'As for there being a "Buddhist" solution, I think that the world is huge, and if some issue is a "world issue", it is a vast issue too. So is the case with this war and the present world situation. No one religion can hope to provide ready solutions. All the religions of the world need to cooperate to find lasting solutions to such problems. Which I think will come about if everybody practises compassion, non-violence and loving kindness.'

His mature response makes me wonder about how he deals with his own not-insubstantial problems. 'The problems you refer to have been minor,' he says, his being radiating quiet strength. 'I do not feel them to be personal at all, although they have brought a lot of difficulties to my people and those who believe in me and are dedicated to me. As far as dealing with these is concerned, as a religious person, I pray and dedicate my merits so that these problems are resolved. Personally, I try and do everything as peacefully and truthfully as possible.'

I cannot but marvel at his poise in the face of the overwhelming mistrust and suspicion that has been directed against him. I think how agitated I would be if placed even for a moment in his situation. He has weathered crisis after crisis and is in the middle of yet another one, and yet has the stillness of mind and thought to remain mindful of others' well-being over his own.

I am eager to know more about this seventeen-year-old. For exercise, he jogs on the roof of his monastery, and there is an exercise bike that is also put to use sometimes. His sensitive eyes are luminous as he tells me about his flute-playing and the occasional verses he composes. At an official level, his dreams are taken as signs of future happenings, and translated into painting by a master thangka-maker. 'If there is any element of truth in what I have dreamt, then there are certain things in my dreams related to the future of Tibet, and the future of the world,' he says, but refuses to give details. 'Since these dreams and the paintings are too detailed, I don't think I can tell you about it right now,' he says, veiling a sacred ritual from my curious gaze.

I have already overstayed my time limit. At the point of being hustled away, I quickly sneak in a question about his future plans, about Rumtek, the rest of the world. 'Yes, the plan is there but not yet the reality. There is always hope.'

The memory of that meeting stays with me for the young refugee's quiet optimism, and the feeling of looking into a deep, still pool of water where every crag and stone at the bottom appears crystal clear. The Karmapa, as indeed all Tibetan refugees who have made Dharamsala their home, challenges the belief that you need anything to be happy and calm and warm and giving. You can give something, of yourself, even when your hands and pockets are empty. You can blaze forth into the inkiest night. And you certainly can be free in exile.

This is the humbling message of the refugees of Dharamsala. They have nothing; they are dispossessed of their homes and land; their lives have been torn away from them. Many have lost husbands and wives and children in the political upheavals they have had the ill fortune of becoming trapped in. Life is hard, as Thondup said to me, and it is not only economic hardship she is talking about. Even though some have made a success of their hotels and small businesses, there are several others that barely get by. And all their hearts, regardless of their financial condition, must struggle with the dull ache that comes with loss, death, chaos.

Yet there is remarkable resilience and a sense of oneness, of standing behind one another and finding the path ahead. The sangha has come together. For instance, when the Tibetan Children's Village was set up in Dharamsala in the early years of exile, it was not only the children that found nurture and sustenance. Women whose children had died in the exodus were encouraged to become mothers to orphans, an upaya (the Buddha's term for skilful means) that fulfilled the needs of both.

Tibetan refugee women especially have shown remarkable adaptability in foreign surroundings and circumstances. Every day in Dharamsala I see strong, confident Tibetan women of all ages setting up shop, dealing with customers while handling their children, crafting objets d'art, running organizations and restaurants, buying and selling with aplomb. Being here in Dharamsala has given them the opportunity to stretch their wings, and contribute substantially to the well-being of their families and society.

The Karmapa himself has shown considerable facility in dealing with the trauma of exile. The second time I met him, I noticed a perceptible change in his attitude towards his own condition. He voiced his growing frustration with the Indian government's refusal to allow him into Rumtek monastery, or even lift the curbs that kept him, literally, from stepping out into the world. With hindsight, I wonder whether the strongly worded statements of that interview had something to do with sending out a message to his detractors. Perhaps he had learned the crucial role the news media played in the country of his refuge, and saw me as a representative of the same (which I was at the time) and wished to use the opportunity to make widely known his sense of disappointment. Spurred by the memory of my first encounter with his wisdom, I tried to engage him in questions aimed at revealing his inner journey. This turned out to be fruitless as he would rather speak about the annoyances that plagued his life, and so the interview proceeded accordingly.

Though troubled by the contrast between the young man's earlier equanimity and the stance he now adopted, I reminded myself that he was a political personage along with being a religious one. The Dalai Lama had perfected the integration of these two diverse roles such that the equipoise and compassion that were a result of his spiritual practice flowed into his political role and enriched it. Though the Dalai Lama wore multiple hats, he was able to be the same person in all of them. And he made it seem effortless too! I didn't realize how much stamina of spirit this required, how concentrated and steady an awareness of oneself at all times, until I stumbled upon what appeared to me a rift in the Karmapa's personality.

In the years since, the Dalai Lama seems to have taken the young man under his wing. The Karmapa does represent the young generation of Tibetan leadership and will benefit immensely from the Dalai Lama's personal example and guidance. He has been part of recent 'Mind and Life' conferences with the Dalai Lama and western scientists, with the Dalai Lama saying that he would like the younger generation to take over so that the ground-breaking dialogue can continue beyond his lifetime. I am sure the Dalai Lama feels similarly regarding his other initiatives as well, whether it is the dialogue with China, enlightened governance, promotion of interfaith understanding or ecological sensitivity.

When I meet the Karmapa in 2004, there is a new

assuredness in his demeanour. He still speaks through a translator, and not knowing English seems to be the greatest stumbling block to his assuming a more active role in the 'Mind and Life' conferences. 'The Buddhist path is of investigation, as is that of science. So I understand the synergy between them. As far as contributing is concerned, I don't think I can right now because I don't know English and that limits my understanding somewhat. The first step is to understand, then to contemplate, and then only can one contribute,' he says. We are back in the same room where I first experienced his depth and stillness all those years ago, though it appears brighter now and less oppressive due to the welcome absence of the paranoid security force.

Much has changed around the Karmapa. The Gyuto Ramoche Monastery in Sidhbari, which was a bare concrete structure earlier oddly symbolic of its prime resident's uncertain situation, has now grown into a well-maintained complex that houses some 300 monks. Their living quarters and the building for a Tantric university have come up around the monastery. These buildings ring a huge quadrangle where the Karmapa gives weekly public teachings. Everything is new and smart and spiffy, and trimmed with maroon and gold emblems.

How rapidly this young man's fortunes have turned, how fluid reality is. In barely four years, an entire universe of activities and followers, cycles of learning and teaching, has evolved around the Karmapa. The irritants may refuse to go away, but he *is* getting to taste some of the freedom that he so desperately wished for. Maybe because life never becomes exactly perfect, our minds just need to *find* the perfection that gleams at the heart of every moment.

Our meeting is short because it isn't an official interview. I just want to meet him and know what he is up to. Like other

Tibetan refugees, he is beginning to find the benediction in the obvious limitations of Dharamsala. This world that has grown around him is a happy one, with monks studying on rooftops in the sun, the new energy of the university, a dwindling security presence, and a growing sangha of followers that come to him even though he cannot visit them.

I find myself wondering what the future holds for the young Karmapa. I think his inner stability will stand him in good stead as it has all the Tibetans who continue in their own ways to cope with the experience of refugeehood. The Karmapa will be a significant leader of the Tibetan diaspora in the years to come, and is even now an inspiration for the young Tibetans to whom he is a peer. How he deals with his own problems, how well he is able to bring to bear his substantial spiritual training upon his leadership, and whether he is able to arrive at a balance between his traditional office and the demands of the modern world, will ultimately determine the quality and extent of that inspiration.

3

Serendipity

A bazaar runs through McLeodganj. There are actually two strands that run parallel to one another, separated by a row of shops that open into both. A pagoda-like structure stands in the middle of the entire hullabaloo, studded with prayer wheels big and small that eager hands of passers-by keep in near-perpetual motion. The lower bifurcation of the bazaar, on your left as you walk in from the bus stand, is the more crowded. A Tibetan charitable hospital stands where a path connects the two arms of the bazaar. At this cusp begins the local subzi mandi, where expensive vegetables are piled high on bamboo baskets. The potholed street is muddy—and squishy where vegetables have fallen off and been crushed before the beggars lounging about could grab them.

Walking through this main bazaar can be disconcerting. There is an overwhelming feeling of a culture up and eager for consumption. There are shops laden with Tibetan jewellery and posters urging you to 'Save Tibet', a passionate plea that somehow seems incongruous in this overtly commercial atmosphere, like Che Guevera's image on T-shirts and coffee mugs. Old articles of everyday utility and worship, rendered useless because the lifestyle they belonged to is destroyed and left behind, are up for sale as artefacts. Mass-produced thangkas hang in bunches from nails driven into shopfronts. Apart from the Tibetans, local Himachali residents too own businesses in the bazaar, happy to capitalize on the international popularity of this alien culture transplanted in their midst. There are even a couple of shops set up by enterprising Kashmiris that sell pashmina shawls and promise 'antiques' and semi-precious stones to the not-so-discerning tourist.

Music shops sell audio tapes and CDs of monastic chanting, and feature Tibetan 'pop stars'—dreamy-eyed young men in jeans, glossy-lipped young women in jeans—on garish, prominently displayed posters. Though jeans seem to be the clothing of choice for young Tibetans, as for youngsters everywhere, chubas are still what most Tibetans will wear to work or on formal occasions. These hang in suspended animation from the roofs of tailoring shops awaiting their owners, which might at times be a western woman who has become enamoured of this graceful dress. There are plenty of shops selling cheap T-shirts, jeans, trousers and skirts, and it is not unusual to come upon expensive, internationally manufactured mountaineering gear piled casually in ramshackle shops, left behind or sold cheap by departing trekkers.

Tucked among these establishments are shops that sell 'dharma books' and others affiliated with various Tibetan cooperatives and welfare organizations. These give an inkling of a different heartbeat under the come-hither tactics of commerce. The bazaar even has a small movie theatre which routinely screens 'dharma films' focusing on Buddhism and spirituality and those that highlight the Tibetan cause. I check its film schedule, which is scribbled on a blackboard up front, every now and then. One blustery evening, I visit it to watch a remarkable film on death and dying in Buddhist cultures, squinting at the small screen while sitting on a bottom-crushing seat, amid an audience made up entirely of foreign visitors.

Only when I am looking for presents to take back home do I seriously trawl the bazaar for the promises of 'riches at reasonable prices' that shopkeepers shout out at me whenever I pass them. But I do not have the deep pockets of the 'dollar buyer' and return empty-handed from the bigger shops with their exorbitant prices and faux knick-knacks fashioned to thrill with the exotica of the orient.

I leave behind the yak bells and butter lamps and assurances of 'authentically from Tibet' and look in on the smaller establishments, the proceeds of many of which go to refugee institutions. The products they showcase have been made by Tibetan craftspeople banded together under organizations formed to save the culture in exile. At a shop that is run for the Tibetan Children's Village, I go through an endless pile of small carpets with flaming dragons and bold floral motifs and a stack of mini-thangkas until I find one with a geometric mandala design. Excited, I take it out of the dinginess of the shop to look at its colours in the sun, and find it to be entirely off-centre!

Entrepreneurs too poor to afford a pucca shop in the bazaar set up their wares on the wayside by open drains. On tables covered with plastic sheets, topaz, lapis lazuli, jade and amber twinkle brilliant-hued in the sun. Are these real, I wonder, looking deep into the golden fire of a topaz. Indeed, what *is* real? Is this reality, which we conjure up with our desires and needs and dislikes, real? All those who come to Dharamsala, who are walking around me in this bustling bazaar, are looking to access a different reality, aren't they? Or perhaps not so much a different reality as a different *view* of reality. For that which is, is. How we look at it can change what we find in it, how we are in it. Our very way of being, perhaps our being too?

What we might need to do is cock our head a bit, and look from a new angle, and yet another, twist and turn and focus the light beam right into the heart of the topaz. Or the jewel of reality.

In Dharamsala, you may find both these jewels . . .

Whatever the place, wherever on earth, how distinct is its early morning manner from anything it may become later in the day. Dharamsala appears sleepy and uncertain in a grey light tinged with blue, as I set out towards the bazaar. That which was busy and vibrant yesterday has completely disappeared, as if swallowed by the interim darkness. The clamour of crowds has been replaced by chattering monkeys that swing from trees to land with a loud clatter on tin rooftops and, instead of sparkling jewels, the bazaar streets are awash with delicate pink flowers that swirl down from trees in the morning breeze and sometimes catch you on the head, sometimes right between your eyes if you happen to look up into the sky.

It is not yet seven—the perfect time to get fresh Tibetan bread. The previous night, I had inquired after it and found I needed to walk towards the bus stand, the one place I know with some certainty on this, my second day of stay. I am yet to visit the main temple and other such Dharamsala must-sees, which I am saving for later when I am a bit more settled into my life here.

I reach the point in the road where one arm swerves to my left, and the other continues on towards the bus stand. A portly middle-aged Tibetan woman has just arrived at this bend, and is busy untying a huge bundle that contains her wares for the day. I ask her about the bread, just to be sure, and she points me into the curve in the opposite direction from where I am headed. I decide to trust her and walk down the way her finger points.

For a long time, no bread appears. My head tells me to turn back towards the bus stand, but my feet want to keep walking. It is a pleasant enough walk, with the road on my right skimming the edge of this mountain and looking out into the valley below. I can see the snaking tarred road that brought me up from lower Dharamsala. Lorries and buses are slowly making their way up the mountain on that road, bringing supplies and a fresh batch of groggy passengers. I follow their progress until the road swings to the right and disappears from view.

On the left, I have passed closed shops and some flashy multistoreyed hotels that are clearly new additions to the topography. They sit uneasily propped against the hillside, their boxlike architecture more suited to flatlands than to curvaceous hills. How much more building will these hills take, I wonder, before they begin disintegrating in landslides and rivers of mud every monsoon?

In front of a new hotel that announces its name in loud gold and fluorescent green, a cavalcade of taxis is depositing sleepy Bengali tourists. It is Durga Pooja time, the greatest festival in goddess-loving Bengal. A time of the year when you can find the Bengali tourist wherever you go—heaving up the vertical incline to Kedarnath in the Himalayas, waddling into the sea in Goa, taking in the scenery and shore temples at Mamallapuram.

The clutch of families has climbed out of the taxis yawning and stretching. They begin counting their bags and haggling with the drivers over the charge from Pathankot, the nearest train station to Dharamsala, sure they are being cheated. I walk a few paces more and there are the breadwallahs, sitting before a gate that is huge by McLeodganj standards. I have reached the central temple, the Tsuglag Khang!

To my left, the sun climbs over snow-streaked Dhauladhar peaks. It is finally light.

This is what explorer-adventurers would call 'serendipity'—discovery through happy accident. The word belongs to an era when Europeans were busy 'discovering' that the world actually stretched beyond Europe and contained lands and cultures and peoples that were, surprise!, very different from themselves.

Travelling has changed much since those times. Chances for serendipity have rapidly diminished, and though the heart of the traveller may secretly long for discovery by accident, of chancing upon the unknown and surprising its secrets out into the open, she knows better than to hope for it to happen too often.

Yet there are journeys that cannot be pre-planned, where there may or may not be footsteps to follow. You may have to wear your own path into the ground. There may be dense undergrowth and brush and chaparral that obscure the way ahead. Even so, unable to coddle away the inner call, you may find yourself setting off on the unmapped journey within your self. And then, perhaps, you will come to Dharamsala. And with some luck and serendipity, find yourself at a gate that will lead you beyond the known.

Standing before its entrance, I realize that the Tsuglag Khang, along with the Dalai Lama's residence that stands cheek-by-jowl with it, is the nucleus of Dharamsala. My finding it like this could well be the effect of the sense of direction inbuilt in the place that drew my feet to its magnetic centre. This is where all roads that run through Dharamsala must converge, where its centre lies though it may not be the geographic or gravitational centre. Those that come to Dharamsala cannot but be drawn into this, its core space.

The bread smells good and fresh, but this moment holds

in it other things to do. I enter the compound and am faced
with a maze of gullies and steps that lead into various levels.
This feels like an ancient city, contained within the walls of a
fortress, every aspect of life packed in and being played out in
a small space encircled within a periphery. The building is
plain concrete, and has the quality of uneven construction
that comes with unplanned additions over the years around
the prime structure. It is strictly functional and new, suggestive
of an ancient tradition that has lost its old homes and now sits
in uncomfortable adjustment in new addresses.

The sacredness one feels here is not the product of
ambience or ancient architecture but more a condition of one's
own heart and mind.

The Tsuglag Khang that stands before me is a poor replica
in scale and magnificence of the original seventh-century
structure in Lhasa. Its name is translated rather quaintly as the
'central cathedral', and the Lhasa version is also called the
Jokhang. For the refugee community, Dharamsala's Tsuglag
Khang is more than a symbol of hope. It is the repository of
what for a persecuted people has meant nothing short of a
miracle, a sign of the possibility of preservation in their rapidly
changing world.

It dates back to the Cultural Revolution of the 1960s which
attempted to replace old, 'superstitious' faiths with the new
credo of communism, by force where necessary, to catapult
China's 'backward' peoples into the modern era. Studies of
this period detail the atrocities committed to perforce root
out a way of living and replace it with one that was drastically
and brutally different. In Tibet, which had been overrun by
the People's Republic of China in 1949, this madness took
the form of large-scale destruction of monasteries and temples
and the defrocking of monks and nuns, among other things,
all in the guise of 'liberating' the Tibetan people from an

'oppressive religion and its clergy'.

Looking to create the greatest impact of the revolution in Tibet, the Red Guards decided to storm the Jokhang—the huge, centrally located temple of Lhasa where several generations of Tibetans had worshipped Avalokiteshwara, the bodhisattva of compassion, of whom the Dalai Lama is considered an emanation. By this time, the Dalai Lama was already in exile in India, and had been denounced by those that controlled Tibet and were in charge of its destiny. They now sought to impose a monoculture upon Tibet which, despite the deceptive vitality of its red emblem, was depressingly and uniformly grey.

In their plan to devastate the temples and monasteries of Tibet, the Red Guards were following the example of brutal conquerors through history who destroyed places of worship to make a political statement of power. A culture's religious totems hold the faith of its people and are symbolic of the continuity of their way of life. Shattering them is a potent psychological tool to devalue a people's faith in themselves and their culture and, very crudely, of telling them who the boss is.

So it happened one day that the unfamiliar clatter of the Red Guards' boots was heard in the courtyard of the ancient temple that was used only to respectfully soft footfalls. Then the mayhem began. Images before which butter lamps burnt day and night, and which held in their gilded hands raised in the benedictory mudra the aspirations of an entire people, were smashed with rifle butts and bare hands. Magnificent thangkas that smelled of sweet incense were ripped away from the walls and burnt in bonfires, where precious texts joined them. Finally, the boots kicked the shards and broken pieces of revered statues out into the street for all to see.

The rape of the Jokhang was complete.

Where is the miracle in all this? The objects of faith had been destroyed, but not faith itself. A sacred space had been violated, but could the boots kick out the altars from people's hearts, where the lamps of knowing and believing burnt bright on this, the darkest night?

As it happened, after the Red Guards left, tear-filled eyes scanned the heaps of smashed statues and gently furtive fingers prised through the rubble, looking for survivors of the carnage. They found two faces—one peaceful and the other wrathful—aspects of the Avalokiteshwara statue that had held court in the old temple, which perhaps reminded the finders of the cyclical nature of life, its all-inclusiveness where the good and the bad are part of one weave, integrated into the fabric of life in which we find ourselves wrapped. There was peace; now there is conflict. And then perhaps, there will be peace again?

As the wheel of life turns, the old dies, and its essence reincarnates in the new. Old bodhisattvas cast away their worn-out bodies and are reborn as chubby-cheeked babies, young again to serve suffering humanity, believe the Tibetans. So did the smashed statues of Jokhang. The pieces extricated from the rubble were smuggled out of Tibet and reached Dharamsala in 1967. When a new statue of Avalokiteshwara was consecrated at the Tsuglag Khang in 1970, it was with the pieces of the old one encased in its womb.

The bodhisattva had in a way kept his promise to return eternally, until all beings were freed from samsara. He now sits in this concrete structure in Dharamsala across from the residence of the man who is considered his living embodiment. His thousand eyes scan those who gather before him for signs of their suffering, his thousand arms ready to reach out to those that need his help. He holds within him an ancient sacredness and, in his upraised hand, the promise of the new.

The throng of early morning visitors to the Tsuglag Khang sweeps me into their flow. They are mostly devotees who have come to pray, since it is still too early for tourists to be up and about. One of the first things I notice is people engaged in ritual prostrations in the corridor, where they hold their hands together in namaskar, take it to their foreheads, lower it back in front of their chests and then slide full length on the floor, arms stretched out in a ground-hugging namaskar to the deities. The process is strenuous and reminds me of the torturous moments I spend every day going through the surya namaskar that is part of my yoga routine. The only difference is I repeat the asana four times, while these men and women seem to prostrate endlessly. Some use pieces of wood smoothened to facilitate the sliding motion, while others have only thin pieces of cardboard cut out from tea cartons tied to their hands. The slide forward is visibly difficult for older people, and I am reminded of my mother's arthritic knee as I watch them painfully go through the motions. Acquiring merit was never meant to be easy, was it?

The miraculous Avalokiteshwara appears to my right, facing north in the general direction of Tibet. I peer through the glass doors behind which the bodhisattva rests, and cannot make out much for the darkness. A thick chain with a padlock ensures no one enters this enclosure. Is this to shield the statue from desecration? But the bodhisattva is among devotees here. Why not throw the doors open and let the prostrators look deep into his eyes as they arise from the ground?

Out of the direct line of prayer, I find an entrance to a hall, an open one this time. I enter, leaving my shoes by the door. As my eyes adjust to the dimness within, a world of wondrous treasures gradually crystallizes out of the darkness. The contrast with the functional plainness of the external structure is striking. The walls are lined with the most exquisite art, and in the centre is a three-foot-high statue of a seated Buddha— the guy who started it all.

Mesmerized, I step into what appears to be a cave of untold treasures. The wooden floor creaks loudly under my weight, and the solitary lama-in-attendance giggles at my mortified expression. I smile back politely, and then proceed with the utmost caution, trying quite unsuccessfully to make my body glide as lightly as a feather over this smooth, polished surface.

The walls are painted with stunning images which are protected from grubby, curious fingers by glass sheets. I make out Vajrayana deities, their consorts straddling them in delicious yab-yum, sexual union, depictions. They sprout all over the walls in fecund profusion, encircling the central figure of the immovable Buddha. Variously hued Taras, female bodhisattvas, dance bare-breasted across the walls, holding their hands in yogic mudras loaded with encrypted meaning. Their skeletal, ghoulish versions bespeak of the Tantric strain in Buddhist Vajrayana, where smashan sadhana, charnel ground practice, is a tool for cultivating detachment by keeping death close.

Warm-toned deities in yellows and ochres and reds follow pale ones in quick succession—their colours perhaps symbolic of their assigned realms, the many hells and heavens whose detailed delineations abound in Vajrayana texts and are articulated in intricate detail in thangkas, and which are, ultimately, indicative of our own states of mind and being. Hell is right here, in the mind that is restless, conflicted, harsh, as is heaven, in the state of being that is at peace, calm, friendly. In a day, how many times we oscillate between heaven and hell, our unaware mind blown in and out of these realms by storms raised by reactionary feelings run amok. The self then absorbs the colour of the emotion of the moment—blue in melancholy, red in passion, yellow in joy? The being with the still mind is also the one who is colourless, radiant in golden bronze—the Buddha, immovable at the centre of chaotic profusion.

The wall on the left has a sequence of yogis, some meditating, others holding slim rectangular manuscripts in their gracefully tapering fingers. These I suspect are the Indian siddhas, adepts who over a period of time helped establish Buddhism in Tibet. The biggest hero of them all, Padmasambhava, widely held to be the introducer of the Buddha's dharma in Tibet, gets to be gilded into a statue here. Others are on the painted panel, earnest and learned, teachers venturing into a faraway land. Many of them are wearing pointy orange-coloured caps with long ear flaps, something one may still find priests and pandits sporting in rural India.

Piled high before the bodhisattvas, gurus and deities are offerings in brass bowls, what would be prasad in a Hindu temple where it usually consists of sweets or fruit distributed to the congregation after a worship ritual. One would expect to find tsampa in the offering bowls here, which is barley flour favoured by Tibetans, or sculptures carved from thick yak butter and used as decorations and offerings during Tibetan festivals. Well, the bowls are instead stacked with boxes of chocolate cookies, pistachio and cashew biscuits, jars of jam and peanut butter, even toffees and sticks of chewing gum! The luridly coloured plastic packaging of this prasad comes as a shock to my eyes that have been wandering over the mellow tones of the wall paintings, which are gentle whispers compared to the loudness that lies offered before them. Suddenly, the world of advertising and marketing, of jazzed-up inane stuff no one really needs but is aggressively manipulated into buying, has invaded this other world where

beings exist solely to be compassionate, and where sex is a
metaphor for universal oneness.

Now that I have been jolted out of my reverie, I can perhaps
be a little irreverent? I imagine the yoginis getting off their
frozen-in-time copulatory straddles and extending delicate
fingers to sample a cookie! Or perhaps a siddha sagely
chomping on a piece of gum, his cap's side-flaps moving in
rhythm with the bovine movement of his jowls! I want to
laugh so hard that I am glad the lone lama breaks off his deep
chanting and turns to me.

'Where are you from?' he says. 'Delhi,' I answer, and he
almost gratefully slips into Hindi. 'What were you chanting?' I
ask him after making some perfunctory small talk. 'Oh, we
have different mantras and texts—this one is written by Guru
ji, you know Guru ji?' he says, using the Hindi honorific, 'ji'.
I respond, 'Yes I do. He is who Tibetans call Guru Rinpoche,
the Indian yogi Padmasambhava, who brought the dharma
to Tibet?' 'Yes, yes,' he nods, perhaps relieved that he
doesn't have to give me a summary of the history of Tibetan
Buddhism.

A pause, then he says suddenly, 'You know, there are so
many mantras we have to recite, by this teacher and that, but
they are all paths. Not one is the goal. Like you came here
from Delhi. You took one path, you could have taken an
entirely different path and still reached here, you know?'

He looks at me expectantly and I nod silently. Folding my
hands before him, I take my leave, breathing in the freedom
of relativity he has just shown me. There is this samsara, this
imperfect world of pulls and pressures and material successes
and failures, and embedded *into* all of this is the web of paths
that we need to uncover to come here, to Dharamsala, and
begin finding the truth about our selves. For is the bodhisattva
only here, in the Tsuglag Khang, painted on its walls,

established as statues? Or is he an evolutionary possibility available to each one of us?

Walking out of the darkened cave, the bright sun blinds my eyes.

Later that day, I drag a chair to the wide veranda in front of my room at the guesthouse. Clouds have been gathering for much of the morning, putting to rest the morning's promise of a sunny day. A chill has crept down the Dhauladhars astride the clouds, and I have drawn my grandmother's hand-woven shawl around me. The elfin Tenzin keeps me silent company from his perch by the wide windows behind me. I watch him draw red fir trees crowned with fluffy clouds that he colours a deep cerulean blue. After I have admired his drawing with appreciative noises, since we don't share a common spoken language, he runs in happily, eager to share his creation with his mother.

I continue sitting at the balcony, watching the play of the ever-moving clouds. Ever so often, they suddenly part and enable a glimpse of the clear blue sky underneath. The clouds of confusion that shift just for a moment to afford a peek at what our true nature is like—vast, open, free. That is what the lama in the temple did for me. The brief exchange catalysed a shift in perspective that was as spontaneous as it was perhaps serendipitous? I had spent the previous night in an unfamiliar bed, lonely and afraid, angry with myself for allowing fears and self-doubt to drain me of my joie de vivre.

Like an honest mirror, Dharamsala had shown up the inner confusion I had been determinedly ignoring, hoping ostrich-like it would go away if I didn't look up from the sands of unknowing. Dharamsala had forced my head out and up, blown away the sand from my eyes and knocked them open. There was nowhere to run, or hide. Here I was, waiting to experience the place, and Dharamsala had inaugurated our relationship by making me experience myself. As soon as I reached here, all the baggage I had brought with me came unstuck. The insecurity, lack of confidence, fear of being alone were strewn all about me like so much dirty laundry.

What else could I do but pick the pieces up, and set them free in the Dharamsala sky?

Dharamsala caused none of these conflicts; what it did was to bring me in sharp focus to myself such that I couldn't ignore the inner turmoil any longer. The cloud had burst, as it sometimes does over Dharamsala, drenching everything and everyone in unexpected wetness and fog. It had showered all over me too that morning, but with benedictions and blessings. Feet that moved on an unfamiliar path as if drawn by a magnetic current, a curiously serendipitous discovery, and then the treasure trove of a sacred sanctum with the wise lama within, who in a few words in broken Hindi showed me the core of the creative endeavour. A beam of light illuminating relativity, yet another aspect of the jewel of reality, of this created world.

'Just walk,' I tell myself as I begin wondering which way to go. 'Just walk, and who knows where you may reach?'

4

Wanderers

Apart from its literal translation as 'home of dharma', Dharams(h)ala also means a resting place for travellers. Across India, a dharamshala is a place that offers free or cheap lodging to pilgrims and peripatetic sadhus. You can arrive in a temple town or temple complex in any part of the country, and there will be rooms available with a mat on the floor to rest your worn-out body and simple food to appease your hunger. In a land where people travelled on foot for months on pilgrimage, dharamshalas were a necessity and building them a sure-shot route to gaining some quick good karma. Dharamshalas would at most times be chock-full of sadhus and lay pilgrims, and were no doubt hubs of religious discussion and instruction. In this day of millionaire gurus and swank resorts in the name of ashrams, one still finds people queuing before a dilapidated dharamshala in pilgrimage towns like Hardwar and Rishikesh, waiting to meet a sadhu of particular spiritual attainment who is passing through.

Dharamsala is also a dharamshala in this sense, a stopover on the spiritual highway, a caravanserai for those wandering in search of paths within, where you can safely set down your knapsack for the time being, and perhaps find a salve for blisters suffered on the demanding trek you have undertaken from old notions, and maybe your nation, to get here. There is nourishment to be had for that within you which is hungry for understanding, and there are guides who may help shine a light on the way ahead.

Thus Dharamsala is not only a refuge for the politically dispossessed, it is also a refuge for those wandering spirits who come here from all corners of the earth seeking truth, knowledge, and the holy grail of Buddhist students—nirvana. Over the decades, it has acquired a reputation as a place where guidance is available to all those interested in delving deeper into their selves, to understand the reality of existence. There has grown here a sangha, a community, of seekers of inner truth. It is fluid and less defined than the other sangha that has found its place in the Dharamsala sun, that of Tibetan refugees. For seekers wander in and out of this variable sangha according to their circumstances, financial resources, visa expiration dates and the value they place on the insights they find here.

Some come for a month or a year, time taken off to 'find themselves' before returning to, or embarking upon, the hurly-burly of a career. Some come back year after year, or as often as their life situations permit, to this dharamshala where they can rest from their whirlwind routines, rejuvenate their travel-weary selves with a dip into ancient wisdom, from which they can take back pearls and practices to make their daily lives more meaningful. Then there are those who stay on forever, who join the sangha in the most obvious sense by exchanging their jeans for monastic robes, and their cars, careers and homes for the vows and voluntary poverty of the novitiate monk and nun.

This multifaceted seekers' sangha of Dharamsala brings into the twenty-first century a tradition that extends far back into time when individuals began to wander away from established society and religion, and searched and researched into the many-hued world they encountered within themselves. Some found God in the image of themselves, others an immanent divinity, and yet others a vast void from whence arose creation. One of them found something quite unique—the cure for human suffering!

That young man was Siddhartha Gautama, prince-turned-wanderer, whose renunciation of family and aristocratic career and subsequent wandering mirrored many such journeys made before him, and held the seed of many more that would follow over the centuries. When Siddhartha left the privileged life that he had been born into and that had been carefully planned out for him, he was honouring his restive spirit by following an enduring convention of Indian spirituality—that of the sramana. Sramanas were seekers who existed on the fringes of society unbound by its rules, and wandered in 'search' of God, themselves, deeper realities—an inner seeking reflected in actual wandering.

Each one of us who is searching for meaning and depth is a modern-day sramana. This search often leads within, either through an external agent like a guru, or through one's own intuitive awareness. In our own ways, whether through meditation, yoga or positive action or through trying to live as consciously as we can, we are trying to experience quietude, balance and peace within, and simultaneously trying to manifest these in our living, relationships and work. I say 'trying' because this is the most difficult thing in the world. It is in this process of searching and travelling that we grow.

Dharamsala is the rare place that offers one the opportunity to be a seeker. It is where we can bring our ennui and expect some answers, some new directions. This rare prospect attracts seekers from all over the world. As they invariably turn towards the wisdom traditions of the east in their journeys, the example of Siddhartha Gautama surfaces as a possible roadmap to follow. Because the path he evolved is now enjoying a worldwide resurgence and is traversing new territories, the story of

Siddhartha and his subsequent life as the Buddha are fairly well-known. He thus emerges as a spiritual peer for the modern-day seeker. And Dharamsala is an important point of connection with Buddhist seeking in today's world.

One may wonder what connects the person who lived two and a half millennia ago to a twenty-first-century seeker. The elements of the quest—the questioning, the acknowledgement that something is amiss in one's regular life, the mental and emotional churning to find a way forward—are as true today as they were in Siddhartha's or any other time. Also, if we look at Siddhartha's life without automatically categorizing it as 'history', we find how it could have easily unfolded in New Delhi or New York circa twenty-first century, rather than Kapilavastu circa sixth century BCE.

The intense young Siddhartha lived in an age not unlike our own. Not only because trade and commerce flourished, but also because there arose an attitude of questioning the dominant religion, Vedic Hinduism, which had degenerated into a maze of intricate rituals that the priestly class of Brahmins claimed only they could decipher. Like the seekers of today who are disenchanted with established religions and feel that these have for the most part lost their mystical moorings, and are thus unable to connect with them at the deepest levels, serious spiritual seekers who abounded in the India of sixth century BCE felt Vedic Hinduism had nothing to offer them in terms of either practices or a meaningful world view.

This hunger for spiritual experience was happening at a time of immense prosperity, much like today when the most materially affluent societies are also fertile ground for internal questioning and ferment. Siddhartha's society was a rich agrarian one. And it was perhaps the abundance of wealth and the 'good life' that prompted many young people to delve into what lay beyond the material world. Prosperity frees minds of survival concerns, enabling individuals to explore and evolve other aspects of their potential.

There started in the seventh century BCE a reform movement that began adopting new paths towards spiritual goals and examining those that had till then existed at the periphery of religion. In our times too, there has occurred a great hunger for the spiritual among the predominantly materialistic societies of the west, and the twentieth century particularly has seen a movement towards eastern wisdom traditions aimed at exploring self and reality in ways that dominant established religions do not.

By the time Siddhartha was born, this movement had become widespread and powerful and was increasingly engaging in fierce debates and public disputations with ritualistic religion. It is possible that these voices had an impact on and attracted Siddhartha as a young prince.

At sixteen, Siddhartha was married to Yashodhara, a princess of great beauty. It is said that he lived a life of indulgence; nights of revelry flowed into days filled with all kinds of pleasures. Perfumed, oiled, clothed in the most expensive of silks, Siddhartha sported and hunted, patronized artists and made love. By material standards, ancient or modern, young Siddhartha had it all.

And then . . . what?

By the time he was twenty-nine, the prince began to wonder whether this was all there was to life. He began looking around for avenues to deepen and engage his mind. An awakening probably occurred, which brought him the realization of the untapped potential that lay within him. Expected to live a nobleman's life, Siddhartha began to acknowledge his own need to move beyond it.

As his mind ripened in contemplation, it became necessary to cast away the identity that bound him to constructs he had begun to see as obstructions to his inner exploration. The titles afforded him by birth and relationships—nobleman, son of a chieftain, husband and father—were beginning to feel like unnecessary, cumbersome bonds that tied him to a particular personality and precluded the possibility of something more, something beyond.

Walking out of his marital home one night, he left behind his beloved wife and newborn son, along with all the riches and comforts that had gradually come to mean nothing to the young seeker. With his sword he cut away his hair and along with it his identity as Siddhartha Gautama. He gave away his jewels and valuable clothes and changed into the mud-coloured robes of a sramana.

A penniless, possessionless wanderer now, he hit the road on the adventure that would change him forever, that would eventually lead to an ineffable experience under a tree in a nondescript town in east India called Bodhgaya.

As I look at the wanderers on the streets of Dharamsala, young and intense and others who are older and equally intense, who have arrived here driven by an urge to know and seek, I cannot but think of them as latter-day Siddharthas. Many come from materially abundant homes and societies as did Siddhartha, often with university education and careers that promise even more abundance. Yet they cannot wish away their itchy feet that want to go find a purpose greater than earning more and spending more, that come from wanting to know why a climbing career and possessions graph do not automatically translate into greater happiness.

It is not only consumerist materialism that causes this wanderlust. Once you have begun feeling restless and discontented, you look around for answers to your ennui in your culture, among your peers. And what do you find? With a rational-scientific world view having become the primary influence on how people live their lives, the avenues available to the angst-ridden seeker of deeper realities have become limited. Established religion has suffered greatly under the scientific-rationalist onslaught, and the comfort of unquestioning faith is simply not available to many a modern mind. For in the world view that prevails, material reality is the *only* reality and everything that even hints at an alternative view of human consciousness and the possibility of its evolution is looked upon with suspicion and dismissed as belonging to that much-maligned realm of 'religion'.

Where do you turn in these circumstances? To the psychiatrist who will analyse your ennui as a 'problem' and try to patch you up and fit you back into your society, or to the pseudo 'gooroo' who will demand a suspension of your logical mind and a deferential following of his designer brand of truth? Or do you set off, looking, seeking, searching, sramana-like into the world, guided by a map of places and people to turn to in your wanderings, made by those who felt the itch before you?

The quests that have brought these seekers to Dharamsala are strands that radiate out from a web of sacredness that is at once primal and new, and thus timeless, and is woven out of innumerable inner journeys and their insights and realizations. This web is not limited to a particular geographical area or to a certain set of people—at the fundamental human level, it binds us all. When we feel the urge to know the truth of life, when we begin to stir from the slumber into which we are born, the node we occupy on this web becomes activated. We begin to throb with the thirst to know, and become sensitive to the messages being transmitted over the web. Thus begins a quest that is as old as the history of humanity, and when it awakens within us, it is with a latent, unspoken memory from the collective unconscious of all those who have gone before.

In this worldwide web of sacredness, there has come into being a golden chain of the seekers of Dharamsala. When wanderers return to their homelands, they go bearing in the folds of their well-worn clothes the lingering aroma of the place, and in their open hearts and minds the imprint of the wisdom they received here. They then become introducers of Dharamsala, like the explorers of yore who encountered new lands and carried back with them stories and specimens of flora and fauna and silks and spices, along with maps that detailed the sea and land routes they followed to get there. Similarly, the seekers of Dharamsala carry back with them the jewels of insight, which they scatter along the way to mark out their path so that kindred spirits can follow the trail in future.

In this way the chain forms, one link leading into another, one journey feeding, overlapping, others that start from where it left off, with older seekers guiding their spiritual compatriots to places and traditions that have been significant to their own quests.

The golden chain of westerners, especially Americans, in Dharamsala can be traced to a visit by the celebrated Catholic monk Thomas Merton, in 1968. Merton was an earnest seeker of truth who was eager to make his spiritual journey flow beyond the confines of his own religious tradition. As he began to study eastern wisdom traditions such as Zen and Taoism, he felt such a strong affinity with them that he described his maiden trip to Asia as 'a homecoming'.

These were the early days of Tibetan Buddhism's encounter with a larger world that knew next to nothing about it. Zen was the preferred form of Buddhism in the west at this point, having been popularized by pioneering scholars such as D.T. Suzuki and the writings of the Beat Generation poets. There was little awareness of the Buddhism of Tibet, which was regarded as magical and ritualistic. Merton arrived in Dharamsala with this prevalent misconception, and initially even refused to meet the Dalai Lama whom he thought to be nothing more than a bureaucrat.

What happened next is narrated by Jeffery Paine in his book *Re-enchantment: Tibetan Buddhism Comes to the West* (W.W. Norton & Company, New York, 2004). During an early morning photographic expedition in Dharamsala, Merton ran into Sonam Kazi, the Dalai Lama's official translator at the time. What followed was a conversation that changed the way Merton viewed Tibetan Buddhism. He received just a glimpse into its depth, but it was sufficient to whet his appetite for more.

Merton sought out Chatral Rinpoche, a lama whom most avoided because of his unpredictable behaviour—the kind that yogis often employ to separate the grain from the chaff, the serious seeker from the thrill-seeker. The two got along famously and, by the end of their meeting, Merton entreated him to teach him advanced practices of the tradition. Chatral Rinpoche asked him to do the groundwork first—prostrations, mantra recitations and so on in units of a hundred thousand— and Merton readily agreed to devote a year of his life to get this over with in order to move on to more advanced practices.

Jeffery Paine deduces that Merton was really interested in the methods of Tibetan Buddhism that were practical ways of deepening one's spiritual practice. Merton was beginning to become acquainted with concepts that formed the core of Tibet's Buddhism, such as the bodhisattva ideal (working for enlightenment not for oneself but to help all sentient beings), tonglin (taking on the suffering of others) and dzogchen (holding that one's nature is innately perfect—we are already the Buddha we wish to be, we just need to realize it). These pointed to the highest ideals that a practitioner or indeed a spiritual tradition could aspire to. Not surprisingly, Merton became exceedingly excited about Tibetan Buddhism and even fantasized about returning to Dharamsala to devote the rest of his life to its study.

Merton's momentous encounter with Tibetan Buddhism in Dharamsala could not be complete without an acquaintance with the biggest lama of all—the Dalai Lama. Merton confessed that his real aim was to further his knowledge of the step-by-step inner development outlined in Tibetan Buddhist practice. The Dalai Lama readily agreed and, descending from his seat, squatted on the floor to demonstrate to Merton the various postures needed during practice. He went on to instruct Merton in meditation and other basic techniques he needed to get along with his practice.

For Merton, his Dharamsala trip was turning out to be quite a breakthrough. He felt he had discovered in Tibetan Buddhism a hitherto unknown form of mysticism with a meticulously charted path to inner growth. This was what was needed to revitalize the spirituality of the west, which Merton felt had lost its purity and meaning in the increasingly materialistic environs it found itself grappling with. In his notebook, published posthumously as The Asian Journals in 1973, Merton wrote with unconcealed elation about what we could call his serendipitous discovery, 'The Tibetan Buddhists are the only ones at present who have a really large number of people who have attained to extraordinary heights in meditation and contemplation.'

Merton however could not act on his intention of devoting

himself to a deep study of Tibetan Buddhism—he died just a few weeks after leaving Dharamsala, electrocuted in a freak accident in Thailand. But his enthusiasm about Dharamsala's lamas and the promise the place held for the modern seeker became widely known with the posthumous publication of his diaries from this, the last great journey of his life. It stirred enough interest in his homeland and among those who considered him a spiritual peer to begin a gradual trickle of visitors to Dharamsala.

Walking through Dharamsala's lanes, I observe with some amazement the diverse collection of humanity that has gathered into its folds. The seekers around me seem to represent almost every corner and continent of the globe. Yet there is something familiar about them, a commonality that unites them despite the obvious differences of physical appearance and language and cultural identity. That, I feel, is the light of a shared purpose of inner seeking and transformation that glows within them and balances their dissimilarities to draw them together in this sangha of Dharamsala.

I glance sideways at the tall man walking beside me. His strides are easy and sure from roaming these streets for twenty years. In this gathering dusk, his lama's robes have erased any angular edges from his form, so that he appears an ambiguous floating cloud of maroon. His expressive hands with their tapering fingers are tucked into his roomy shawl, a parting gift from a beloved teacher, further accentuating the feeling of formlessness around him.

Right at this moment, he is looking back at me, his sparkling blue eyes peering quizzically from behind his round spectacles. He has just asked me about my interest in Buddhism and my own spiritual quest, and I need a moment to catch my breath from the steep climb and gather my thoughts into something pithy and intelligent. I have been asked both these questions often enough, so one would assume I would have a standard response ready at the tip of my tongue. Not quite so, for each time I need to answer them something new has happened and my responses must be reconfigured accordingly.

We have recently emerged from the Tsuglag Khang complex where, over a couple of hours, this American lama has fold by fold unveiled before me the tapestry of his spiritual life. I barely know him, yet here we are in a room whose wide windows open to the arch of the sky, chatting about that part of life which is the most difficult to lay bare before any other except perhaps one's spiritual guide. Anywhere else, I would hesitate before assuming this intimacy with anyone. In Dharamsala, it is what comes most naturally. Here when two strangers meet, they seem to fall effortlessly into conversations about their personal journeys, how they got here, their guide lamas, their practice problems and, at times, the practical issues of cheap yet decent accommodation and restaurants whose food is least likely to give you stomach-cramping dysentery. Here too the veterans will be looked upon as providers of information, of the inner and outer maps needed to get around Dharamsala.

This American lama is a Dharamsala seer, a veritable mapmaker of landscapes within and without, I think as I listen to his story.

Tenzin Choerab, as he is now called, started life as an American kid oddly interested in meditation. When other children his age were idolizing baseball players or rock stars, he was pinning a poster in his room that had 'meditation' emblazoned across it. His intent must have been keen enough for, while attending college at Berkeley University, California, he found he had a roommate who meditated. The young philosophy student finally made a beginning by learning to focus on a point between the eyebrows.

It was the 1950s, and slowly and surely angst was setting in among the young in the US. After the Second World War, the economy had revved up and its ever-expanding girth and rapacious appetite had meant greater prosperity for American citizens. The Baby Boomers did not have to grapple with the economic hardships their parents had faced. What this generation craved was meaning, substance, depth. Our young student's yearning for something so far removed from his familiar milieu, at a time when spiritual practices of the east were still not understood in the west, shows how the young were looking beyond their culture and continent for solutions to what they experienced as the overwhelming meaninglessness of life.

It was still decades before our young man would venture into Dharamsala. He did make it to India though, in 1958, and joined a guru and his disciples on a pilgrimage to Amarnath, the natural ice lingam Shiva cave-shrine in the Himalayas. Afterwards, he accompanied the group back to the guru's village in Gujarat, where they were instructed in the nuts and bolts of meditation.

As the lama before me speaks, I imagine the power of such a trip for the young American student. It must have seemed several dimensions of reality removed from the world he had come from. The discrepancies of place, geography and culture were only outer manifestations of the inner fracture the young man must have felt, between two very different ways of thinking and perceiving the possibilities and potential of life.

This guru, whatever may have been his level of spiritual accomplishment, was nothing like any teacher the young man had ever encountered. The guru lived austerely, his simplicity made possible by a controlled will that realized that outer accumulation often results in, and from, inner confusion. Moreover, he was one in a long line of thinkers that placed the goal and success of life in self-realization, and who had redrawn centuries ago the parameters of human life around spiritual advancement rather than material success.

It was a way of thinking in diametric opposition to all that the young American had been taught to believe life was and could be. Each day he spent in the ashram he learnt the value of watching the mind rather than allowing its movements to take over. He realized he didn't really need too many 'things' to live. His wants could be whittled down to the basics—food to sustain his body rather than cater to his taste buds, a pair of clothes he washed and wore, a mat to sleep on. Anything more seemed unnecessary. He pitched in with the ashram chores, swept and cleaned and cooked and washed. As the days wore on, he felt a dropping away of the baggage he realized he had been carrying only when he felt it dissolving. Gosh, there had been so much of it! Expectations, ambition, likes, dislikes . . .

Then, the time came for the young man to leave this sanctuary and venture back into the world he had left behind. Light years seemed to have passed. He looked upon everything with new eyes, and wondered whether his Indian training could survive the million degrees that separated dusty Gujarat from urban California.

Eventually, as human beings are wont to, he readjusted to his environment. But something had fundamentally changed in him that couldn't, wouldn't, go *back* to what it had been before he had set out. The sramana spirit now inhabited a niche in his being and surfaced occasionally to enable him to choose paths that would not have occurred to him otherwise.

The returned wanderer felt a strong disconnect with his philosophy course at university. What he was looking for was an answer to the question that had been ringing in him long before he went to India, a question that grew out of his ennui but went beyond it. It was the classic query that had launched many ships into the dark, stormy waters of inner questing— that echoed in our young man's ears as it had in countless others of a like spirit before him.

'Who am I?'

He had expected the philosophy course to be the closest to what his culture had to offer in response to this ancient human cry. What he found was a course of study entangled in structures and constructs, whatever wisdom it might have had to offer buried under dead, heavy theories that didn't connect at all with the living, breathing human being. The student came to a decision as he completed his major—instead of looking for signs of life in a dead tradition, he would tend to the living. He would study medicine.

So he enrolled in medical school. He also met a warm, loving woman and they were married as soon as he graduated. He was happy and, at last, fulfilled. He didn't feel the itch any more, and he felt—this is it!

Subdued for the moment, his sramana spirit watched and waited. The world had never satisfied anyone, not for long at any rate. And so it bided its time until the moment came for it to assert itself once more.

The lama grows quiet. His ginger tea lies before him, cold and ignored. He shivers and draws his shawl closer around him. I wait for him to pick up the thread once more.

The life he and his wife made for themselves was comfortable and filled with the light of love. He had become interested in the Buddha's dharma, and had begun a course of study with a Tibetan teacher. This teacher had spent several years meditating in the mountains above Dharamsala and was the first link in the chain that would eventually lead this American here.

As time turned, so did circumstances. What had been carefully woven unravelled. His wife was diagnosed with cancer to which she eventually succumbed. Sad and bereft, he instinctively turned towards the culture where he had once been unconditionally happy. His sramana spirit awoke and he experienced the itch as he had never felt it before. For now, it came with the knowledge of impending death, of an experience of chaos and void that gave it an edge of urgency. He felt the first noble truth, the inevitability of suffering, so keenly in his bones that he knew the second, third and fourth noble truths that told how to deal with it would also be equally and resoundingly true.

He needed to go to India. He needed to know more.

As this thought formed, the doctor came to know of a request made by the Dalai Lama to western physicians. It was the mid-1980s, and there was beginning a series of dialogues aiming to bring about a synthesis of Buddhism with modern science, in which the Dalai Lama represented the former. He now wished to see whether the ancient Tibetan system of medicine could be integrated with the western one to form a technique of health care that combined the gentleness and holistic vision of the former with the vigour and knowledge of the latter. What a perfect coincidence, thought the doctor as he gladly volunteered for the project.

The lapsed sramana left his job as assistant professor of medicine at a reputed university and travelled to India once again. Only this time, he headed straight to Dharamsala, where the headquarters of most things Tibetan, including medicine, were located.

From then on, his life followed a twin track of seva (service) and study, which would ultimately merge into one. He began work on the project at the Men–Tsee–Khang, the Tibetan medicine centre in McLeodganj, and simultaneously began studying the dharma in earnest. As the harsh winters rolled into cool summers and the snows on the Dhauladhars melted and formed again and again, the sramana quietly followed the cycles of meditation retreats and study prescribed by his teachers.

Dharamsala became his cave, his world shrunk to its periphery. It wasn't a solitary cave though, for his work had transplanted him right in the midst of the Tibetan sangha and, as time passed, he became somewhat of an elder in the other sangha of Dharamsala, that of seekers. The warmth of connection was thus not lost; in fact it was of the essence to an important aspect of his study of Tibetan Buddhism—the learning of a love that was not bound to any individual identity and so flowed everywhere. A love that could never again be lost, simply because it had nothing to lose.

The blue eyes are serene as they turn from the sky towards me. 'I have loved and been loved greatly. My mother was an exceptional woman, and so was my wife. Both women died young, but the love never dies. It has expanded astronomically,' he says, and his eyes expand to take into them the sweep of the sky, the mountains, the whole earth. 'The quality of love is different. There are no strings for anyone, not even oneself, it is much more unconditional. There are fewer expectations of people, of the love. The power of love is greater, isn't it, if you don't expect anything back?'

I nod silently, trying to feel the great big love this man has learnt here, where he has no one, and yet, everyone. With a mind twisted into wanting love for love, that feels cheated if love felt is not returned in equal measure, that has prettified love and tied it up in satin bows and smothered it in chocolate, I try to understand this love so free, so far, but somehow so familiar, like the long-forgotten taste of mother's milk.

'Love is deliberately cultivated in Mahayana Buddhism so that it goes out to all beings, to alleviate their suffering. That kind of love becomes much more powerful,' he says. From suffering to suffering he has travelled, from struggling with his own to taking upon himself all of creation's. When you learn to love like that, what else is there to learn? I would have gladly walked away at this point, my heart full, but there was another bend in the road the lama wished to take me to.

Over the years, the Dalai Lama became one of his teachers and would pitch in with suggestions on directions to take in his study. 'I would consult him on whether I could go for a particular retreat, and he would check for a moment and then tell me—' 'Check with what?' I ask, interrupting him in my curiosity. He smiles, and says, 'With his inner eye. I feel he has always been able to read my mind.'

Perhaps intuiting his state of preparedness, the Dalai Lama readily agreed to what the sramana requested next. After a three-year retreat, the sramana felt it was time to wholly commit himself to his spiritual adventure. Though he had lived an ascetic's life ever since his arrival in Dharamsala, he now felt ripe for formal ordination into the Buddha's sangha.

Much to his amazement, and great delight, the Dalai Lama invited him to Bodhgaya, the site of the Buddha's illumination, to receive his vows. To be ordained into the sangha at the very place where it all started was simply too good to be true. The memory makes his eyes sparkle with the intensity of stars in the Dharamsala sky on a cloudless, fogless night.

That was two years ago. Life as Tenzin Choerab, the name he received during his ordination, has been pretty much like what it was before. Dharma study and working on an integrative healing paradigm are the twin poles of the axis upon which his life in Dharamsala turns. One melds into another, as he attempts to bring aspects of his spiritual experience like meditation into play in his work as healer of body, mind and emotions.

Although I know it is the wrong question for a monk who is attempting to efface the ego-self, I ask it anyway. 'How far do you think you have come, on this journey that began all those years ago as a kid interested in meditation?'

He doesn't answer right away. Perhaps he is worried about getting home in the dark, for he has a long way to walk and has tarried here with me too long. Or perhaps he is struck as we sometimes are when something is suddenly pointed out to us, by how far he really has come, to be able to be here in this chair and talk about all that he has been. I am overwhelmed by his journey; he isn't. 'I haven't learned much,' he says thoughtfully. 'I'm just scratching the surface.'

Later that night, I look at the stars from my balcony and think of the brightness that glowed from within the lama's eyes. As if on cue, another pair of bright eyes materializes before me, reminding me of the easy-to-find everyday magic of my life here in Dharamsala. Picking the twinkle-eyed little Tenzin on to my lap, I think of the other Tenzin I have spent the evening with. One among so many wanderers who halt their caravans and pitch their tents in this oasis of dharma. Some move on, hustled by their desires and needs, or like Thomas Merton, into the mouth of kala, time that eventually devours all. Others stay, like Tenzin Choerab. And find how unbelievably light being really is, when there is nothing to hold on to, not people, not relationships, not even your name. Neither your self. Perhaps there is no permanent self, after all?

Isn't it obvious in the way we move from one 'self' to another? Not in the sense of dying and then being reborn as a different person, but right here in this very space between birth and death. We go through so many cycles of being and becoming. As Tenzin Choerab did, from doctor to healer, from successful professional to impoverished wanderer, from one great love to another, greater love. Cycles that may encircle one another and are inextricably intertwined, but don't seem to afford any one foothold to place your particular personhood. As the sramanas wondered, 'Who am I?' at this instant I wonder, 'Where exactly in this muddle of circles and cycles, is "I"?'

I think about the vast, impersonal, un-individual, non-self way the lama has learnt to love. A love that is unbound by the contours of self and other, that flows everywhere like this night wind that is upon my face.

Little Tenzin is curled in my lap, asleep. His mother comes to get him, and I carefully hand him over. She smiles gently at her sleeping child. I smile with her, at her.

5

The Presence

The twin icons of Tibetan identity-in-exile in Dharamsala—the residence of the Dalai Lama and the Tsuglag Khang—stand next to one another atop the crest of a mountain. Midway down this mountain runs a path that hugs the base of these structures, encircling them in an embrace made warm and sacred with countless prayer flags, prayer wheels and mani stones whose hardness is etched with the beloved mantra of the Tibetans—Om mani padme hum. This path is the new Lingkhor, the circumambulation whose original makes its way around the Dalai Lama's old home, the Potala Palace in Lhasa. Like so many monastic, cultural and social institutions of old Tibet, the Lingkhor has also found its echo in the ground of Dharamsala.

'It is a great morning walk,' Pema the guesthouse caretaker tells me when I ask him about the sacred circuit. 'It is not too steep either, so you won't have much trouble walking.' He has obviously little confidence in my mountain-walking abilities. But it has been a few days since I began gadding about Dharamsala, and the body is finally showing signs of adaptation to slopes and steepness. 'Oh, I'm sure I'll manage,' I mutter dourly and then can't help breaking into a smile, for puckish little Tenzin has chosen this moment to giggle at me from behind his father's legs.

Father and son offer to point the Lingkhor out to me on their way to the little one's school. We set out on a strange morning when a stronger-than-usual sun is scorching grey clouds into fiery orange. We are joined by Tenzin's little classmates and other schoolchildren dressed in the bright blue uniform of the Tibetan Children's Village. As we near the branch in the road where they must continue straight ahead and I need to turn, Pema points out the way for me to go as he shepherds his untidy herd of little ones. Their laughter and chatter is audible in the early morning quiet for a long time after they disappear from view.

The Lingkhor appears as a branch-off from the main road, the tar and concrete of which disappears into the smaller, narrower way paved over with stones. On my right the rock face is freshly washed with snowy lime. A little ahead, a man with a can of whitewash is liberally splashing it on to mark the sacred route.

Almost instantly, the eye is drawn to masses of smooth stones and shiny slates of all shapes and sizes that line the path at waist-height. They are engraved with the mani mantra, and are coloured in the elemental colours of blue, white, red, green and yellow. Water, space, fire, earth, ether, which coalesce to give shape and form to the physical world. My eyes follow the letters of the unfamiliar script of the mantra, repeated over and over, indecipherable yet unexpectedly familiar in its Sanskrit-like appearance. I become conscious of a fragrance creeping into the air, of pine mixed with incense, from who knows where? The body falls into a quiet rhythm, legs in tune with heart in tune with Om-ma-ni-pad-me-hummmm . . .

I sense this mantra under every breath on the path. Mostly older Tibetans are out at this time, while the younger ones are probably setting out on other paths to schools, offices, businesses, shops. Almost everyone on the Lingkhor carries a prayer wheel in one hand and a rosary in the other, the one sending out with each rotation the mantra hidden in its heart into the Dharamsala air, the other turning bead by bead with every whisper of the mantra upon the person's breath. The progress is slow and painful for some who hobble along with a cane for support, placing one foot cautiously before the other.

As the path curves around the mountain, I come upon a tiny makeshift room. Mani stones are scattered about the entrance, their paint drying in the sun. Inside, an engraver is absorbed in his work, carving the curvy letters of the mantra upon rough stone surface. He notices me, his eyes looking up for a brief moment before going back to the unbroken rhythm his hands have kept up through the distraction. He is obviously used to such intrusions from curious passers-by and is well practised in ignoring them. I look around at his handiwork that is at various stages of progression, and pick up one round river stone with just the syllable 'Hum' carved upon it in Tibetan.

'How much for this?' 'Not for sale to you,' he says gruffly. 'Commissioned by someone?' I guess. He nods, and with a sweep of his arm indicates all the stones that have been commissioned and therefore aren't available to me. They form the bulk of his work.

I look around, fascinated by the stone–mantra interface. Seed sounds pregnant with energy and meaning have sprouted among these stones, some from riverbeds, others from mountainsides. The mani mantra is many-layered in meaning as well as functionality, ranging from holding in it the mystical core of Tibetan Vajrayana to being the simple phrase repeated several thousand times to invoke the blessings, and good karma for future births, from the bodhisattva Avalokiteshwara. Though it has been translated rather simplistically as 'Om, the jewel in the lotus', it actually refers to a coming together of

method (mani) and wisdom (padme) to transform (hum) the
ordinary body, speech and mind of the practitioner into that
of a Buddha. As the mantra travelled from India to Tibet, the
sharp Sanskrit mellowed upon Tibetan tongues. So what you
now hear muttered under breath on the Lingkhor is 'Om mani
peme hung' as supplicating eyes turn above, not to imaginary
heavens populated by celestial deities, but towards the
residence of he who is considered the living bodhisattva of
our times.

At the engraver's, I select a small, flat, four-sided pebble
with just the first syllable, Om, scratched upon it. Holding it
in the folds of my fist, I walk on.

Several times in Dharamsala, I am reminded of the strands
that bind Tibet, in culture and spirit, to India. This is but to be
expected, since the dharma travelled from here and subsequently
became the core around which Tibet erected not only its
religion but also its society, language, script, its identity. Of
course this identity is uniquely Tibetan, but when I come
upon familiar flavours, like the form of the script, I cannot
help but feel a kinship that is close and familial, like cousins
made aloof by distance-induced amnesia.

The very idea of clockwise circumambulation of a sacred
site, which is what we are doing here on the Lingkhor, is a
connecting point between the amnesiac cousins. Called
'pradakshina' in Sanskrit and 'kora' in Tibetan, it means drawing
a full circle around the deity with one's self, carrying one's
prayers in one's being. Like the flame that is waved around
the deity during ritual worship, in circumambulation we *are*
the flames, kindling in our being the benediction we associate
with the deity. Whilst the deity in Indian temples is the idol
in the womb of the sanctum, on the Lingkhor it is a human
being who has in effect been cast out of his sanctum, and who
found a new home here in Dharamsala from where his

sacredness has wafted forth anew.

Resting at the rain shelter in the middle of the Lingkhor, where a million prayer wheels turn (well, maybe not so many but they seem so), and where I finally find the source of the perfumed air in large vats of glowing juniper incense, I think of a small kora parable embedded in a Tibetan writer's short story of the same name ('Kora' [Full Circle], by Tenzin Tsundue).

A fly sat on a crumb of cow dung being carried away by the rainwater flowing down the street. The streamlet took it to the end of the village where a stupa stood. The streamlet then went around the holy structure taking the fly on a circumambulation and finally joined into a nearby tributary. The fly was born into a human being in its next life, blessed with an opportunity to hear the words of the Buddha. Thus a scripture says.

Only, it is not a stupa built around the bones of the Buddha that we encircle, but a man who claims to be as human as all of us. His presence here in Dharamsala has sanctified the place into a kind of modern tirtha, pilgrimage, where pilgrims of all nationalities and persuasions gather to be around him so that perhaps they too can touch the hem of the robe of free-flowing joy and compassion that seems to billow about him at all times.

The Lingkhor lets me out right in front of the twin entrances to the Tsuglag Khang and the Dalai Lama's residence.

Across the globe, the word 'Dharamsala' inspires an instant connection with the Dalai Lama. The moment it was allotted as his temporary home in exile in India, this nondescript Himalayan village began its ascent on the world map of sites of spiritual significance. It didn't happen overnight but gradually, like the Dalai Lama's own rise as lovable guru-philosopher-hopegiver in the world population's hearts and minds. As representative of a culture that was all but expected to fall into immediate decline, and from a part of the world that the average world citizen had never heard of, the Dalai Lama didn't have much going for him when he set out to make the case for Tibet in the world arena. Today, a Nobel Peace Prize and an ever-growing global following later, not many among the general news-reading public can claim not to have heard of him.

When the Dalai Lama fled to India in 1959, he was the dispossessed ruler of a secluded mountain region that occupied the place of myth and fantasy in popular imagination. It was the Shangri-La of the east, and accounts by explorers true (Alexandra David-Neel) and false (M. Helena Blavatsky) had reinforced this magical image. Little did anyone know that this embattled land littered with monasteries and temples and ruled by monk-kings was also where a powerful tradition of spiritual transformation had been preserved and had thrived through the presence of a large community of teachers and practitioners. Tibetan Buddhism, as Thomas Merton discovered, was not about ritual, magic or even religion as commonly understood. Its path of systematic self-transformation, from flawed human to perfected Buddha, was the real jewel in the lotus that had somehow survived in the muck of the world.

When the Dalai Lama left Tibet, so did several reincarnate Rinpoches, teachers, and old texts with commentaries in Sanskrit and Tibetan. A giant bodhi tree of tradition had been uprooted, and its seeds desperately sought ground to grow new roots in, so that the forces of destruction could be trumped by the assertion of inevitable continuity, and the wheel of wisdom set in motion by the Buddha could continue its rotation. Many of them found this opportunity in Dharamsala.

Along with a refuge, Dharamsala provided a launch pad for the dharma to spread its wings and fly to distant lands. In an odd way, exile became the impetus that propelled Tibet's Buddhism into the modern age. The event that caused immense hardship and heartbreak to the Tibetan sangha was paradoxically also the hand that uncorked the bottle and let the genie out. For a long time, since the middle of the seventh century when it had arrived upon the desolate plateau, the dharma had remained locked within the kingdom's impenetrable borders. It was an isolation that proved to be nourishing as it facilitated the unimpeded development of a uniquely Tibetan strain of the Buddha's dharma, perfected through the Buddha's preferred method of growth—self-trial and experimentation.

As the world stepped into the twentieth century, it had few such untouched oases. Tibet too was at last forced to acknowledge the world beyond the Himalayas, beyond the tableland on which it was perched. It was a world that was being rapidly changed by wars and revolutions. Old powers were deposed, new ones enthroned. Entire ways of life were lost forever. New ideologies liberated the masses, and then shackled them anew. Religion lost its meaning, God lost his. There was only one certainty in this new world, and that was Change. Fast, furious, constant. It was a modern worldwide manifestation of the ancient Buddhist truth—nothing is fixed, nothing is permanent.

These winds of change forced Tibet's doors apart and let themselves in. The Tibetans were blown out of their cloister-like plateau and scattered all over the world. That which was secreted away was now flung out in the open. If one is to believe an eighth-century Tibetan prophecy attributed to Padmasambhava, things were actually going according to plan. 'When the iron eagle flies and horses run on wheels . . . the dharma will go to the land of the red man,' the yogi had reportedly prophesied. In the twentieth century, there were aeroplanes in the sky and cars on the roads. It was indeed time for the Tibetans to emerge from their splendid isolation and go forth into the world.

How this was done can best be described as a saga of extraordinary adaptability. The shock of modernity could well have wiped out the ancient tradition, had its purveyors not shown great courage and openness towards the unfamiliar. The Dalai Lama, and several teachers who travelled to the west (the land of the 'red man' of the prophecy) in those early years such as Lama Yeshe, Chogyam Trungpa, the sixteenth Karmapa, among others, were faced with the dilemma of explaining themselves to cultures so alien to theirs that they could well have come from the moon. Each did it in a different way, using different modus operandi. They developed the vocabulary to speak to the west by understanding their mores, morals and manners, as well as their psychology, medicine and science. And as they were introduced to these remarkable people who could literally make happiness out of nothing, more and more in the west became interested in the dharma.

Of all Tibetan teachers, the Dalai Lama is perhaps the most charismatic and widely known. The 1989 Nobel Peace Prize as also the international availability and popularity of books compiled of his thoughts and teachings may be the most obvious reasons. I also feel it is because he manages to be happy despite heavy odds. In an era of growing cynicism, when dissent and protest have become synonymous with violence, the Dalai Lama has stood firmly by a peaceful freedom struggle.

What's more, he refuses to hate or badmouth the enemy, or even give in to language that divides the world into 'good' and 'evil'. Where we have come to expect nothing better from politicians than self-serving rhetoric, the Dalai Lama's daily prayer is: 'For as long as space endures,/ And for as long as living beings remain,/ Until then may I too abide,/ To dispel the misery of the world.' Where we can't dream of any version of happiness unconnected with material goodies and high-paying jobs and lovers and relationships, the Dalai Lama *is* happy sans all these and more. Indeed, he has lost home, country, much of his immediate family and many from the larger family that includes all Tibetans, and has seen all that was the most sacred and dear to him reduced to rubble. He knows that there is a very real chance that he may never lay eyes upon the mountains that circle Lhasa ever again, in this lifetime at least. Yet, he smiles, and exudes a genuine love and concern for all those he comes across—bellboys in hotels, elevator operators, fundraiser organizers, new refugees from Tibet, politicians, Hollywood idols . . .

While the main motivation for the Dalai Lama's visits abroad may have been to raise awareness about Tibet, the widespread interest that slowly arose in Tibetan Buddhism ensured that a lot of his time was also spent speaking of the dharma and giving teachings. The Dalai Lama himself repeatedly emphasizes universal human values of compassion, a warm heart and responsibility towards the well-being of the earth and all its creatures. He places these values over and above religiosity of any kind. There is no sense *being* a Buddhist, he has asserted, but in becoming a good, kind human being. This has been his message to those who come to him desirous of converting to Buddhism, star-crossed with its potential for changing their lives. The Dalai Lama gently points out that it is ultimately important to get the essence and, once that happens, it does not really matter if the outer form is labelled 'Christian', 'Jew', 'Muslim', 'Hindu' or 'Buddhist'.

You may attribute the devotion of the Tibetans flicking their rosaries along the Lingkhor towards the Dalai Lama to cultural conditioning, blind faith, what have you. But even one as me, who has no grounding in Tibetan Buddhism, can feel the power this person exudes that is connective, integrative, kindly and benevolent. With an expansive laugh, he includes an entire room, an entire auditorium into a circle of love where we are one, human beings all, seeking the same things, part of the one vast weave of life.

There is an air of temporariness about the temple of Tsuglag Khang and the Dalai Lama's residence in Dharamsala. Perhaps it's the way everything seems hastily put together. It is evident the builders were not out to build monuments or palaces, just something practical and appropriate to house the sacred— idols, thangkas, the man.

The functionality of his residence underlines a hope of return, that this doesn't need to be more than a provisional structure in exile, a temporary stopover. The Dalai Lama has lived here since the land was allotted in 1960, though he has now shifted to a new house within the same compound. For most of us, to be forever in transit would tremendously strain our nerves. Used to seeking security and solidity upon which to base our ideas of ourselves, what would we do when everything is as stable as a house of cards? When the rug of stability may be pulled from under our feet any second?

This is the kind of uncertainty the Dalai Lama has continuously faced for the last four decades and more. We could liken the unpredictability of his situation to a traveller perpetually stranded at an airport, called Dharamsala in this instance. Instead of collapsing under the strain, he has by all appearances thrived. There is nothing strained about his manner, no shadow staining his smile. Rather his presence is filled with lightness and good energy, the kind that comes with a clear mind and a loving heart. How has he pulled this off?

Perhaps by realizing the eternality of transience, the impermanence that is truer than any solidity we may seek or imagine. That it is actually the solidity that is the mirage, unattainable in anyone's life no matter how wealthy or powerful he may be. Sooner or later, entropy will take over the seemingly imperishable, and the dance of constant change will play itself out. Once we stop resisting change and the impulse to hanker after any kind of permanence, we can imagine how free we will become. Chains binding us to the destiny we imagine for ourselves, or to an identity we claim as 'ours', will fall away. And then, perhaps, we could be as free as the Dalai Lama seems, no matter what our circumstances are dishing up in that instant—pain, suffering, exile.

The Dalai Lama's residence in Dharamsala exists amid great natural beauty. In benevolent weather, the gardens around his home are full of fragrant flowers, mountain bird melodies, the chirping of insects, and incandescent fireflies. The path upwards undulates gently and is lined with such a profusion of bushes and flowers that one might even fail to notice the onerous presence of policemen and their barracks near the entrance.

I have never been near the Dalai Lama's personal quarters, which include the temple he prays at every day that he is here, but I have been within the complex in the vicinity of his old residence, which has been converted into a space for meetings.

What does he see when he looks out of his window, I wonder.

A snowy mane of mountains, of the same extraction as the Himalayas that gird Tibet. Perhaps the deep valley on the other side of McLeodganj. It must be a view very different from any that he may have enjoyed from the roof of the Potala Palace in Lhasa or his summer home, Norbulingka, in Tibet, both places where much of his childhood and early youth were spent. That view has now disappeared forever from the landscape of Tibet, and exists only in the memories of its former residents.

By all accounts, the old Tibet no longer exists. Overrun by industry and railway tracks and extensive mining, the precarious ecosystem of this the highest inhabited plateau, the 'roof of the world', struggles to survive. The spirit of the ancient civilization struggles even more, gasping for air amid repression and cruelty, some of which is express and some subtle, insensitive change.

Lhasa, the fabulous city of fables, an outpost of the Buddha's dharma, is now a Chinese city with neon lights and skyscrapers, pubs and prostitutes. Development projects to 'modernize' the city have resulted in the demolition of several old residential quarters, and drab cement apartment blocks have apparently replaced the stately wooden houses of old. Even the Lingkhor is a ghost of its former self.

The Potala, which housed several bodhisattva lama–rulers of Tibet, is sad in its de-sacralized state. The thousand-roomed palace survived the brutalities of the Cultural Revolution and perhaps the outward structure is the only thing that did. It is now a tourist hotspot, its one-time sacredness its USP and its lamas turned into tourist guides who will take you around for a few yuan. Is it an empty, soulless place, only the shell reminiscent of times past? Or is it a structure suspended in time, awaiting the moment when a living bodhisattva's magical touch will bring it back to life?

It is dawn at the Tsuglag Khang. I have been hanging around near that part of the temple courtyard that shares a wall with the Dalai Lama's residence, looking at people circumambulating the temple. Two bushy-tailed black dogs appear on the scene and walk around the temple clockwise—the correct direction to draw the sacred circle. 'Reincarnations?' I smile to myself, as another possible one appears. A white-haired Caucasian woman in Tibetan nun's robes is beating a tambourine, loudly chanting 'Om mani peme hung', as she circumambulates. Her clear, tuneful voice washes over the temple in gentle waves, which lap around the courtyard and flow on beyond. The prostrators for once look up from their labours and seem startled.

My thoughts turn to those who have been introduced to the possibility of a different way of being by the Dalai Lama. On the Tibetans, his impact has been tremendous. With the power of his traditional office, he has drawn the diaspora together and inspired them towards assimilation in the modern world through necessary reforms in the feudal character of Tibetan society, all the while encouraging them to keep alive their roots in their culture and the dharma. Tenzin Gyatso is the first modern Dalai Lama of Tibet, who has climbed down from his godly pedestal and established a direct relationship with his, and indeed all, people. This has resulted in a deeply personal connection between him and Tibetans who in Tibet would catch a glimpse of him only on rare occasions. The reason there is a profusion of Tenzins of both sexes in

Dharamsala is that parents have ensured his blessings upon their children by christening them with his first name. Their fondness for this person decidedly goes beyond tradition or duty; I sense in it genuine affection for a man who is gentle and wise, and has a heart as wide as the sky.

Thinking of the trail of Tenzins that has steadily formed around me in Dharamsala, I head out of the Tsuglag Khang complex. A petite woman waylays me with the question: 'Do you speak English?' She is beautiful and very young. I nod, and she seems relieved. 'Can I meet the Dalai Lama?' 'Where have you come from?' I ask her, trying to hide how thrown I am by her question. 'Ukraine,' she answers, blinking her intensely blue eyes. 'I've just gotten off the bus from Delhi. I want to know if I can meet him?' So moved has she been by the Dalai Lama that she has travelled this whole distance, from Ukraine to Dharamsala, to be near him. Over time, I meet many like her, who have come here because they responded to the Dalai Lama, and have made the long pilgrimage to Dharamsala to explore for themselves what he calls his 'religion of kindness'.

I tell the Ukrainian girl I don't know if she can meet him, though I want to be able to say, 'Of course he is right there across this courtyard. Of course you can meet him.' But I know that even when the Dalai Lama is in town, his schedule is normally so packed and fixed months in advance that you need to be a head of state or somebody terribly important to get an audience with him so promptly. There is just too little of him to go around.

So perhaps it is best to connect with his wisdom instead of his person, something the Tibetans seem to be able to do with their devotion to the bodhisattva element *within* the individual, to the 'Presence' which is what 'Kundun', one of the Dalai Lama's titles, means, to the jewel of compassion that sparkles from under the leaves of the lotus.

And perhaps it is best to walk the Lingkhor and think of the cycles and circles of life, and how at the centre of every whirlpool, chaos and maelstrom there is always a still point.

6

Bridges

The Dalai Lama's presence in Dharamsala has made the place a modern tirtha in more ways than one. Though the word 'tirtha' has come to denote a place of pilgrimage, its literal Sanskrit meaning is 'ford' or 'bridge'. In the traditional sense it stands for a spot that is a point of connection between different dimensions of reality, where the divine realm collapses into the human and possibilities for transcendental experiences increase manifold. Being at a tirtha is thought to be similar to standing at a portal between worlds, where you may enter another dimension of being that is different and perhaps more intense than the one you normally inhabit. Indeed this break from the regular mind space of random thoughts and concerns into a space where the flow is concentrated and balanced can happen anywhere, in the middle of your kitchen, for instance, or while bathing your baby or tending your plants. Wherever the portal opens, there is your tirtha. The shift has to occur within, no matter where you stand.

Attributing special energies to particular places is a universal human predilection, and perhaps Indians have been fonder of it than most other cultures. Every village and town will have a sacred space and each geographical region its major and minor tirthas. They may be linked to rivers, lakes, mountains, even old trees or unusually shaped rock formations, and each will have a special story assigned to it that has to do with miracles, healing powers or manifestations among human beings of deities, so that the place is thought to have become divinized and a bridge to the mystical for ordinary folk.

Dharamsala's energy is very much that of an Indian pilgrimage spot, where there are avenues for inner enrichment and the spiritual lies embedded in the mundane world. There are deities, living and otherwise, to be circumambulated and, if possible, emulated. What is unusual is that Dharamsala is also a tirtha in the sense of being a ford between disparate facets of human existence and reality. At an overt level, this is evident in the cosmopolitan character of the place, where different nationalities rub shoulders and exist in one space. The ford also comes into play in the exchanges between seekers and teachers, and when old knowledge speaks to dilemmas generated in the modern world.

In the last decade and half, Dharamsala has become a bridge of another kind through an unusual ancient–modern experimental dialogue that spans the gulf between spirituality and science. This synergy has happened in large measure due to the Dalai Lama's willingness to open up his tradition to modern minds so that it can be interpreted in ways that can be of benefit to humanity today. For Buddhism to remain relevant in the contemporary milieu, not only as a spiritual tradition but as the way of life that it has been all along, it needs to be stirred and challenged by new ideas. It needs to be able to speak with the situations and circumstances of today. Else it may find itself replaced, as many other established religions have been, by new isms and ideologies that may be based less on careful self-analysis, like the Buddha dharma is, and more on knee-jerk reactions to the frustrations of the world.

Moreover, it was felt by scientists who came in contact with Buddhism in the 1970s and 1980s that, if there could ever be a bridge between science and spirituality, it would be the easiest to build upon the girders of Buddhism. There are several reasons for this. One of the most significant is that the Buddha had dispensed with a Creator-God theology and had instead encouraged engagement with problems of the present, of the human condition. So Buddhism did not come with the metaphysical baggage that would have made a dialogue with scientists—who are required to be rational-minded by their profession and often turn out to be atheists—impossible.

Buddhism also has inbuilt controls to nip in the bud the institutionalizing of dogmas. For one of its basic understandings about the nature of reality is the impermanence of all things and phenomena. Nothing is eternal, or perpetual, nor does anything have an inherent character of its own. Reality is a play of phenomena that arise in interdependence with one another. Everything is linked with everything else. And so when any one factor in this vast, interlinked web changes, all others cannot but be affected. Thus constant flux is the nature of everyday reality. This viewpoint also precludes dogmas, unshakeable tenets, and leads the Buddha to declare that no one should follow anything he has taught until the student has checked the veracity of the teachings through personal experimentation and analysis. 'Be lamps unto yourselves,' was his final instruction from his deathbed, emphasizing this as a cardinal rule for anyone who wished to correctly follow his path, any path, to truth.

This was the Buddha's version of what we today refer to as the 'scientific temper', that is, not taking anything for granted, and accepting only that whose truth can be proven logically through empirical evidence. Practitioners of the Buddha's path have applied this scientific temper to explore the true nature of reality, both outer and inner, while modern science has mostly externalized the quest. Science has also made the process of investigation all about finite measurements and phenomena qualifiable through sensory evidence alone, which has limited its understanding of the human mind and of phenomena that lie beyond the physical realm. It is also why Buddhism and science developed so differently despite tapping a similar human energy—that for exploration and ultimately for improvement, for knowing what we didn't before and using it to better ourselves and the human condition.

The fundamentally altruistic aim of knowing not just for the sake of knowing but for utilizing knowledge for a larger good prompted several scientific initiatives in the last couple of centuries. Two thousand five hundred years ago, the spiritual quest that begot Buddhism also germinated from this aim, where Siddhartha set out to find not personal salvation but an end to human suffering. It was fitting then that this became the driving motivation for the progenitors of the Buddhism–science dialogue—the Dalai Lama, the late neuroscientist Francisco Varela and the entrepreneur Adam Engle. The latter two began dreaming up such a dialogue separately around the same time and, discovering one another's intentions serendipitously, decided to present this proposal jointly to the Dalai Lama.

They couldn't have chosen anyone more appropriate. For the Dalai Lama is an amazingly modern mind, open and aware, who allows the winds of new, diverse modes of thinking to enter and blow freely through his mindscape. This does not mean he is any less of a Rinpoche. On the contrary, he is a 'holder' or protector of the teachings of his lineage and has spent a considerable part of his life engaged in practice, rituals, prayers, retreats and teaching. Rather, his openness seems to flow from the Buddha's injunction to empiricism above attachment to a teaching or doctrine. The Dalai Lama has remarked on occasion that he would abandon doctrinal beliefs if he found evidence to the contrary, and cites the example of aeroplane travel having given him proof that Mount Meru does not actually hold up the centre of the earth, as held in scriptures of Buddhist cosmology.

This attitude has led the Dalai Lama to embrace the challenge presented by science, something rare in teachers of religion and spirituality, who may find it a threat to their closely held beliefs. One has to let go sufficiently of attachment to one's tradition, as well as the tendency to regard it as the supreme truth or the 'best way', to cultivate this attitude.

Perhaps his facility with technology has helped the Dalai Lama come to grips with the methodologies employed in scientific research. He has often reminisced about tinkering with pieces of machinery as a child in the Potala, and helping restore two cars his predecessor had imported into Lhasa. I remember seeing a photograph from some years ago, perhaps when there were less demands upon his time, of him hunched over a worktable in his residence in Dharamsala, working with great absorption at a watch's intricate machinery. He has felt enough affinity with technology to have said, 'I would have been an engineer, if I had not been a monk!'

It is easy to imagine the enthusiasm with which the Dalai Lama may have welcomed the idea of participating in an actual dialogue with science. The Mind and Life Institute was set up expressly for the purpose of organizing these dialogues, the first of which was convened in 1987 in Dharamsala. Since then, each conference has been constructed around a particular topic with the participation of scientists engaged in relevant branches of research. Anticipating hesitation among members of the scientific community to be seen dialoguing with a religion, it was decided to keep the meetings semi-private and release the proceedings later in the form of books.

Till 2004, twelve 'Mind and Life' conferences had been organized, of which eight took place in Dharamsala. History of sorts is being created in this little mountain town, as it becomes the ground for a unique contemporary interaction. In an era that has seen a dramatic rise in exclusivist and fragmentational energies the world over, in politics, religion, even branches of study that become increasingly narrow and specialized, these dialogues are a movement in the opposite direction, towards holism and integration. Bridges are being built, based on mutual understanding and openness, and facilitated by the gentle wisdom of the Dalai Lama.

October in Dharamsala can be quite temperamental. The monsoon is officially over, though it rains most afternoons. Winter is still not close enough to bring out heavy woollens, but as evening crawls into night, the rising chill makes you wish you had some. During the day, walking in the sun can make you throw off your light jacket and sweat it out in your T-shirt. It is almost as if the weather doesn't wish to let you be, and this constant needling is like the periodic whack in Zen meditation, to keep you wholly focused on the present.

It was such a temperamental Dharamsala October that played host to 'Mind and Life XII' in 2004. The theme was 'Neuroplasticity' with the tagline 'The Neuronal Substrates of Learning and Transformation'. One of the most exciting fields of recent research in neuroscience, neuroplasticity refers to the brain's ability to change in response to training and experience. When I came to know of the topic, it occurred to me that this was something eastern spiritual traditions including Buddhism had believed in for centuries and the radars of scientific research had now picked up.

Self and mind as dynamic entities that come into being through interrelated factors such as conditioning, perceptions, reactions and so on has been deeply studied in Buddhism. The very fact of their changeability renders it possible for the mind and self to evolve towards a more balanced existence. We begin from ignorance, and, as we uncover truths underlying the phenomenal world, we learn and change. This process of transformation can be a conscious effort aided by spiritual practices that still the mind and focus it on the process of learning and realization. That neuroscience had picked up on the changeable character of the brain (which it places as being synonymous with 'mind'), after decades of using for it the analogy of a computer with fixed functions, made me feel that a potentially stimulating dialogue was looming on Dharamsala's horizon.

When they are held in Dharamsala, the 'Mind and Life' conferences take place in a wooden-floored hall at the old residence of the Dalai Lama. There are large bay windows all around. Above hangs a series of richly coloured thangkas of Vajrayana deities. A corridor runs around the hall with windows opening outwards on to the Dhauladhars.

Walking up the steep, curving path to the conference hall, one passes through the gardens that fringe the low functional buildings in the Dalai Lama's residential complex, thriving with an abundance of flowers and birdsong. A cold breeze stirs down from the perennial snows of the Dhauladhars and ruffles the heads of flowers and leaves of pine, releasing their fragrances into the air.

The security presence on the sidelines gives way to the

more gracious maroon-robed monks and Tibetan officials who usher me into the hall. I am early, and chance upon the crew that is here to film the proceedings on behalf of the organizers setting up their cameras and sound equipment. Wires snake their way around the room, lying in piles, climbing walls, running round chairs and over the central table around which the scientists and the Dalai Lama will sit on comfortable, well-worn sofas. I sidestep the wires, looking for the chair that bears my name. There are many more chairs now than I remember from the 2002 conference, which also took place in this very room, and they take up every inch of space in the hall and extend out into the corridor.

I take the opportunity to glance at other observers' chairs in the room and find many of them filled by the Mind and Life Institute's benefactor foundations, and old hands of this dialogue like the author Daniel Goleman, who has moderated an earlier conference and turned two of them into books (*Emotional Intelligence* and *Destructive Emotions*), the Hollywood actor Richard Gere, who has attended most of them, the American Zen practitioner Joan Halifax, who participated in the fourth conference on 'Sleeping, Dreaming and Dying', among others. There are more Indian names this time unlike 2002, when I was one of two Indians. There are a lot more journalists, perhaps brought on by the institute's greater comfort level with media reports on the dialogue after the first public session at Harvard University in 2003.

The hall fills up as we near the opening time for the morning session. Each of the five conference days has been divided into morning sessions, where a participating scientist will make a presentation on a topic related to the main theme, and afternoon sessions, which are given over to discussions. This is not a rigid structure though, and at times the Dalai Lama will spontaneously share his reactions and views during the presentations. The atmosphere is convivial and warm, as old friends and acquaintances greet one another and newcomers are introduced all around. I have located my chair in the corridor, just behind a bay window. I sit down and look into the hall—the mute spectator who witnesses, observes, records.

The participants are in their places. I recognize the trio that will act as the Dalai Lama's interpreters—Geshe Thupten Jinpa, who is an ex-monk and currently teaches religious studies at McGill University in Montreal, B. Alan Wallace, who is also an ex-monk and now president of the Santa Barbara Institute for Consciousness Studies and author of a great number of books on Buddhism, and Matthieu Ricard, a monk at Shechen Monastery in Nepal with a PhD in cellular genetics from his pre-monastic years. Together, they act as facilitators of the dialogue, using their comprehensive knowledge of Buddhism, their familiarity with scientific concepts, and their fluency in both Tibetan and English to help cement links when they appear tenuous.

The Dalai Lama's seat is at the head of the table, in the shadow of a gold Buddha seated in samadhi, eyes half closed in contemplation. To the left sit the rotund teenaged Kyabje Ling Dorje Chang, who is affectionately called Ling Rinpoche and is the reincarnation of the Dalai Lama's senior tutor, and Ugyen Trinley Dorje, the seventeenth Karmapa. Behind them is a contingent of monks who have been studying science as part of their monastic curriculum for the last five years upon the Dalai Lama's instructions. His intention in including the young is to enable the continuance of the dialogue beyond his own lifetime, and ensure that it is not solely dependent upon his person but finds sustenance through the participation of the larger sangha.

The chatter in the hall quietens. The Dalai Lama has entered and prostrates three times before the Buddha statue before walking towards the participants. As he is introduced to them, he extends to each his hand in a warm handshake. I think of a passage in his autobiography, *Freedom in Exile*, where he recounts the life of royal seclusion led by the Dalai Lamas of old. The air of sacrality in which they remained cocooned at all times was such that most people never looked into their eyes. And here is our Dalai Lama, shaking hands all around with great affection and aplomb! It is indeed a precious opportunity for all of us who have come to be here from various corners of the world.

In his introduction to the conference, the Dalai Lama draws attention to the common ground on which this dialogue is based. 'When we say "Buddhism", people may think of it as a religion. It is so, but if we look closely, Buddhism can be a science, for its tradition, especially the one laid down by the Nalanda masters, is one of investigation,' where 'Nalanda masters' are the Indian scholars from the ancient Buddhist university of Nalanda, who travelled to Tibet over a period of time with scriptures and teachings of Buddhism.

A gentle bridge between the two traditions is formed right at the outset, when the Dalai Lama introduces a contemporary version of the Four Noble Truths of Buddhism. The traditional ones are the inevitability of suffering; its root in craving; the possibility of its elimination; and the way to do this by following the Buddha's eightfold path. While the old ones still hold good, the Dalai Lama gives new ones that are especially meaningful for this dialogue: 'Buddhism is a science that tries to explain the nature of reality, even particles, like modern science. This is the first new noble truth. The second is the knowledge of mind and emotions—once we know that disturbance is not outside but within us, we can act accordingly. The third is the philosophy that has sprung from this core knowledge. And the fourth is the technology—how to use it to strengthen positive emotions in a beneficial way.'

Over the next five days, all four of the Dalai Lama's new noble truths are brought into play. Of particular interest to the scientists are the mind training disciplines of Buddhism, the 'technology' aspect of it. Latest neuroscientific research has discovered the inherent ability of the brain to change in structure and system throughout one's life—through the birth of neurons, formation of new connections between neurons (synapses) and even the strengthening and re-formation of existing synapses. New evidence has also shown that mental training can lead to greater brain plasticity—a view that is as old as Buddhism itself. A point made by the psychologist Richard Davidson, coordinator of this conference, when he says, 'Of all topics in modern neuroscience, this is one that has significant capability of interaction with Buddhism.'

Some tensions surface fairly early. Dr Fred H. Gage from the Laboratory of Genetics at Salk Institute outlines the role of the hippocampus in the brain in generating new neurons, and the importance of finding newness through experience in brain neuroplasticity—something that gets impaired during stress and depression. Matthieu Ricard points out that the ancient Buddhist view that 'the mind can override external situations' is based on a 2500-year-old experience, while western behavioural sciences have largely ignored the role of mental training.

Also, when Alan Wallace describes Buddhist techniques such as withdrawing the senses and bringing the mind to subtle consciousness as a 'mental manipulation of physical reality', there is resistance from Helen J. Neville, professor of psychology and neuroscience at the University of Oregon, Eugene. 'Scientists and Buddhists have great appreciation for evidence,' she says. 'Why then do you speak of consciousness as existing independent of the brain when there is no evidence of it?' Her comment lets loose a flurry of counterarguments until the Dalai Lama intercedes and reminds all of the true purpose of their getting together. 'The aim is not to browbeat you into believing us. It is to learn from one another. So let us bracket this issue of independent consciousness for the moment.'

I see how crucial the Dalai Lama is to this process, in ensuring that the dialogue remains true to the spirit of collaboration in which it was conceived. When there is an argument over an issue such as this, he withdraws from the melee and quietly and without judgement watches the proceedings. And when the dialogue has broken down, he steps in and with a hand that is at once firm and gentle steers the process back on course. As he has done now, with a smile that brings everyone together in its warmth.

In these moments, he *is* the bridge.

At a mid-morning tea break, I find a young man and a woman clutching their cups, looking lost among people who all seem to know one another. Familiar with that feeling, I go up to them and introduce myself. They are from Switzerland, and are here to teach science to monks at Tibetan settlements in South India. 'I think this is my karma,' says the young man, whose long, golden hair is dreadlocked and ponytailed. He has been meditating for some time, vipassana actually, and was teaching in a school when he overheard people talking of an invitation for science teachers to join a project funded by the Swiss government and initiated by the Dalai Lama. And he signed up. The woman is more of a wanderer, and had come to Dharamsala three years ago. 'I was thrilled to find this opportunity to come back, and maybe continue with my dharma studies?' she says, her soft voice thrilling with excitement.

As the conference continues, new evidence is presented that experience not only transforms the brain but modifies how genes become expressed in us. Till recently, the gene was God of modern biosciences. Now the position stands revised and in the 'nature versus nurture' debate, the role of the individual's environment has come to have equal rating, which means we are not rigidly pre-wired for anything; there is always scope for change and renewal. Michael J. Meaney, professor of medicine at Douglas Hospital Research Centre, McGill University, says, 'Neither gene nor experience can influence development independent of context. Experience requires translation through processes associated with bodily function that commonly includes brain activation . . . inevitably influenced by the genome . . . Alas, gene and experience are inseparable.'

Dr Meaney connects this with the passing of traits from parents to children, not only through genes but also through behaviour. 'Parental behaviour affects genetic expression,' he says. 'For instance, when the parent has been exposed to stress, the offspring will show increased response to stress in adulthood.' He outlines an interesting experiment where two sets of baby rats were studied—one set had been licked to a greater degree by their mothers than the other. The ones that had been licked more showed appropriate stress response, as opposed to less licked babies, who displayed high stress responses. The Dalai Lama finds in this validation for his own belief in the tremendous power of 'genuine love and warmheartedness'.

Parenting, and its long-term impact on children, turns out to be a recurring theme during the conference, with more than one scientist taking it up as the field where they would like their research to be applied. Helen Neville, who has researched human developmental plasticity and found that 'stimulating environments lead to enhanced brain growth, learning and intelligence', speaks about optimizing human development through attention training, something that child lamas in Tibetan monasteries are automatically provided from a young age.

The discussion turns to 'neuro-ethics'. Says Professor Davidson, 'We have ways in which we can optimize human development. How should access to these be determined? There are two ways of looking at this presently—one is the principle of "no child left behind" where you try and provide these to as many as possible, and the other is to identify the brightest and put the resources behind them.'

Issues of ethics are often been raised in the 'Mind and Life' dialogues for, as the Dalai Lama has said, 'With the ever-growing impact of science on our lives, religion and spirituality have a greater role to play reminding us of our humanity . . .' Now, he points out that Buddhism emphasizes equality because all beings have Buddhanature—equal potential to achieve nirvana. But at the practical level, the Buddha gave different teachings according to the capacity of practitioners. So in application, different needs must be kept in mind and ministered to accordingly. Those with greater potential can be provided a boost to develop this, while making sure that the 'majority of the population is at the same level. The minority that is at a higher level should keep increasing.'

Dr Meaney interjects, 'This sounds like the Marxist dictum of equality of opportunity, where everyone has equal access.' 'This is why I call myself half a Marxist!' says the Dalai Lama and roars with laughter. Everyone joins in, perhaps feeling the keenness of the joke. Instants like these act as a quick change of gears where one dips into a lighter state of being, even if just for a moment, and returns refreshed. I observe how the Dalai Lama often takes recourse to humour, not only to alleviate sombreness but also as a device to diffuse tension. His belly laugh rings out often during the conference and, each time, facilitates yet another gentle bridge into a lighter, more open state of being for those in the room.

The discussion on neuro-ethics turns towards methods. The brains of young children are being imaged in neuroscientific research and information about future vulnerability to disorders is becoming known, which could become the basis for discrimination against them. What would be a responsible attitude towards this?

The Dalai Lama prioritizes motivation—the sure-fire check for good ethics in Buddhism. He refuses to answer in black or white terms, for in a universe constructed out of cause and effect there really is no space for absolutes. 'You have to look at this case by case,' he points out. 'For example, if someone has a contagious illness, to ignore this fact would be foolish. But to use it to ostracize that person and remove him or her from the human ranks is entirely wrong. The illness must be isolated but not the person.' The scientist's own motivation is crucial in this matter. 'If one can ensure one's own altruistic motivation, that the knowledge is being gathered for the child's good so that preventive measures may be taken, then that is pure motivation. If, however, the information can be used negatively, then it is wrong.'

But how to ensure this purity of motivation? 'By establishing the foundation of one's actions in genuine affection,' says the Dalai Lama. 'You don't need expertise or high education to do this. Even rats, of which Dr Meaney spoke, can understand and show affection. So this is a natural instinct in all of us. If we act out of compassion, it is positive even if it outwardly appears harsh. And if there is any other motivation, even though it may seem beautiful, it is unethical.'

Many scientists request private audience after the day's proceedings end at five o'clock every evening to discuss issues further with the Dalai Lama. Daniel Goleman tells me that these tête-à-têtes often help break the ice. 'Most scientists who come are not Buddhist practitioners, nor is it a requirement at all,' he says, as the setting sun leaves its ochre imprint on the Dhauladhars. We are sitting in the veranda of the guesthouse where the scientists and observers are staying. 'Some are quite sceptical, and understandably so,' he continues. 'There are those who have not been as willing as we would like them to be to engage in dialogue. Some might think that they have to come here and teach the Dalai Lama their point of view, whereas actually this is a collaboration of different perspectives.'

Matthieu Ricard tells me something similar, about the kind of middle ground that 'Mind and Life' conferences tend to come to rest at. 'I have noticed in this and previous meetings that the best brains in the world of science come here not really knowing what to expect. They are almost always pleasantly surprised to see the depth of Buddhist philosophical thought and how vast and complex it is. So a meaningful dialogue is built quickly, more than what many of them expected in the first place. And His Holiness is always very eager to know and learn. The scientists discover that they can talk to him not as a beginner but even about the deepest issues, of ethics, of the natural world.'

One of the more engaging presentations for me as a seeker comes right at the end—in Richard Davidson's account of his experiments with meditators. He begins from the premise that voluntary emotional regulation, in the form of 'down-regulation of negative emotions and intentional cultivation of positive emotions', has a definite impact on mental health—the replacement of the negative with positive being key. This is part of contemplative practice in Buddhism, where compassion and other positive mind states are activated through single-pointed concentration upon them.

Professor Davidson recounts the testing of eight adepts, monks from Shechen Monastery in Nepal including Matthieu Ricard, who had each spent 10,000 to 60,000 hours in meditation, and comparison with a control group that learned meditation shortly before the experiment. In one experiment, the monks were asked to generate a meditative state followed by a neutral state, so that changes in the brain could be studied. 'The monks showed greater signal in every part of the brain compared to the control group, especially in parts of the brain related to attention. Over time, the signal in adepts remained elevated through rest and meditation.'

The next part of the experiment had to do with the voluntary cultivation of compassion. Ricard was the subject of this experiment and, as he generated a mind state of compassion, it was found that gamma activity, which shows recruitment of neural resources and occurs with mental effort and motivation, gradually began increasing. In fact so large was this increase in gamma signal that it had 'never been seen before', said Professor Davidson. Interestingly, the part of the brain linked to motor activity also became activated, which could be seen as the intention to act upon compassion.

In his concluding remarks, the Dalai Lama says that the conference had corroborated his 'personal conviction in the value of compassion and lovingkindness and the need for their active cultivation'. The science student-monks have some interesting comments. Says one, 'I felt a greater sophistication on the part of scientists in their dealing with brain and psychological activity.' He is reacting to the brain–mind divide that has often proved to be a stumbling block in the conference, with the scientists bracketing the two together. Says another, 'In Buddhist tradition, the fundamental motivation for any activity is to help other beings. I felt the scientists have a similar motivation.'

The day draws to a close and everyone lines up to receive the customary white silk katas (scarves) as blessings from the Dalai Lama. As they crowd together for group photographs, I walk out into the garden and breathe deep of the perfumed air, thinking of the sustained effort that has kept the dialogue going since 1987 despite the odds, the prejudices against religion and spirituality that modern science harbours. Gaps, fissures exist, but so do the golden seeds of shared wisdom, carefully nurtured by the Dalai Lama and others who have become his associates in this process. And the dialogue continues, with sincerity and commitment, mindfulness and sharing, over bridges past and present, some here in Dharamsala, others elsewhere around the globe.

The warmth of the day recedes with the sun. The Dhauladhars loom ghostly and grey in the twilight. People emerge from the conference hall in twos and threes and begin the descent on the spiralling path that will disgorge them into the busy bazaar, and then back to their hotel for this last night in McLeodganj. They talk with warmth and promise to remember those who have become friends on the sidelines of this dialogue, bound by the unique synergy that they have participated in. In the dim light, their faces appear animated, if a little tired. Their last words are of farewell, and of assurances to continue the collaborations that have begun here in this small hill town in a nondescript corner of North India.

The day is done, a chasm spanned, and it is now time to rest and dream of shared futures.

7

Co-worlds

If you come to Dharamsala as a tourist hungering for sights to see and pose in front of for family photographs, you may well be disappointed by the lack of choice. Sure, there is the Tsuglag Khang and the bazaar and the temple of Bhagsu, but that's about it. You can probably see these in half a day, and spend the other half hanging out in the bazaar. Even if you don't mind buying curios and would like to check out every shop in town, it will take you up to two days in all. And if you want some Himalayan scenery, there are other spots in the region that fare higher on the natural beauty index, such as Dalhousie and Manali. Even motoring or walking to one of the suburbs of Dharamsala—Naddi or Forsythganj—might be a better idea.

What even the most casual visitor's eye will notice about Dharamsala is its overwhelming variety of people—a great multiplicity of culture and its various indicators like language, food, attitudes and so on packed into an untidy jumble and placed precariously upon the ledge of a mountain. Here many worlds coexist and cohabit, and in this sense have become 'co-worlds', the 'co' signifying a coming together, a commingling and, in practical matters, cooperation, coordination and collaboration. Their 'co-ness' encompasses these and one more—complexity. The knit is as ribbed and layered as it is many coloured and faceted, and the fabric that has thus come to be is riotous and robust, if somewhat uneven and unmatched.

The character of most places tends to be in tandem with the larger region in which they exist. Historically, towns and cities came up in areas of safety, greater availability of food and livelihood and opportunities to trade. The growth of cultures is slower than that of settlements and is more organic, evolving through needs of survival, interactions of human beings with one another and with nature, and through responses to influences and new ideas that blow in from the world beyond. The areas of influence of cultures may be circumscribed within a geographical region, hemmed in by natural barriers like seas or mountains, or they may push these boundaries by travelling to new lands like many old cultures did, sometimes with goods in traders' caravans, sometimes as ambition encased in sword sheaths, as stories on tips of tongues, as religion's texts carefully wrapped in silk.

The Tibetans, who contribute to Dharamsala's co-worlds through their varied in-exile identities, are no strangers to the movements of cultures. Significant aspects of what is now their identity came into being over a period of time owing to precisely such movements from India to Tibet. What is unprecedented is the transplantation of culture that occurred, from Tibet to Dharamsala and other Tibetan settlements, in the twentieth century. Earlier, it was a gradual movement of religion, scholars, teachers and texts from monasteries and universities of Buddhism in India, over the Himalayan passes, into Tibet. These inputs of knowledge were presented, accepted and then given time to become assimilated in the soil of the existing culture of the plateau. It all happened in the natural flow of time. There was all the time in the world to learn, and check out for oneself, in the spirit of the Buddha's own example, the validity of his teachings. Like rainwater, the spirit of the new tradition seeped into the ground and from thence moved into the underground reservoirs that fed Tibetan culture. And when it sprang up as new growth, it found the cultural ground made soft and fertile by a long period of nurture.

Transplantation on the other hand is abrupt. There is violence in the uprooting of something and supplanting it elsewhere, though the gardener's intention might be to enhance its prospects of growth in the long run. The transplantation of Tibetans didn't happen of their own volition, nor was the motivation of those responsible for it altruistic in the least. For Dharamsala, which became the ground of this transplantation, it has meant the replacement of *its* old cultural identity with an entirely new one, one which is not quite in sync with its regional culture.

When the Tibetans were given space to settle in Dharamsala, there already existed a town populated by Himachalis, the people native to Himachal Pradesh. The place had been an old British Raj cantonment that had rapidly lost importance since the country's independence. It had none of the looks, or what travel brochures are fond of referring to as an 'old-world charm', that had turned its sister Himachal towns into boisterous tourist spots. A Tibetan writer said as much to me, with some indignation, in response to my thought about Dharamsala's many worlds. 'Dharamsala *is* the Tibetan community,' he insisted. 'There was no Dharamsala worth the name before Tibetans came here. Tell me, would you or anyone else be writing about Dharamsala if it were not for the Tibetans?'

True, to an extent. Undoubtedly it is the Tibetan community's presence that set into motion the currents that have now transformed Dharamsala into a cosmopolitan spiritual–cultural hotspot. People who may not know of major Indian cities would have heard of Dharamsala, a tiny dot in size and population when compared to the many burgeoning metropolises in the country, and this is primarily because it is where the Dalai Lama lives. But I don't agree that the whole story of Dharamsala is solely that of the Tibetan community. A closer look will reveal a weave both complex and diverse, where the co-worlds don't only happen to exist in one space at the same time in the sense of a random clutter or a hotchpotch, but are also integrated and braided *into* one another in interesting ways.

What makes the 'manyness' of Dharamsala so conspicuous is the smallness of the geographical area available to it. The vertical topography of mountains makes it hard for places to really spread themselves out as they can in flatlands. Every inch of space has been obtained by cutting away at hillsides, and there is only that much a mountain will allow of its natural verticality to be made horizontal before its strength begins to give way. Hill towns face greater space shortages with smaller populations in contrast to towns in the plains simply because they cannot keep expanding indefinitely. Dharamsala has spread out though, with people tapping nearby suburbs and villages to build residences and institution buildings. This has relieved the pressure of population in the epicentres at both McLeodganj and lower Dharamsala, but only marginally, for spiralling real estate prices still indicate a high premium on the available land here.

Walking through any part of Dharamsala, upper or lower, will afford a visual illustration of the co-worlds I speak of. Those walking on the road with you will include Tibetans of varying age groups. Maroon-robed monks and nuns will appear intermittently. Then there will be the visitors—the wanderers—of diverse nationalities. The Himachalis will be definitely present. If you are doing this survey while the Indian 'tourist season' is on, mostly in the summer months of May and June, you will find Indian tourists on the road too, and sometimes couples on their honeymoon out to get some fresh mountain air.

I would place the population composition of McLeodganj at any given time as roughly half Tibetan, and a quarter each of Himachali residents and travellers. Among these, the Tibetans and the travellers constitute more of floating populations. The former because new arrivals from Tibet form a steady trickle into Dharamsala before they are repatriated here or elsewhere, and Tibetans who trade in woollen garments are away during winter months and return in summer like migratory birds. The population of travellers (other than the seasonal tourists) is more unpredictable, and somewhat nomadic in its behaviour. It consists of those that are drawn to spiritual sustenance in Dharamsala, like nomads in deserts to oases, and end up making homes here and staying on for extended periods of time. Until finances run out or visas expire with such finality that Indian officialdom cannot be coaxed to resuscitate them. They may then try to return after some time to renew their Dharamsala lives, or give up and make their own little Dharamsalas wherever they are, with some help from internationally itinerant lamas and Rinpoches.

With much squeezed into little, an intermeshing of these co-worlds is inevitable, for they don't have the luxury of individual spaces to inhabit. The 'co-ness' of diverse humanity that naturally occurs in any human habitation, be it a village, city or nation, is consequently magnified several times over in Dharamsala. This compression of different worlds, even different historical time zones, into one space can be quite striking if somewhat bewildering to one unused to cultural fusion.

In Dharamsala, the co-worlds of Tibetans, Himachalis and the visitors bump into each other, sharing space and boundaries. The result is a composite culture that provides for some unusual sensory experiences. Taste-wise, there is a range of eating places where tandoori chicken and parathas coexist with pizzas and pasta, momos and thukpa with croissants and German bread. The spoken sounds of many languages float through Dharamsala's narrow lanes along with Bollywood film music, Israeli rock and Tibetan pop music, and temple bells mingle in one's auditory nerve centre with Tibetan mantras chanted deep and guttural.

Some of this fusion comes from plain good business sense. Signs in Hebrew and restaurants announcing 'kosher food' are meant to attract a particular kind of customer. Trade has often led to intermingling of cultures—all are equal in the tumult of the bazaar, for one's rupee is as good as another's—and its effect here has been to make the place culturally diverse and given over to a composite identity. So you have Himachali shopkeepers who have picked up a smattering of international languages to reach out to the diverse kinds of customers they get and, one imagines, have given up the general Indian distaste for toilet paper, which has become a ubiquitous, prominently displayed presence in shops all over Dharamsala alongside bottles of branded mineral water.

Food is the other great uniting force, and in Dharamsala one sees how expressive a medium it can be of both diversity *and* fusion. People come together over food—to eat, to cook, to buy and to sell. Because it is so basic to life, it makes for a powerful point of human conjunction. In Dharamsala, because of its large population of visitors who are not cooking for themselves, food unites people through need, taste and commerce—seen in the proliferation of restaurants and eateries all over town. Most are Tibetan-run, and the ones with the international menus have been started by visitors in collaboration with Dharamsala residents. Where the owners and cooks here might be Tibetan, the recipes are authentic Italian or Israeli or German. There is something about eating a Tuscan pasta dish cooked by Tibetan hands in a simple table-and-chair restaurant that is a uniquely Dharamsala experience.

Watching Dharamsala's co-worlds in action, growing and lying alongside one another, makes me wonder about how 'co' they really are. Communities separated by ethnicity, religion, language and/or ancestry have lived beside one another all over the world for ages. Even so, human beings have always found ways of demarcation between themselves and 'others'. Whether the determinant is economic status, social hierarchy or a claim to godly sanction, difference has been kept alive and complex. Each point of difference has sharpened the degrees of otherness between human beings; for instance, we feel the one who may share our skin colour but not our language is less 'other' than one who shares neither, and so on. We in India have taken the determining of difference very seriously and have perfected it into an intricate system of castes, sub-castes, sub-sub-castes which is as complicated as it is artificial and cruelly oppressive.

Thus, mere existence in one place does not imply a co-ness of worlds. Communities that have lived for generations in the same neighbourhood and have shared backyards and clotheslines and gossip have only required a spark to ignite subliminal feelings of otherness and send centuries of mutual existence up in flames. In India, such periodic 'communal' riots have shown how the 'co' of coexistence can degenerate into the 'co' of communalism that is its exact, ugly opposite.

Why does this happen? One obvious reason is the shallowness of the 'co' element that has not progressed beyond a cosmetic togetherness. Even though the communities may have shared the same living and working space for centuries, their hearts and collective psyches have remained divided. Exigencies of survival have forced them to band together and may have precluded open warfare, but that is as far as it goes. Their perception of the otherness of the other remains embedded in their attitudes and is passed on from one generation to the next.

Contemporary Dharamsala is an attempt at co-living. Because the coming together of its divergent communities is a fairly recent phenomenon, it offers a ready opportunity as an observatory for the processes of both co-ness and difference. With this intention, I begin to question Dharamsala's co-worlds. It all *seems* very 'co', but is it really so?

Seeing that many of its residents are either cultural Buddhists or are studying Buddhism, I wonder whether I could really ask one seeking nirvana—literally, extinction into nothingness—how they stick to their community lines in their daily lives.

A mental red light flashes, warning me against falling into stereotypes. Though it is one that is consciously or unconsciously perpetuated by the Tibetans themselves, can we really categorize an entire people as 'spiritual' just because they are Buddhist? Young Tibetans particularly find this stereotyping constricting. Some years ago one of them had made a film set in Dharamsala that featured Tibetan youth and was rebelliously titled *We Are Not Monks*. Even so, the teaching of non-duality, of accepting an innate equality of human beings where all have the same potential to evolve into a Buddha, may have seeped into the cultural attitudes of Tibetans. The thing to do would be to look for it in their co-equations and identify its influence on community relations in Dharamsala.

Where does the ghetto end and the sangha begin?

The ghetto is conceived of fear and is born of persecution and distrust and the need to limit a community, which is perceived as a threat, within a circumscribed space. The ghetto may be a community's own creation driven by the need to seek safety in numbers, and one that is still rooted in fear and an apprehension of persecution. Being in the ghetto makes the community feel safe and protected. It is their space where they can be themselves. The ghetto is defined by its boundaries, by what is kept out and what is allowed in. Its walls, which are built upon the community's hearts and minds, are barb-wired and well secured.

'Sangha' is a Sanskrit word that means community. In the Buddhist sense, the sangha implies a community of seekers oriented towards the common goal of spiritual evolution. Yet from the Buddha's time, the sangha has also stood for a vision of a society based on harmony, equity and a balanced exercise of power. The Buddha's own sangha was Dharamsala-like in the sheer diversity it packed in. People from all castes and socio-economic groups had been accepted into this sangha and there are records of altercations and dissonance among them, unused as they were to sharing the same living space. Realizing the need for regulation, the Buddha organized his sangha along the lines of a republic.

The sangha is defined not only as a collective of monks but as a way of living in community. Its boundaries are porous and easily permeable. Elements of difference and diversity are quietened in the inner realization of a universal oneness. The sangha forces one to face the other, who is no longer at the other end of a high security wall but right here with you in your cloister. 'Engaged Buddhists', who bring a contemplative perspective to bear on the issues of the world, talk of the whole world as one sangha. Nature and all its forms are part of this sangha. The whole of humanity is in this sangha. Everything is webbed together, we just need to become sufficiently aware of these connections to realize the ideal of the sangha in our everyday living.

Is Dharamsala then a ghetto, or is it a sangha?

I think the honest answer would be that it is partially both. To some extent there is a ghettoization of communities. Perhaps the Himachalis feel their town usurped and their numbers reduced to a minority, but they do acknowledge the immense recognition Dharamsala has got because of the Tibetan presence. They have also benefited from the tourist economy and escalating land prices. One direct example of commingling was the story of two Himachali brothers who had studied at the Tibetan Children's Village and even won prizes in Tibetan language tests! Though their numbers are not large, non-Tibetan children are admitted at Tibetan schools and thus come to know the Tibetans with whom they share their land and space.

Dharamsala is the only home that many Tibetans who live here have known. They are directly invested in its well-being, especially its fragile ecological health that increasing pressures of population and dwindling forests and rainfall have endangered. One day I visit an appliqué thangka maker's workshop in the Tsuglag Khang complex. There, entertaining a roomful of young Tibetans sewing together patches of brocade and silk into Buddha images, is a radio tuned in to a local station. Soon there comes on a song in English that bemoans the sad state of the local ecosystem with the lyrics 'Oh, oh, oh, what happened to McLeodganj?'

It is a concern that has inspired residents' initiatives in the last few years. Seeing that plastic mineral water bottles form the bulk of non-biodegradable waste in Dharamsala, an aptly named 'Green Shop' in McLeodganj sells boiled and filtered drinking water to tourists for a nominal fee. At a coffee shop en route to the Tsuglag Khang, the Tibetan owner tells me about the collective effort made by residents to put in place a waste-disposal system. 'We won the contract from the municipal corporation and were able to bring some order in the collection and removal of garbage,' she says. But they lost the contract the following year, and now the garbage trucks visit the main dumpster only once in a while. No one is clearing garbage off the streets where it falls into open drains and chokes them. 'I have to carry garbage from my home in plastic bags and throw it in the main dumpster. And the streets are always dirty now. We get so many visitors from around the world and they say, "This town should be clean, it is a sacred place." I feel like telling them that this wouldn't be so anywhere else in the world. It is dirty because it is in India.'

Her frustration comes from the prevalent feeling among Tibetans of rampant corruption in Indian officialdom, a view that many Indians share with them. She makes this remark to me because it is not a 'Tibetans versus Indians' matter for her. I have expressed concern over a local problem. She knows I will understand.

Living together in a cramped sangha requires a certain generosity of spirit. This is often in evidence in Dharamsala and keeps it sufficiently moored in the sangha space. It takes the form of charity to monasteries and voluntary participation in social welfare projects, but its most heart-warming instance occurs in the cheerful support given to castaways, particularly beggars and mangy mongrels. An academic from Delhi university who spent time in Dharamsala researching the effect of exile on the Tibetan community tells me that she has come to feel that Dharamsala is not only a refuge for the Tibetans— it is so for all kinds of marginalized people and creatures. Her remark makes me think that, perhaps by accepting all manners of refugees, Dharamsala's primary energy has become one of acceptance. Its promise of a safe haven draws not only bedraggled Tibetans over Himalayan snows and spiritual refugees over continents, but anyone in need of comfort and security who is close enough to sense its call.

The beggars of Dharamsala are like beggars anywhere in India. Their favourite spots seem to be near the Tsuglag Khang and the Lingkhor. Most of their business comes from Tibetans—not many pass by without dropping a coin or placing some food before them. This can be attributed to the Tibetan community's practice of dana (giving) as a way of gaining spiritual merit. Though it is an old Indian tradition, I find Tibetans to be more graceful and happy givers than their Indian counterparts. They may have little to give, but when it is shared it is with genuine gladness. Once at the Lingkhor, I sat down to rest at the midway point. An old woman came up a moment later and sat beside me. She took out a small packet of biscuits from her chuba pocket, tore it open and offered me some. I declined, but she wouldn't hear of it. I was touched by this simple act of sharing and found it replicated many times over in different ways in Dharamsala.

Generosity of spirit also translates into a generosity with space. Everyone seems to get their little patch under the

Dharamsala sun cramped though it may be, whether it is the beggars by the wayside, new émigrés from Tibet or spiritual nomads who wish to stay on for a while. This inclusiveness is another sangha characteristic, where all are equally welcome to join in, however different you may be from the existing residents. Where the ghetto will sift and sieve and reject the non-like ones, the sangha accepts and embraces.

Whether you wish to stay in Dharamsala for a month or a year, or forever, a range of options is available to you. Guesthouses work for only those who stay for a shorter time span. Those in for the long haul prefer to rent a place that can serve as home. And if something suitable is not available in McLeodganj, or if it is too expensive, suburbs like Sidhbari might offer good options. Once on my way to McLeodganj by cab from the railway station at Pathankot, my co-passenger was an American who had done precisely this. He and his wife had built a house in Sidhbari in a small community of similarly placed individuals. He worked as a meditation teacher and travelled to McLeodganj sometimes to teach. The income generated was meagre, and needed to be supplemented with stints in the United States, moonlighting as a management consultant. In this way, he would return periodically to a career and society he had given up to make a life in Dharamsala that was more meaningful for him, but which also needed money to sustain. 'Dharamsala is no utopia,' I thought to myself then, as I imagined the strain of living two mutually discordant lives, like trying to balance on two boats simultaneously in a fast-running stream. 'You can't survive on pure prana energy here; you need all that you need elsewhere too!'

Some spiritual nomads do seem to manage with the bare minimum. It is possible in Dharamsala to live a yogi's life—materially austere and spiritually rich. One such was a statuesque Spanish woman who was not an ordained nun, nor did she seem headed in that direction. Her main motivation in hanging about Dharamsala was to be near the Karmapa, with whom she felt a spontaneous connection the very first time she met him. She was taking Buddhist philosophy classes at the library, and living there as well. It turned out that the library provided accommodation to select students for longer courses of study. She got a paltry grant from her father in Spain, which she managed to stretch out until the next one came. She would also, whenever she could tear herself away long enough, return to Spain to earn some money selling jewellery she designed. Doing so didn't seem to stretch her as it perhaps did the American management consultant, for she seemed to have learned to balance her needs with her resources, keeping her focus all the while on her true purpose for being in Dharamsala—her spiritual practice. This balance kept her life from being fractured into the 'spiritual' and the 'non-spiritual'.

Her Dharamsala life was largely solitary, though she gathered friends and teachers along the way. When her tenure at the library ended, she lived wherever she could within her tight budget. She was a nomad within Dharamsala, her roots here sprouting from the core of her being and anchoring her in the spirit of the place. The American on the other hand had found a stable centre in Dharamsala to which he wished to return forever, from wherever his survival needs took him. Both are as much a part of Dharamsala's co-worlds as the Tibetan or the Himachali, perhaps more so because they are here *out of choice*. Others may have come to be here by birth or circumstance, but the settlers and nomads come willingly to be part of Dharamsala's sangha. This makes them responsible for making it work, and their efforts at co-ness are sincere and born out of gratitude to the generosity of the other worlds that have accepted their existence alongside their own.

It is a cold, cloudy morning. At the appliqué thangka workshop, the master thangka maker is handing out the designs for the day. The faces of his young apprentices are pinched with the cold. They get busy working on different parts of a massive thangka, and I peep into the colourful world flowing from under their fingers. On a wide platter before each one, there are small heaps of cloths of varied texture and material and colour. Black cotton for the hair, ochre silk for the skin, red thread for the lips, gold tissue for the robes . . . They must pick the correct piece according to the formula, and stitch it on to the blank piece of cloth in their hands.

Isn't Dharamsala like this appliqué—different patches mingling together with shared boundaries and on one ground? Their boundaries are porous, like stitches where even the finest ones have minuscule gaps between them. Up close, the patches appear disparate and vibrant. As I take a few steps back, the whole Buddha arises into view, being worked upon by different hands. What was a patch of black a moment ago is now his hair matted into the ascetic's knot. His robe swirls under an entire row of needles, and his eyes are emerging out of nothing even as I look.

This then is Dharamsala. The community lines exist, but are often elastic and permeable. Nomads and seasonal visitors are welcomed and taken care of. There is a genuine co-ness among the many worlds as in the patches of the thangka, despite the friction that is inevitable in human diversity. The sangha exists and, one hopes, will continue to realize its innate oneness in the co-energies of cooperation and collaboration.

8

Sustenance

'So, where are you having lunch/dinner?'
Conversations among travellers exploring new terrain often begin and/or end with this question, along with its variants: where will you eat, how do you know the food there is good, or more importantly hygienic, is it expensive, let's try something new . . . For you are far away from home and kitchen, unless you rent a place that has one. The majority of travellers to Dharamsala don't, which is why food is big business here and the bazaars are lined with eateries and restaurants that offer a wide variety of cuisine—Tibetan, Indian, Indian-style Chinese, 'fast food', Israeli and assorted European.

From the moment I come to know that the guesthouse I am staying at does not provide any meal options, not even tea or drinking water, I am gripped by what can best be described as 'food anxiety'. It is known to infect the low-budget traveller who cannot afford to stay in upmarket hotels with room service, or in other words food at the other end of a phone line. Such travellers must learn to access the skills of their hunter-gatherer forebears that lie dormant in some dusty corner of the collective unconscious of the species, and sharpen them for immediate use.

Lying back in bed one quiet night in Dharamsala, I realize

how basic needs, when they are easily and effortlessly met, tend to become invisible. How many times in my life have I gone hungry, I think as my stomach growls, dissatisfied with an insubstantial dinner. And how many times have I really paid attention to the satisfaction of a simple meal partaken in response to genuine hunger?

Travelling on a shoestring budget means an instant reconnection with, and an appreciation for, food. And by this I don't necessarily mean an appreciation for *good* food. Just food, plain, stomach-filling, digestible, not too unhealthy, food. In Dharamsala food is stripped of the other functions it fulfils at home, as regulator of the day for instance, which is planned around mealtimes. Here there are no mealtimes, nor beverage breaks. Instead there are points in the day when I find myself hungry. Then I go out and eat. I am rarely hungry after sundown, and have my main meal at midday when I am the hungriest.

I am learning something of the hunter-gatherer's life—find food when hungry. Eat your fill, and get on with other things. On paying attention, I find I am programmed to crave food at set times during the day—the 'mealtimes'. Also, I don't really need a lot of the food I would normally consume in the course of a day. The mind gets hungry even when the body may not. Realizing this relieves my food anxiety somewhat.

Interestingly, the pattern I fall into, of eating midday meals and little or no dinner, is the ideal food consumption routine prescribed for monastics in the Vinaya—rules of living in the Buddhist monastic sangha. Because of the Buddha's firm belief in the middle path, the food rules for Buddhist monastics are not as harsh as those of other monastic traditions, such as the Jain munis, who most often will have one meal a day and that too only as much as will fit in one palm. The Buddha knew from personal experience that physical mortification is of limited utility on the spiritual path, having spent six years as a young ascetic in self-flagellatory penance where he would sometimes restrict his food intake to one grain of rice a day. Having worn his body out and still nowhere near his goal of ultimate understanding, he finally ended the harsh penance by accepting a bowl of rice and milk. Revived, he sat down under the bodhi tree for the contemplation from which he would emerge the Buddha.

Would the starving ascetic have made it through the last lap of his spiritual journey without the nourishment provided by the bowl of rice and milk? It seems the Buddha himself didn't think he could have—a belief that found expression in his lifelong commitment to the middle path in all matters, particularly those related to the spiritual life, as well as his conscious avoidance of harsh extremes.

The Tibetans have taken to the middle path well, and it is so in matters of food as well. Their traditional diet has evolved from the needs of high-altitude living, so that there is an abundance of meat, yak's butter and tsampa, and a scarcity of wheat and rice, lentils, fresh vegetables and fruits. The diet of exiled Tibetans has undergone inevitable change because of a wider choice of foods in places where they now live, like Dharamsala, and the unavailability of some ingredients like yak's milk and its products. The change in climate has also necessitated dietary modifications, such as the substitution of butter in tea with milk. Their meat-eating, which has often been questioned as a violation of the Buddhist injunction to non-violence, needs to be seen in a cultural context where meat was the primary source of protein, as also in a middle path context that shuns extremist interpretations of the Buddha's teachings.

Dinner time at my guesthouse is merry and raucous, with the inmates cooking together in the common kitchen on the roof. Several rooms in the guesthouse are rented out to working, single Tibetan men. I know their workday is over when guitars begin humming in the balcony, and mouth-watering aromas waft in from the kitchen upstairs.

Little Tenzin loves these song-filled evenings, and is often to be found on the terrace with a guitar that his doting parents have bought him 'all the way from Delhi'. He cannot hold the full-sized guitar in his tiny hands, which proves not to be a problem for he always manages to bully one of the tenants to hold it up for him. Tenzin will then strum the guitar quite regally, sitting upright on a chair, with the young man holding it squatting near his feet. I am convinced this little boy is a reincarnation of an aristocrat of old Tibet, so lordly he appears.

When his dinner is ready, HRH Tenzin gets dragged in by his mother. He is soon out again holding a bowl of food, having wailed his way out of sitting inside. Because his buddies have drifted away towards their own dinners, I am paid a visit. Seeing no corresponding bowl in my hand, Tenzin holds out his own with the unhesitating generosity of children, and motions to me with his spoon to tuck in. I spoon some food into his little mouth and lead him back towards the family's room, from where light and laughter and food odours spill out into the dark corridor.

Being vegetarian limits my eating choices in Dharamsala, especially when it comes to Tibetan food where the popular dishes and delicacies incorporate various kinds of meats. The vegetarian options tend to overuse chopped cabbage and onion. I have had some watery thukpa variations, a soup filled with noodles and vegetables, which can be quite tasty if the vegetables are properly blended together in the broth. Thenthuk is another soup dish with flat, thick noodles that I enjoy eating hot combined with tingmo, plain soft bread that tastes great when soaked in soup. Vegetarian sections do exist on Dharamsala's menus and are kept there by travellers like myself who have opted for gentler ways to sustain their bodies.

One of the best Tibetan dishes I've tasted in Dharamsala has not been in McLeodganj but in Sidhbari, outside the Norbulingka crafts centre. I was the only customer at the shack, and pointed out thukpa on the menu to the Tibetan cook who spoke neither Hindi nor English, the only languages I am proficient in. I sat outside on a bench listening to water singing over stones in a river that flowed close by and watching darkness descend rapidly upon the white-crested Dhauladhars. When the food was ready, the cook brought out a wobbly wooden table and plonked a steaming bowl before me. I slurped up the tasty thukpa even as night insects came buzzing around the bulb over my head.

Perhaps the proximity to natural beauty improved the dish's taste? I do get influenced by such things as ambience, and am susceptible to the charm of a meal distinguished by a gurgling stream nearby, or by the warmth of the preparer. By this standard, the most spectacular meal I must have had in Dharamsala will have to be a lunch at Naddi, another of the suburbs. It was in the veranda of a hotel that jutted out from the mountainside, so that one felt almost suspended in air with the valley below and the mountains rising sharp and sheer in front. The food—parathas with mango pickle and curd—was nothing remarkable, and I wouldn't remember it if I hadn't eaten it watching high-flying eagles lazily circle the peaks before me.

Eating in the noise and dust of the bazaar may not be in the same league aesthetically, but that is where Dharamsala's most interesting eateries are located. Restaurants with names like Snow Lion (Tibet's national emblem), Lhagyal (from *lhagyal lo*, a slogan that means 'victory to the gods') and Amdo (the Dalai Lama's home province) beckon you with the promise of authentic Tibetan food. I have many a bowl of pungent noodle dishes in their uniform interiors that almost always consist of formica-topped tables and wooden chairs whose padding is worn out from having borne far too many posteriors than they were upholstered to.

In the bazaar streets, shopkeepers fishing up mounds of samosas and pakoras at roadside shacks are joined by Tibetan men and women selling momos (steamed or fried dumplings with meat or vegetable filling). Momos have joined the legion of street foods in India through the efforts of enterprising Tibetans. In Delhi I have eaten momos in swank restaurants, dingy shops and by the wayside. But nowhere have they tasted like they do here in Dharamsala—fresh and real, with the unmistakable flavour of home cooking.

One evening I spot a couple doling out momos at a bazaar street corner. Their steamed vegetable momos come with a potato and spinach filling, which must be sampled in the interest of novelty. I turn into the little paper dish handed out to me and allow the world of taste forming in my mouth to shut out any distaste at the open drain and pile of garbage right next to where I am standing. The momos are soft and succulent, and warm and soupy at their core. The elderly man who is serving them watches my obvious delight with corresponding delight of his own, and presses more upon me like a fond uncle feeding his favourite niece. And so, food is transformed into something much more than sustenance—a way of sharing warmth with a stranger.

I have another yummy momo experience in Dharamsala. I emerge hungry at noon from the philosophy class at the library. There is a cafe a few steps down where many people from the class are heading for lunch. I spot a woman at the bottom of the steps with the telltale steel container of a momo-seller, and immediately know what my lunch will be.

The woman lives nearby, she tells me in elementary Hindi, and gets up early each morning to prepare her batch of momos for the day. She also sells flat, diamond-shaped noodles served cold and dripping with a fiery chilli-garlic sauce, which are more like a snack than a proper meal. I sit beside her on a rough wooden bench, and ask for steamed potato momos followed by a plateful of spicy noodles. While I eat, the seller gets a regular stream of takeaway orders from the Tibetan government offices located in the same complex, the Gangchen Kyishong. This is a hotspot for Tibetan style fast food, and soon the original momo-seller is joined by another woman who sets up shop alongside. She doesn't seem to mind the encroachment on her territory, and both fall into a gossipy huddle which they interrupt only to prepare the orders.

The momo-sellers' camaraderie seems based on their shared experience as women whose entrepreneurship helps feed their families. Such women are responsible for many of Dharamsala's eateries; they run them at any rate, planning menus, cooking and serving, and overseeing the till. One such eatery opened during my stay, on the way from McLeodganj to Naddi, a short distance from the Tibetan Children's Village (TCV). The elderly couple that owned it had arrived from Tibet with nothing more than the wife's culinary skills, which were indeed formidable. Though I had some difficulty explaining the vegetarian concept to them, they finally understood my order thanks to the translational skills of the TCV staff that formed their main clientele. The food was delicious, and I think I finally got to know, after hundreds of meals, how thenthuk and thukpa are really meant to taste.

Many such family-run eateries manage to do quite well, and are able to raise themselves out of poverty. An unfortunate fallout of their prosperity is that the task of cooking is immediately turned over to non-Tibetan hired help, and the food ends up feeling restaurant-ish instead of tasting like robust homemade cooking from a Tibetan matron's kitchen.

This phenomenon is indicative of a class consciousness where you don't work with your hands if you have enough money to hire others to work for you. Because the old hierarchy is not applicable any more, a social upgrade based on the materialistic standards of the modern world has become possible for the Tibetans. Life in exile has brought new opportunities for upward mobility. For Dharamsala's world of food, it could mean a sad loss of taste.

Dear Guest, our Vegetarian Kitchen is trying to provide you with the freshest possible ingredients available; we therefore keep our menu small. Each day we are serving special dishes that reflect the freshness of the market. For these daily specials, please read the board.

The main purpose of this restaurant is to provide young Tibetans a vocational training. Therefore bear with us for any mishaps.

Please note that we are located within the monastic compound. We therefore have to request you to refrain from smoking (also outside), taking any other drugs as alcohol etc, as well as to behave respectfully. Thank you for your consideration.

So says the back jacket of the menu card at the Namgyal Café, which nestles next to the monastery whose name it bears within the Tsuglag Khang complex. The cafe is just one room with six tables and numerous chairs crammed around them with difficulty. It opens into the blue Dharamsala sky on two sides. I am sitting at one of the seats that widens out into the mountains, which appear at eye-level due to the cafe's elevation.

It is noon, not really lunchtime for most people as yet, though my hunger pangs have signalled the time for my main meal of the day. I have ordered a vegan pizza that will be cheeseless and consequently lighter than others on the menu.

I mull over the peculiarity of discovering vegan dishes in Dharamsala. The vegan diet has never caught on in India despite its large population of 'cultural vegetarians'. Nor can it hope to, for we all love our milk, curd, cottage cheese and milk-based sweets with a passion that has caused one of the best-loved Hindu gods to figure in his childhood tales as a butter- and curd-stealing cowherd. Yet here in cosmopolitan Dharamsala, a vegan pizza is sizzling in the oven even as a young trainee steward asks me whether I am sure about that slice of chocolate cake I want to sneak in for dessert. 'It will have butter and milk,' he says, anxious to protect my vegan purity. I assure him I'm just trying the vegan pizza for the heck of it, mainly because this is the only place I have come upon till now where I can sample one!

The pizza takes a long time arriving, which I discover at subsequent meals here is part of the adventure of supporting restaurants that provide 'vocational training'. The young staff members are cheerful if inept, and charmingly unperturbed by their own lack of coordination. The vegan pizza when it finally comes tastes like cardboard. I quickly turn my attention to the gooey chocolate cake, which is thankfully not vegan. Drawn to its friendliness I return to the Namgyal Café often, and find its other pizzas and pastas absolutely delightful and true to their promise of 'freshest possible ingredients'.

At lunchtime, the cafe fills up rapidly and soon there is an assortment of nationalities grouped around the tables, their voices filling the tiny area like so many babbling streams. I catch snatches of conversation from which 'sunyata' or 'Shantideva' or 'anatma' leak out, and I know that I am among serious students for whom mealtimes need not interrupt dharma discussions.

Cafes in Dharamsala provide much more than food; they make available space for its sangha to meet and engage in exchanges of thoughts, ideas and opinions. Meals are often a pretext for philosophical banter that meanders from late brunch to a later dinner via several cups of strong, black coffee. Food becomes incidental to sustenance of another kind, that which feeds the mind's hunger to know. Co-travellers on the inner path get a chance to share experiences and insights, along with slices of cake and pots of tea. This opportunity to congregate and communicate with like-minded friends is invaluable to the spiritual life, and is one way in which the sangha of seekers forges bonds and fulfils the needs of its members for support and encouragement—I would call it 'food for the soul' if it wasn't an absolutely ragged and done-to-death cliché!

Dinner at Pema Thang Hotel's restaurant one evening reveals another meaning of soul food. The spacious restaurant is jam-packed with a party of enthusiasts from Europe that is in Dharamsala on a reconnaissance of the spiritual services on offer. They have spent the day meeting monks and touring monasteries and now have a clutch of questions for their Tibetan guide, which range from the manner of draping robes by monastics, to soul and God, and Mahayana Buddhist views on death and dying. The aroma of food sizzling on hotplates seems to whet their appetite to know more, and the questions run on through the length of the meal. As the clatter of forks on china dies down and the empty plates are relinquished, it is with a satisfaction that has come from something more than a full stomach. The hunger for answers to life's dilemmas has been allayed for the time being, and the possibility for a true and decisive appeasement glimpsed.

What more can you hope to get from a dinner?

9

The Library

'Visualize all sentient beings in the mire of samsara, struggling in pain, crying out for succour yet unable to help themselves. Feel their suffering, and lovingkindness towards them. Express this metta and karuna in the form of a desire to attain Buddhahood for their sake, to free them . . .' says the young translator as the geshe looks amusedly at the earnest faces around him. His eyes travel from one face to another, all thirsty for a sip from the ocean of wisdom they are sure surges within him. The new ones fidget, uncomfortable as yet in sitting cross-legged on the ground. A veteran teacher of Buddhist philosophy at Dharamsala's Library of Tibetan Works and Archives (LTWA), the geshe can easily distinguish the old hands by their air of being much-travelled-in-the-east, lotus positions and loud chanting in Tibetan. After all these years, the sight is still incongruous enough to set off a brook of laughter silently burbling within him.

The room that spreads out before his high seat is large and airy. This, the first class of the day, is about to end. Sunlight streams in from the wide windows to the geshe's right, where a golden Buddha statue glitters upon its altar decorated with fresh flowers and bowls of water by a few chosen students in the morning. The geshe is an old monk whose name has become subsumed into his title—Geshe—a degree roughly equivalent to doctor of philosophy awarded at the end of a long and rigorous course of training at Tibetan monastic universities. Geshe-la looks out of the window that opens on to a sunny courtyard, and his kindly face settles into an expression of quiet absorption. His sagging, wrinkled skin seems to tauten along with his spine, as he readies to conclude this class on the fourteenth-century Tibetan commentator Tsong Kha Pa's text on the 'gems of mind training'.

From the back of the room, I watch as the translator's smooth, young face also tightens in anticipation as he listens attentively to geshe-la. The young man probably prides himself on being able to get through translating a piece without having to turn to the geshe for help, which is proof of his excellent mind-focusing abilities. As he begins to configure the geshe's metaphysical Tibetan into simple English, his eyes slowly move away from the teacher into a half-closed concentration into nothing—an expression mirrored on several faces in the room.

I am wedged between a big, much-tattooed American monk, who looks like he would be more comfortable in a biker's gear of leather and angry attitude rather than the single-cloth maroon robe and its vows, and an older Scottish woman whose fingers constantly twitch around a rosary of fake sandalwood beads and with whom I have walked that morning. Behind me, a young Tibetan woman furiously takes down notes as the geshe speaks, as opposed to the majority of the class that begins writing during the translation. She is one among a handful of lay young Tibetans who have joined this class to 'understand the dharma better', she tells me. They seem an aberration among non-monastic Tibetans who for the most part are not involved in dharma study, the prescribed rituals and Om-mani-padme-humming seemingly enough for their spiritual needs.

I am the only Indian in the room.

The class finishes as usual with chanting in Tibetan, which I can join in because I have a booklet published by the library that helpfully renders the mantras in Roman script along with their translations. When the chanting is done, everyone waits respectfully for the geshe to depart. The old monk has some trouble getting up after the prolonged sitting. To steady his wobbling frame, he seeks the support of his wooden desk. I marvel at the enfeebled body that houses a mind which soars forth steadily like the peaks of the mountains that loom over the library. The young interpreter proffers his arm, and all of us bend forward from the waist as the geshe hobbles out of the room.

The guru is gone. The students watch ravens squabbling in the courtyard as they wait for the next class to begin.

Namo guru bayah!
Namo Buddhaya!
Namo dharmaya!
Namo sanghaya!

I seek refuge in the guru
I seek refuge in the Buddha
I seek refuge in the dharma
I seek refuge in the sangha

We chant this refuge mantra at the beginning and end of each class, only, it is in four jewels instead of three—the guru has been added in Tibetan Buddhism to the original triumvirate of Buddha, dharma and sangha. I wonder whether this happened because the Buddha was no longer the prototypical teacher, having been elevated out of the human realm of samsara by his nirvana. Each class follows a cycle—chanting the refuge and other mantras in Tibetan, the lecture, questions from students and then chanting the same mantras again that one did at the beginning.

Cycles that complete a full circle soothe the human mind with a suggestion of stability. The mind latches on to this rhythm of the classes, and looks forward to its comforting constancy. Perhaps any such crutch will do at this point when I am learning to divest the mind of its habituated patterns by recognizing the comfortable ruts it makes for itself, which ultimately express themselves in the way I am, the way I live. All of us in the class are trying to make ourselves afresh with this watching and recognizing and dropping and leading away. We are making an attempt to find a new 'I' amidst all the clutter and noise and untidiness within, a peeling away of the petals of the lotus to reveal the jewel at its core.

Is that jewel no-thing? Is the sanctum empty after all, and the 'I' a smokescreen that clouds that truth?

The prayers we chant carry reminders of the intent we must keep through our inner journey, and on which is contracted this class and indeed the whole of Mahayana Buddhism of which the Tibetan Vajrayana is a significant offshoot. It is the intent of striving for enlightenment, for seeking the ultimate resolution, not for personal gain but for the benefit of all beings. The supremacy accorded to this altruism by Mahayana is one among many fault-lines along which the sangha of the Buddha's followers split around a century after his demise.

When this separation occurred, the Buddha's path was rapidly acquiring the characteristics of a theistic religion. There was a part of the sangha that persisted in preserving the original teachings as they were, while others wished for the path to become dynamic and accept changes they felt were inevitable, like the idolization of the Buddha and the development of rituals. The Second Council of the sangha, convened some 100 years after the first one had been held a year after the Buddha's death in 483 BCE, brought the schisms out in the open. Thereafter two schools of Buddhism were recognized— Mahayana, which embraced change, and Theravada, literally, 'the Doctrine of the Elders'.

In a case of one-upmanship, Mahayana followers would refer to Theravada as 'Hinayana' or 'the lesser vehicle', thereby setting it up in opposition to 'Mahayana', which in Sanskrit means 'greater vehicle'. When Buddhism entered Tibet several centuries later, it was bestride a third yana—Vajrayana. Going by the names alone might give one a sense of progression, from lesser to greater to a seeming zenith, with a notion of the latest being the best. Actually, they can be seen as extensions of the same idea, offering a palette of practices to seekers according to their diverse needs—an idea that is well accepted in Indian spirituality which maintains that there can be as many paths to realization as there are seekers.

So one can assume that seekers who come to Vajrayana are amenable to offering the fruits of their spiritual labours for the betterment of all beings, rather than keeping them for themselves. The detachment that is called for from selfishly desiring spiritual progression is thus not harsh and juiceless. It is sweetened by the connection between oneself and the entire realm of fellow sentient beings that feel and suffer just like us. I taste a raw beauty when I try to imagine this mega-connection with everyone and everything else. I am a speck in this vast created universe, but I am not as powerless as I assume myself to be. I can contribute something to this giant web which I inhabit. By throbbing with compassion and by quietening and stilling myself, I can breathe into the synapses around me the inner power and bliss that are the fruits of my practice within my self. I can change myself. I can also change the world.

That this endeavour is not one's alone, but of significance to a universal community, is a powerful thought that changes the way one relates with one's inner life. The resultant responsibility one feels helps deal with the insidious trap of ownership of one's practice by the ego-self that binds and constricts this, as it does other aspects of our lives. The bodhisattva ideal of deferring self-enlightenment until the point when all beings have been helped out of samsara is closely intertwined with this altruistic intent. In Mahayana forms of Buddhism, the bodhisattvas are sometimes even greater heroes than the Buddha(s), for they are believed to have *chosen* to remain in bondage where they could have easily flown into the freedom of final extinguishment, of nirvana.

How can you choose freedom for yourself when everyone else continues to suffer? This is the question the bodhisattva encourages us to contemplate, we who wish to follow his ideal.

In the class at the library, we offer this dedication: 'By the merit I have gathered from these acts of virtue done in this way, may all the sufferings of every being disappear.'

Before we go about thinking of ourselves as righteous little bodhisattvas, we are brought to terra firma with the confessional declaration: 'From beginningless samsara, in this and other lives, I have unwittingly committed many non-virtues or caused others to do the same. Bewildered by the confusion of my ignorance, I have rejoiced in my own and others' non-virtues. Seeing these mistakes, I declare all this to you protectors from the depth of my heart.'

Then, we request for the teaching: 'With hands pressed together I request the Buddhas of all directions to light the lamp of dharma for those who are groping in the darkness of suffering.'

The second class at the library begins at eleven, and tends to be even more crowded than the early morning one. The German woman who sat next to me on the bus that brought me to McLeodganj from Delhi comes in with a couple of others and, recognizing me, comes over to chat. Her suitcase that was to follow has been lost in transit, and she is now at the mercy of local clothes' shops to tog her up for the entire length of her stay. I have seen some funky, faux-ethnic clothes in psychedelic colours and fabrics on sale in Dharamsala that you could perhaps wear to a rave party or to an evening of 'hash'-ing it with friends. That is where the German woman seems to have sourced her hot purple and gold outfit that is nothing short of a visual explosion in the middle of a staid sea of faded jeans, lived-in and comfortable-looking shirts, and maroon monastic robes.

Still, I think she looks good. I tell her so. She flashes me a bright red lipstick smile and pulls out her copy of the *Way of the Bodhisattva* by Shantideva from her backpack. It is the text we are studying in this class. 'I can certainly do with some more patience,' she says, indicating the part of the text that is being taught at the moment. Her missing suitcase is a case in point, she says. 'I really blew it the day before with the airline office on the phone. And then yesterday, we started this part of the text. It is just the right time for me. Just the right lesson . . .' Her voice trails off and I sense a touch of regret perhaps about her behaviour. 'Hey,' I say softly, 'we can all do with some patience, can't we?'

The geshe has arrived, and he is not the geshe from the morning. This one too is old and kindly, and soon the two geshes morph into one in my mind—a sort of generic geshe who comes in at regular intervals into this sunny room to teach a classful of people in need of learning to be patient. The young translator is gone too, and we have an older American woman who is remarkably fluent in Tibetan. She sometimes tells the old geshe to stop when *she* thinks the piece she has to translate has gone on long enough. I don't much care for her harshness with the old monk, and wince whenever she is short with him. Perhaps this is an Indian-Tibetan cultural thing, I tell myself, this respect for age business. Nobody else seems to even notice her behaviour, which is such a contrast with the respectful stance of the young translator from before.

But I must be patient! The ensuing lecture does much to show how to iron out these creases that form in our minds as we go about reacting to provocations big and small, how to let go of our constructs and contexts sufficiently to become still in the midst of raging turbulence. This part of the text is in the form of a debate, where Shantideva responds to queries that have arisen in listeners' minds from his basic lecture on patience as one of the characteristics to be actively cultivated by the bodhisattva wannabe.

As we go through the rigorous Q&A session, this sun-filled room in the library begins to echo with sounds of debate from Nalanda, the premier Indian Buddhist university of old. Barriers of time and distance recede, and it is as if we are placed in some sort of an eternal continuum that juxtaposes twenty-first-century Dharamsala directly upon eighth-century Nalanda. The ghost of Shantideva, a prince-turned-monk in the manner of Siddhartha Gautama, sits astride our geshe's shoulder and whispers his Madhyamika (middle path) philosophy into the old monk's ears. And we are the feisty interlocutors, such is the correspondence I find between the ancient queries posed by anonymous seekers some 1300 years ago and those thrown up by my twenty-first-century mind right now. For instance, 'The basis of virtue is faith. If someone makes public my faults while ignoring my good qualities, those who know me will lose faith in me. Am I then justified in getting angry?'

Shantideva, 'If that is your reason for anger, you should get equally upset if another is disparaged. Does this happen? No. If we can bear the slander of others, why do we get angry when we are ourselves slandered?'

The seeker responds, 'Others' slander is linked to their faults and qualities that are not connected with me. Their situation is out of my control.'

Shantideva persists, 'The person who is slandering you is also out of control because he is controlled by his emotions, which too are dependent on certain factors. Since this is a situation dependent on other factors, there is no reason for *you* to get angry.'

Okay, the seeker realizes, this tack hasn't worked with the wily old master. So he, and my questioning mind, tries another.

'What if someone vilifies the Buddhas and bodhisattvas, and disparages the Three Jewels and representations of the enlightened body, speech and mind (like stupas and scriptures)?' the seeker wants to know.

This question is startlingly modern in its potential for interpretation for our times, in terms of stiffening religious stances, the intentional hardening of old, quiet religions into political weapons of xenophobia, and the preoccupation of a section of adherents with 'protecting' the purity of their religions.

This time, the geshe has his own angle to add to the seeker's query. 'In Tibet, statues were torn down and Tibetans were told that these statues cannot get up and defend themselves, how will they protect you? This was deliberately done to destroy the people's faith. We also saw the destruction in

Bamiyan in Afghanistan, when the Taliban regime of the time blasted the massive Buddha statues with explosives.'

How does a still mind respond to such grave instigations?

Says Shantideva, 'Instead of responding in anger, we should feel compassion for them because they are creating suffering. If we can stop them in this by using skilful methods, we should. If we cannot, then we shouldn't act violently out of hostility and anger. At this time, we can remind ourselves that the Buddhas and bodhisattvas, the realized beings and the teachings cannot be hurt or be made unhappy by these actions. This is because they have overcome all conceptions of the self. The Buddhas have completely eliminated the self and the bodhisattvas have reached varying degrees of transcending the self. So if thoughts of "I" and "mine" arise, they do not influence their actions. Their [the bodhisattvas'] mind is like the heavy wrestler who has pinned down the weaker wrestler of the ego, which is not dead but immobilized. Where symbols of religion are concerned, they cannot be made to suffer because they don't have consciousness. Those who perform these actions are the ones who truly need our compassion. The objects they target cannot be harmed, but they themselves are being harmed by their own destructive emotions.'

How to feel this compassion for 'the other', especially at the moment when he is venting the poison of his negativity on us?

According to Shantideva, 'This can be done by understanding that their negative actions are either seeding future suffering for them or they are the result of disturbing emotions that have been activated by their negative karma. Understanding that this situation is a result of their own actions, we shouldn't get angry.'

'What about righteous anger?' asks the seeker. The geshe explicates this question with the concept found in some religions of defending the faith, where followers feel they will be handsomely rewarded in the afterlife if they take up cudgels for their religion in this lifetime.

Shantideva suggests caution. 'This is a mistaken belief. They may do so to defend their faith but, from the karmic point of view, only they will have to individually bear the consequences of their negative actions.'

To each his own? This view is characteristically Buddhist, one that can only come from a theology that is devoid of a creator-God and such comforts afforded by other religions. Things are simple. You sow and you reap. There is no grace, no possibility of ducking out of karma good or bad, except through fortifying and training self and mind to withstand whatever life throws our way. This *is* the wheel of samsara. The way to veer ourselves out of it is by turning the counter-wheel of wisdom, of the teachings, of dharma. Here in the library, this is the opportunity that seeker-students have, just as they did in Nalanda more than a thousand years ago.

At this point the Nalanda seeker becomes overwhelmed with the idea of the endless suffering one brings upon oneself through one's own ignorance. Shantideva is quick to point out, 'Others' negative karma makes us feel uncomfortable because it triggers our own seeds of negative karma. If we allow ourselves to become enmeshed in this discomfort, we will be unable to do anything to help the sufferer, for we suffer ourselves. The bodhisattva has no space to feel discomfort because he is totally filled with love.'

Love, then, emerges as the true way of the bodhisattva. It is the antidote to suffering, our own and others'. It is the way out of limited perceptions that hold our minds in their vice-like grip and manipulate us at their will. Love is also the motivation from which the bodhisattva acts; it is the genesis, evolution and culmination of all her dealings in the world.

She is not here to merely live and die. She has paid her dues and has suffered and ached like the rest of us. She has then sweated through the rigours of self-training and has finally pinned under her the cause of pettiness and sorrow—her ego-self, as Shantideva says in the analogy of the wrestler.

She is not free from samsara, not as yet. But she is free to love . . .

How to love was what Tenzin Choerab, the American monk who turned Dharamsala into his cloister, had told me was the one big lesson he had learned during his years of practice. On the long walk to the library, I meet another who has learned to love well in Dharamsala. She is Nancy, the elderly Scottish woman who sat next to me in the class. She comes from the Shetland Islands where harsh winds blow the year round and have stroked her skin into deep wrinkles that run into one another like a network of interlinked waterways. Temperamental weather makes life on the Islands difficult. But that was nothing compared to her own volatile nature and its stormy mood-swings. Weary with herself, she began to visit Samye Ling, a Buddhist centre that was established in Scotland in 1967. Samye Ling is purported to be the oldest such centre in the west, and makes available the opportunity for lay westerners to live there and begin their dharma practice.

Nancy began meditating. On days when it wasn't raining or snowing or blowing icy sleet, she would take her mat out to the porch of her house and sit facing the sea. She would watch the rough waves that angrily crashed against the big rocks of the shore, and feel her own feelings whirling through her and crashing into her mind again and again. They carried a lot of anger, pain and frustration. She would quietly watch them build up and wash over her, and when it was time to go in she would be so exhausted that she had to support her slight frame against the walls.

Gradually things became better. She was able to know a destructive thought when it arose, and take it through the motions without allowing herself to become emotionally engaged in it. When she sat on the porch, she now looked out at the horizon, where the earth met the sky and at which point all tumult ceased. But she felt hollowness in her life. The anger had died down, but had not been replaced by love. It was something she still needed to learn.

'I found out about the library in Dharamsala at Samye Ling,' she tells me as we sidestep the sharp stones that jut out of this short cut path we have veered into on our way to the library. She is nimbler than I am, and I often suppress yelps of pain as the stones dig into the soft soles of my sneakers. 'I was told about the philosophy courses and I thought it would be interesting to travel to India and live among others who are interested in the same things as I am, like meditation and Buddhism,' she says.

The path curves out into the main road and my poor feet are thankful for the smoothness of its tarred surface. 'We must look out for the next short cut,' Nancy says to me, for she is the veteran of this route. 'It will come to the left and I have identified a fallen tree to mark it out.' This is not Nancy's first, second or even third visit to Dharamsala. She is a regular who tries to come every year for a couple of months. And it is not only for the classes.

Coming to Dharamsala the first time was an eye-opener for Nancy. Till then, the only Tibetans she had known were the teachers at Samye Ling. She knew about the Tibetan cause, but did not realize the enormity of the problems of the refugee community until she arrived right in the middle of it. 'I found so much suffering here. Right away, I wanted to do *something*,' she says. She began visiting monasteries and schools and other refugee institutions in Dharamsala. Then one day, she hit upon an idea on how she could help. She would finance the education of young Tibetan monks. 'I met my sons for the first time here. They had been chosen for scholarship and immediately addressed me as "mother".' Her eyes moisten with the memory of that moment. Like all new parents, she felt a huge surge of love for the little boys who had so spontaneously welcomed her into their circle of love. 'Of course they have their own families, and in any case they are training to be monks. But I feel in my heart they are my children,' Nancy says.

The fallen tree has been spotted, and she pauses for a brief while at the turning, rifling through her bag. I wait politely, and she soon looks up and hands me some photographs. 'See, my sons,' she points them out to me in the photos and smiles proudly when I say how well they look. Finding the little monks and supporting them was a leap of love for Nancy. She found she had so much love to share, love that was as spontaneous as the little boys', but which came as more of a surprise to her than it must have to the children.

The little boys are now grown into bright adolescents, and Nancy has consolidated her leap into the unknown territory of unconditional love. Are they here in Dharamsala, I ask her, suddenly eager to see this mother with her sons. 'No,' she says. 'They are studying at the Tibetan settlement in Bylakuppe in Karnataka. I have just come from there.' So Dharamsala is her retreat in a way, where she comes to study? 'Yes, that and the fact that I wish to be near His Holiness the Karmapa. I feel such a strong connection with him.'

The path has become steep and, for some time, both of us concentrate on putting our feet right. Walking the spiralling way down from McLeodganj to the library is an exercise in being anchored in the present moment. There are many by-lanes and short cuts that you may miss if you are not all there. Or you might slip and fall on one of the less-frequented bits. The path requires constant, moment-to-moment awareness, which is just the kind of priming the wandering mind needs before attempting the intense concentration demanded by the class.

The steep path lets us out near Jogiwara, a residential area with many homes and shops. I recognize a Sikh's shop on the way which I had visited some time ago. It had a sign outside advertising the availability of tofu, but all I could see and smell were parathas being fried on a huge griddle. On entering the shack to explore, I found two monks seated on the low benches digging into a pile of parathas. As I sipped oversweetened tea, I found they were actually on holiday from their monasteries and had decided to travel. I hadn't realized you could get time off from being monks, I teased them jokingly. They were not merely having a good time, they said, but were also learning English so they could translate scriptures and take the dharma to a wider, world audience. It was an ambition I would find articulated many more times in Dharamsala, an expression perhaps of the altruistic intent to help others, in this case by conveying the dharma to them?

Nancy and I make another turn, this time marked by criss-crossing water pipes. I ask her about the Karmapa as we start descending a stairway. 'Of course, my interest in Buddhism pre-dates my experience with Him.' She refers to the Karmapa in a way that implies awe-filled capitalization. 'Initially, I didn't want to go to see Him but went because my friend insisted.' This was when he was a new arrival at Sidhbari and had just begun giving audiences. 'We were waiting for Him in a room. As soon as He entered, the very air seemed to sparkle with dancing particles of gold! I felt very strongly connected with

Him.' Her voice begins to quiver with emotion at the memory.
'Then next year, I was here in Dharamsala but I didn't want to
go to meet Him. I thought that nothing could match my first
experience and I didn't want to be disappointed. And then, a
thunderstorm came to Dharamsala from His direction, as if
He had sent it. At that point, I *knew*.'

As she speaks of directions, my mind wanders up this
hillside where the library is located. Right at the top of this
very mountain stands the Dalai Lama's residence and the
Tsuglag Khang, and we have passed the entrance to the
Lingkhor on our way down. I think how well this fortuitous
and temporary settlement of the Tibetans has turned out in
Dharamsala. Whether by design or serendipity, this one
mountain in a way has come to bear upon itself the composite
sacredness of Tibetan culture and religion and its spiritual
knowledge and, if it were in old Tibet instead of modern
India, it would have come to be worshipped as some sort of a
preserver deity.

We are at the library now. The wide stone-paved courtyard
that stretches out in front of it is warm with the sun and the
contented sleep of dogs. While I instinctively try and avoid
the dogs, Nancy stops by them for a while and lovingly strokes
their supine backs. 'I know,' she whispers to them. 'You are so
old and so tired. It's okay, this is a good place to rest. Be
happy . . .'

I leave Nancy to her little tête-à-tête. She reaches out
instinctively to others without prejudices inspired by otherness
or fleas. To my mind, she is learning to love like a bodhisattva.

The door that is the main entrance to the library is huge and
imposing, as if to declare the specialness of what lies behind

it. The wooden threshold needs to be stepped over, and reminds me of old Indian temples and rural homes. Here, this is symbolic of a stepping in, into the sphere of protected and sanctified knowledge. Somehow I cannot shake off the feeling of entering a temple. Again a cultural thing, I presume. But one day I find something in the library that validates the feeling of sacredness that follows me like a lingering aftertaste during my visits here.

Walking about the library, I come upon a large room lined row upon row with glass-paned bookcases filled with bundles of richly woven cloth. A young man comes up to me and I ask him about this room. It is a storehouse for all the original manuscripts of sacred texts rescued from the monasteries in Tibet, he says. They include commentaries written by Tibetan scholars over the centuries on scriptures of Mahayana Buddhism brought from India. The silks they are wrapped in are colour coded to distinguish the texts from the commentaries.

'You know, in the old days each monastery would have these many texts. And now, this is the sum total of what we have,' says the young man sadly. He is a philosophy student and would like to translate these texts some day, like the vacationing monks I met in Jogiwara. 'Some have already been translated by scholars here at the library and some others are in the process. This is actually one of the ongoing projects of the LTWA, so that more and more people can become acquainted with these precious teachings.' For the benefit of all beings, I add almost reflexively, like an 'Amen' or 'Insha Allah'. The young scholar's serious demeanour relaxes into a smile. 'Sure,' he says.

The 'temple of knowledge' concept that comes into play in my mind as I step into the library is rooted in the exalted position traditionally accorded to all learning, especially that related to eternal truths, to dharma. Perhaps this reverence had to do with the opening of the mind, the expansion of consciousness that would come from knowing the reality of things such as the mechanics of oneself and the larger universe. Unfortunately, because of the recognition of the preciousness of such knowledge, it often became protected, at times too protected, by conventions that placed it outside the realm of common access. It happened in India, and it happened in Tibet, where it shrank into the space of the monastic institutions. The knowledge gathered in sacred texts became veiled in silks and isolated in libraries where only the chosen few could get to it.

As mentioned earlier, the uprooting of the teachers of Tibetan Buddhism resulted in many of its teachings and practices becoming available to the contemporary world. Translation of ancient texts has rendered old wisdom in a modern idiom, and thus provided textbooks to those who wish to follow this path but do not have the scholastic wherewithal to learn a new language to do so. The library is an important node in this translational endeavour driven in large measure by Tibetan scholars. I think it is the best way to guard against future destruction. What is particularized and confined can be easily destroyed; what is as freely available as sunlight and air simply cannot.

This is only part of the marvel that is the Library of Tibetan Works and Archives of Dharamsala. Its phenomenal achievement that makes for its true miracle is that it provides a place for free, honest and rigorous exchange of experiential knowledge of the inner life. It gives us implements with which to chip away at our world-hardened selves in the form of geshes, texts in a language we understand, and courses that are accessible for all alike and one can attend for as long as one wishes to. It is also the hub where the wandering sramanas of Dharamsala connect with one another and the dharma, where they find a direction into their inner lives and a community of co-travellers.

The library is thus a latter-day version of Nalanda (though tiny in comparison), not only because it teaches texts of masters from that university, but also because it is an institution like that one of yore, where an atmosphere of philosophical enquiry is supported by active practice and where discussion and debate is encouraged and fostered. There is no stipulation that this is open only to Buddhists, the registration process is easy and anyone who wishes to join in is readily accepted into the fold.

At the library, it is as if Nalanda has come alive once again centuries after it fell into ruin. And it has happened here in Dharamsala, fashioned by Nalanda's old alumni into a new incarnation that meets the particular needs of these times.

10

Bhagsu

A loud whoosh wakes me up on an afternoon made somnolent by a warm sun, tired limbs and a full stomach. I have stretched myself out in the shapeless puddle the sun makes on my bed, crisscrossed by horizontal shadows cast by the window bars. The sound is the kind that children make when they are pretending to be eagles or fighter planes or Superman or anything else that in their imagination is airborne and swoops around. Upon the chiaroscuro on the bedcover, a moving shadow has joined the stationary ones. It is little Tenzin prancing about on the balcony.

I raise myself up on one elbow and peer outside to see what the fuss is about. Tenzin, still in his school uniform, is progressing across the balcony in little hops not unlike a frisky bunny. His arms are making downward motions with each hop, and his fingers are wiggling in what can only be the international sign for rain. He is emitting sounds that go whooo . . . He is either pretending to be a train engine that is being rained upon or imitating the ghost of the Lady of the Lake, drowned and weed-sodden.

Seeing me peep out, his mother, who is trying to get him to change out of his dusty uniform, smiles apologetically. 'He is trying to be a waterfall. You see, his class went to Bhagsu for a picnic today,' she says by way of explanation. I am fully awake now and am enjoying little Tenzin's rendition of a waterfall, which is actually quite creative. 'Bhagsu has a waterfall?' I ask her. 'I thought there was just a temple there.' And one I haven't paid any attention to because I feel I have been taken around enough soulless temples whose lack of sacredness and dirt and greedy priests I find irksome. I instinctively recoil from visiting temples that are worshipped in, for they are more likely to have lost the stillness of transcendence than the ones that lie in ruins, silence having come upon them perforce by centuries of disuse.

This is a knotty space to be in, for I do recognize that religion and its practice in India is noisy and raucous and untidy and gaudy. The way we worship is the way we live life—as a grand mela. Simultaneous with darshan and pooja is loud revelry and music. There are good times to be had, and some sadness as a pocket is picked and someone loses their hard-earned money or an old woman faints because of the heat. Trade is plied and small fortunes made by the priest in collusion with the mithaiwallah as they recycle pooja laddoos and sell the same lot to different devotees. All under the benign eye of the god/goddess in the sanctum, whose blessings are sought for everything from male heirs to jobs to alleviation of ailments to suitable boys for marriageable girls.

Since one is learning to watch one's mind and recognize tension in thought before it expresses itself in word or deed, I linger awhile upon my recalcitrance towards temple-going that has grown over the years. As a young child, I rather enjoyed the outing and prayed hard with my palms pressed together before my nose to be truly deserving of the laddoos that came as prasad. The ritual of worship during festivals fascinated me with the beauty of flickering clay lamps, mixing vermilion and water with rice grains for tilak, incense perfumed with jasmine and rose and a million other scents that would fill every nook of the house, and the collective chanting of shlokas and prayers.

I suppose as I grew up I realized the gods didn't really appear before you in times of need no matter how hard you prayed, neither would a thunderbolt strike you down if you didn't fast on particular days or if your mind was wandering as your lips moved mechanically in prayer. There was a gnawing feeling that perhaps the idol in the sanctum was God if I believed it to be so, and stone if I didn't.

This disillusionment was accompanied by a growing realization that the sacred was much more profound than the emblems that had been tacked on to it, that it was a sphere of experience that sometimes had nothing to do with temples or shlokas or rituals. That there was something within me, within all of us, that was powerful and deep and primal that resonated with the idea of the sacred. This was what needed to be explored. I felt I needed to divest myself of the symbols to look more effectively for the spirit they sought to represent. And so was unwilling to put myself, and my sense of the sacred, up to the onslaught of callous priests and rituals of devotion that were meaningless to me.

Was I throwing the baby out with the bathwater? The sacred couldn't surely be limited to its symbols, but who is to say it wouldn't be present in them? In particularizing the sacred as 'x' and not 'y' or 'z', was I not falling into the trap of the judging mind that contextualizes and sets boundaries? And therefore buying into a view conditioned by preset notions? If I am to lessen the basic instinct to cling to joy and pull away from displeasure in the cause of moving towards a more balanced space of being, how could I continue to qualify this, or any other, prejudice?

My self-righteous spiritual bigotry lay bare before me on the sun-spangled bedcover. I stared at it wide-eyed, thinking there is so much I don't know about myself.

If I was searching in true sramana spirit, I must look everywhere. And be as open as I can be. That didn't mean I had to *accept* everything. But I must allow myself to *look* at everything without instinctively pulling away.

I open my notebook and a piece of wisdom by the eleventh-century Zen master Yuan Wu, carefully pressed like a love-memento-dried-flower, falls out from between its pages. It joins my ignorance on the bedcover and glints brilliantly as it catches the sun. 'There is no duality between noise and quiet,' says Yuan Wu. 'Even when it comes to extraordinary words, marvellous statements, unique acts and *absolute perspectives*, you just level them with one measure. Ultimately they have no right or wrong, it's all in how you use them.'

The puddle of ignorance shrinks in the light reflected off the jewel. One measure, no right or wrong, it is how you use them. I am ready to level the noise and quiet of Dharamsala with one measure. I have spent much time in its quiet. Tomorrow, I will seek out its noise. Tomorrow, I will go to Bhagsu.

It is Sunday morning. Bhagsu is about a kilometre away from the guesthouse. I am to get on to the road that branches out towards the right from the bus stop. Much to my relief, there are no short cuts that I must remember, nor are there steep, rocky paths to negotiate. 'It is a straight, pucca, motorable road,' Pema assures me, and I can see that he still doesn't think I have it in me to be a real mountain-walker.

It is pleasant walking on the gentle troughs and crests of the road to Bhagsu. Pine trees rise intermittently out of the periphery where the road ends and the mountain falls away.

They must have very deep roots to be able to hold themselves up on the edge. They need flat, but all they got is an incline and they make do with it, curving their own trunks to adapt. Adaptation is the key to their survival, as it is for all nature, including human beings. It is how Dharamsala survives and flourishes—the Tibetan community by adapting wherever necessary to their own new needs and the new rules of their place of refuge, local residents by adapting to a population influx by turning landowners and traders, and the travellers by adapting to new cultures and ways of living. To adapt successfully, there needs to be a willingness to give up. I have given up some of my own notions about myself and my life, of how things should or should not be, to be able to spend this time in Dharamsala.

Sometimes adaptation is necessary for growth. If the tree does not adapt to the slope, it fails to rise from the ground. You either adapt or you stagnate and eventually die away. The adaptive process requires an open mind that must accept what is as it is, and then find ways of being with it.

Having to deal with the challenge of the new, as one of the points raised during the 2004 'Mind and Life' conference on neuroplasticity mentioned, is what pushes the brain to birth neurons and make new connections between them, and depression is defined as the failure to find newness in one's experiences. This echoes the Zen idea of 'beginner's mind' being a characteristic of the enlightened mind. You may have done the same thing over and over, yet each time you come to it with a freshness of never having done it before. The mental shift comes from recognizing that newness and jadedness are both qualities of the mind, and not inherent properties of objects or circumstances or events. There is no flavour or colour to the experience other than what the mind can fill into it. And because we *can* control our mind, we can also find newness in tasks and situations that we may have gone through before but that can become new if our minds can.

Beginner's mind is the keystone of adaptation. To have a beginner's perspective is to experience afresh instead of coming from preconceptions. At this moment, I am headed towards something I have encountered scores of times before. Yet I am trying to do this with a new awareness, one that does not hold the present moment ransom to notions of the past. It is my shot at beginner's mind, and I must come to Bhagsu with a perspective as fresh as these fluorescent green pine leaves that are just beginning to poke through the branches that brush my arms as I walk close to the edge of the road.

Near Bhagsu, the road becomes busy with shops that remind me of stragglers inching behind a wedding procession, hopeful of some coins straying their way from among those showered at the musicians. The name of the temple has leached out from its confines and is now the name by which the surrounding area is also known, which includes a small bazaar and hotels and guesthouses for the low-budget traveller.

A curious mix of the foreign and the Indian meets the eye in the bazaar square, which is more of an oblong. Taxis are emitting a big group of women and children, shepherded by a sole male whose chin has just sprouted its first hair and whose presence is the charm amulet supposed to keep thieves and molesters away. The women are glittering in bright, sequinned saris and gold jewellery, the married ones marked with sindoor in the parting of their hair and a brusqueness that proves effective both in herding their children away from the temptations of the bazaar ('Not now Chintu, after darshan!' to an insistent child in black terylene who just has to have an ice-lolly) and in shooing away beggar children who come running up to the group. The poor adolescent escort looks distinctly uncomfortable as he is mobbed by them and has to be rescued by a tough matron who screams murder at the little waifs.

The group follows the ant-line of devotees that has been steadily trickling into the narrow lane that leads towards the temple's entrance. There are a couple of shops selling flowers and incense and coconuts arranged in leaf trays for pooja. The rest of the bazaar oblong has restaurant-fronts where dreadlocked foreigners with beads in their hair are sitting around strumming guitars and chitchatting over glasses of cold drinks. There is a distinct hippie feel to the scene, a carefree air about the people, a sense of revelry that need not stop for anything, not work or sleep or food or any other exigencies life may present. The blissfully barefoot people here remind me of the Homeric lotus-eaters—their happiness not a product of hard-won inner peace but of an external agent/process that holds them under its spell and dulls their minds into a monotonic euphoria.

The scene appears to me as a realm of Buddhist cosmology where one constantly repeats an action or emotion until that one insight is found that will lead to the dissolution of that particular state of mind. A friend told me a story once that was an old Indian one and had found its way into Japanese Buddhist folklore. An ignorant man was trapped in a hell realm because of his wicked deeds. It was found that just once had he shown a hint of compassion by not killing a spider when he could have done so. This showed that he had a potentiality for positive change, however slim it might be. Thus, a strand of spider's gossamer appeared in his hell for him to climb out towards a less punishing existence. The man grasped the frail rope but saw others also trying to grab on to *his* opportunity. Afraid that the weak line would snap under the weight of so many, the man turned around and shouted and fought until he had shooed all the others away. When he turned back, the line of gossamer had disappeared. He had allowed the possibility of compassion to become extinguished from his heart and, with it, his chance for evolving out of his hell.

We all have our own private hells, don't we—states of mind and being that repetitively emerge when we allow ourselves to become entrapped in cycles of emotional reactivity?

The lotus-eaters of Dharamsala have come here seeking a new high that for a while will ease them out of their private hells. They are chilled out and appear unburdened. It is a lightness one can envy, but its quality is inherently suspect and carries a hint of perniciousness because it has come from imbibing the lotus and not from self-effort and practice. It is a short cut to a blissed-out state that lasts only as long as the effect of the lotus.

What then? You are back in the hell realm, nothing has changed, not in the least your own self which started everything in the first place. The contradictions and frustrations ain't going nowhere until you deal with them. The lotus is very attractive, but it has absolutely nothing to do with the state of one's mind, and the euphoria that accompanies it is plastic and short-lived. The thing is not to confuse the lotus with the *jewel* in the lotus, for it is as fragile as the thread of gossamer and trying to use it to construct a new mode of being as fruitless as the efforts of the ignorant man in hell.

Let's look for the real thing, guys, and keep the lotus for a couple of parties on the way, I want to tell the barefoot blissfuls. Instead, I turn into the lane to the temple.

The temple is an old one, its original stone structure now laid over at places with marble that has already begun to crack and yellow. A shoe-minder sits in the corridor of what looks like an old dharamshala. For a small fee, he will look after your shoes while you are gone. At the moment, his temporary collection includes a couple of expensive loafers among the usual lot of chappals and sandals and Bata men's shoes. I leave my sneakers in his care and walk barefoot towards the temple.

Outside the stone steps that lead towards the sanctum, a huge signboard requests one to leave the shod, leathered and drunk aspects of oneself outside the holy premises. Another sign, this time engraved on marble in Hindi, recounts the legend of this temple, whose complete name is 'Bhagsu Nag':

A demon king by the name of Bhagsu is greatly worried by the drought in his kingdom. It doesn't rain and all the wells, lakes and reservoirs are drying up one by one. He hits upon a plan, which involves stealing water from the snake-god Nag's underground realm. He manages to steal the water but is discovered by the snake-god who catches up with Bhagsu at this very spot where the temple stands. Bhagsu lets go of the water, which gushes forth in the form of a waterfall. Instead of fighting the snake-god in true demon style, he begins to pray to him. Nag relents and lets Bhagsu have enough water that will save his parched kingdom and the rest is allowed to flow on at this point. Because the dispute is resolved amicably, the place is given a joint name [much like joint declarations at modern diplomatic summits]— Bhagsu-Nag.

The legend of Bhagsu and Nag is fascinating in its modern ecological implications. The central premise is a tussle over water, something we in India are becoming acutely aware of in an era of depleting monsoon rainfall and receding Himalayan glaciers. The source of the Ganga at Gaumukh in a neck of the Himalayas west of Dharamsala has receded several kilometres in the last few years. The groundwater that flowed in the Nag's realm in the story and that comes to Bhagsu's rescue is now so severely depleted in parts of India that borewells several kilometres deep are unable to tap into it. Indeed it has been predicted that wars in the not-so-distant future will be fought over water—for there is no Nag to pray to and no mighty Bhagsu to drag a river to slake our collective thirst.

Here in Dharamsala too, the water situation for most part of the year is quite desperate. Forests have thinned and there is nothing to hold the soil in its place. Consequently rainwater is not absorbed into the soil; rather it washes off its topmost layer, thus making it rocky and infertile. The increase in buildings and population has meant progressively greater water consumption, and a proliferation of wasteful practices like flush toilets that literally send much more water down the drain than is needed. This burden that Dharamsala bears can be eased if residents and visitors alike consciously adopt water-saving practices.

Reading the Bhagsu Nag temple's legend has put me in a good enough mood to climb the dirty marble staircase with an open heart. Each step on the staircase has been donated by a patron, as have several marble slabs embedded in the temple's walls. Every donor has got his or her name engraved on to their slab to be preserved in this temple for posterity. Could it be the same spirit that moved 'Swarnlata Puri' of Jalandhar and England to have her name carved upon this small square of marble in Bhagsu Nag as that which causes people to have their bodily remains cryogenically frozen in the hope that they will survive far into the future?

The sanctum is small and stuffy and in complete darkness except for the pooja lamps that glimmer before the deity. It is said that entrances to the sanctum in temples are deliberately made low so they can be entered only with a lowered head— symbolic that the ego has been left outside along with one's footwear.

Some women from the big group are inside. They are holding a newborn to the priest to get its forehead smeared with sandal paste. The baby displays its innate curiosity by immediately reaching out for the fifty-rupee note that his mother and aunts are leaving on the priest's plate. 'What a sharp child! He will surely do some business and make a lot of money,' says the priest, donning the mantle of soothsayer. The women are pleased with the prophecy. They clank eleven rupees more on to his plate, and start withdrawing backwards, their faces still bowed before the deity.

I enter next, and find the deity to be a brassy-looking Nag placed in a hole in the ground. 'Tell me something about this idol,' I urge the priest. It must be my jeans that signal me as a low-paying devotee. Unlike the chirpy manner he displayed with the newborn, he murmurs something under his breath about the idol having risen from the earth. 'How?' I persist. 'The whole story is written outside. Why don't you read that?' he snaps. I get the message, and quietly fold my hands before the idol.

The Nag reminds me of the veins of folklore filled with creatures from the animal realm that throb in our culture. Remembering this negation of anthropomorphism saves me from feeling too bad about the attitude of the uninterested priest who after perfunctorily handing me some sugar balls for prasad has quickly turned to a newly married couple bearing loaded pooja trays.

In the temple's courtyard, the marble slabs appear everywhere, bearing the names of people whose donations have helped transform this old stone temple into a shiny tile-covered one. Even army regiments have some to their credit. The area has a martial past and its Dogra Rajput community has contributed an old regiment to the Indian Army that still bears its name. I imagine the soldiers coming to this temple to seek blessings before going off to war. What if they were to become inspired by the spirit of Bhagsu to pray to their aggressors instead of fighting them? Perhaps that is why the temple does not have an idol of Bhagsu, only of the Nag, despite bearing both their names. Pacifists can be dangerous in matters of war and ambition, and Bhagsu is an effective pacifist who found a satisfactory resolution to his problem without resorting to violence. In the courtyard, I think of Bhagsu and pray to his peaceful spirit in my heart.

On the way out, my eye falls on a table that displays a group of photographs. The most recent one is of a fat swami trying to get his chubby legs into padmasana, the lotus position. His predicament is enhanced by the company in which his picture has been kept. Flanking him are old photographs of emaciated yogis with their rib cages sticking out and an intense fire in their half-closed eyes. I look around for someone to explain this picture gallery. A young man who looks like a priest-in-training, and has not yet picked up the sting that comes in handy while keeping unprofitable devotees at bay, is found. I ask him who these people are. 'That,' he says pointing to the fat swami, 'is the current mahant [head] of the temple. He is in Rishikesh.' So the mahant is leading the good sadhu's life while his deputies run the show here, I think to myself but refrain from saying aloud.

'What about these other yogis? Who are they?' 'This one here is the previous mahant,' he points to a knife-boned yogi whose eyes are rolled back in his head. 'And this one is his guru, and these others are yogis who would sometimes come to live in the temple's dharamshala during winter months when their Himalayan caves became snowbound.' Are there any yogis in residence now? 'No,' he shakes his head regretfully. 'I haven't seen many in recent times. You see, in the old days, this was a quiet place. There was no pucca road, and only pilgrims with true devotion would make the difficult trek. Now it's become so crowded. Yogis need silence for their sadhana. I think they prefer the snows to this racket.' Whoops from the bathing tank adjacent to the temple interrupt our conversation. I understand why the yogis may have retreated from Bhagsu Nag.

The noise of loud, showy devotion and mechanic ritual that keeps them away is precisely what has cleaved the practice of religion in India from its spiritual roots and set it adrift on a sea populated by shiny new temples and greedy priests. The quiet-seeking yogis do not contradict Yuan Wu's one measure. For they *have* already embraced noise—their own. Having to deal with external noise in the same instant in which they are engaged with silencing the noise within, would be too much, don't you think?

The waterfall at Bhagsu is way up the mountain, at the point where the stream gushes over the mountain's neck. The mud path that goes up to it has a sign warning of landslides. The waterfall is neither big nor spectacular. Its water flows down in a thin stream that cuts a valley into the hillside, which is much wider than the current flow of water. Apparently the entire scree strewn with water-smoothed rocks fills up with roaring rainwater during the monsoons. Today, it is filled with what looks like the entire town of Dharamsala, come here to do their week's washing! There are monks who have stripped down to their underwear and are washing their maroon robes. Inn keepers have brought their guests' laundry and some have spread out multicoloured heavy woollen blankets on the larger stones and are pounding at them alternatively with feet and elbows. Everyone is chatting with everyone else despite the hard labour, and their cheery voices and occasional laughter tinge the place with a carnivalesque gaiety. Washing is spread out to dry on grass along the gradient of the fall. I worry about all the detergent being let out into the river. The thin sliver of silver at the top of the mountain has turned a dirty brackish green at the bottom.

I perch myself on a stool at a cafe that overlooks the valley of the waterfall. A French-speaking couple next to me are arguing about going up to the waterfall. The woman's reluctance cannot be overcome, and the man determinedly strides away. I can sense the acrid smell of acrimony hanging over the spot. The woman absently looks up at me and returns my smile with a dour look. I hastily turn to the happy sounds that come from the Tibetan families on their Sunday picnic. They carry flasks and food in plastic baskets and sit on rocky outcrops in the waterfall's scree. They seem happy to be out in the open, even if it means witnessing the extensive washing of others' dirty laundry. Adaptation, I think, and look at the Frenchwoman struggling to get past her tightness. She is unable to see any happiness around her as she undoubtedly mulls over her companion's unfairness in leaving her by herself. She reminds me of my own expectations of others that often crease relationships. Wouldn't beginner's mind be absolutely precious in such situations? If we could come together with a person anew each time we met him or her, without loading them with the burdens of past mistakes and perceived injustices, or even with the desire of repeating old joys?

The sun is getting hot, and I retrace my steps into the market oblong. The place looks more crowded than before because makeshift spice stalls have come up by the wayside. Their collective aroma enwraps me, and leads me towards a woman in a brown chuba who is setting out her wares on a low plastic-covered table.

'Tashi Delek,' she greets me, and looks up with the squint that accompanies weak, long-distance vision. I am fascinated by her wares and begin pointing towards each one in turn to know more about it. She knows instinctively that I will buy and begins explaining the herbs and roots in broken Hindi flavoured with a strong Tibetan accent and sprinkled with the odd English word.

'These are all gifts from the Himalayas. You will not find them anywhere else. This is samundri jhaag,' she points to a white, flaky stone whose name literally means 'foam of the ocean'. 'Soak this in milk overnight and apply on your face. It cures pimples and skin diseases.' I tell her I'll take some.

I inhale deep of the spicy aroma of the herbs that enters my lungs and releases its warm, healing quality within me. The cheap table holds such treasures—knots of brown, tan, maroon, black, holding within them cures for illnesses of body and mind, and, well, bad magic too. 'This here,' says the woman holding up a dried brushlike root, 'is the nazar booti. You tie it at your door with a black thread knotted thrice, and no magic will have any effect on you. You will sleep well, no depression, no tension.'

Suddenly I am a little girl listening enthralled to stories of witchcraft in my Naani's warm kitchen in another part of the Himalayas. Naani's eyes glow like the coals on which she roasts rotis, as she tells me about the spirit that lived in the lemon tree at the back of the house so that no one could go to the toilet at night for its moaning and banging. She got rid of it by burning a panful of red chillies under the tree, and with incantations that weren't let out during the storytelling. Then there was the bad magic cast on her newborn son that made him sick all the time, which was ousted with jadi-bootis (roots and herbs) for which she had to trek into the forest on a moonlit night. During these moments, I imagined her as a kind of superhero with sari billowing in the wind and multiple arms bearing spices and herbs to vanquish evil and sickness.

I am brought out of the past by the Tibetan woman's impatient clucking. I look at other wares on her table. There is shilajit, lumps of tarlike ooze that for centuries have been considered a cure for impotency. The Tibetan woman doesn't show it to me. Instead, she plucks out some mulethi, 'sweet root', that I know from a tonsillitis-ridden childhood when my mother, reluctant to put me on antibiotics, would try one home remedy after another. I pop the mulethi into my mouth. The chewy wood splinters under my teeth, releasing a bitter-pungent juice that instantly reminds me of how much I hated it at the time! I try and arrest the reaction and nudge myself to experience anew. As I let go of the old distaste, the pungency begins to feel warm and soothing. I allow the restorative juice to trickle down to my throat. The comfort of this moment erases the aversion from the past.

Is this how beginner's mind works?

Little Tenzin comes running up to me that afternoon as I enter the guesthouse. He knows I've been to Bhagsu and wants to know whether I saw the waterfall. I wiggle my fingers, hop a couple of times and go whoo . . . He giggles and claps his hands in absolute delight.

Stretching out on the bed for a nap, I think of the journey to Bhagsu. Perhaps I lost some of my equal measure on the way and did get into judging the tinny tenor of the temple and its priests. But instead of strengthening my initial revulsion, the visit has whetted my appetite for more. I have often wondered about the ancient, pre-Tibetan sacredness of

Dharamsala, and the yogis' pictures at the temple confirmed the existence of such. I glimpsed their sacred silence amidst the noise and dust of Bhagsu. Perhaps the noise of other temples of this region will reveal further clues?

All thoughts in my head gradually subside and my eyes become heavy with sleep. Outside, little Tenzin quietly hums like water running over stones.

11

Ancient Sacredness

I am lying on my hard bed, eyes wide open. Above me, around me, is an expanse of darkness. From under the door, sharp knives of light slice through the soft body of the dark. I turn my eyes towards the window. The deodars outside are looming shadows, unknowable now as the tree-selves they were until just a few hours ago. It is the night of no moon, amavasya, and, in this land of no street lights, darkness rules.

I sit up in bed unable to sleep. The blackened sky is studded with a net of stars that appear brighter and closer tonight, now that there is no moon to compete with. Each star is ringed with a halo of its own light, frozen in a point in time that has already passed. To think that in this moment that is *now* for me I am actually looking at the past unfold live in the sky is enough to scramble one's linearity of thought. To confuse the ordinary thinking mind is one way to get it to lower its defences so that one can slip into the unexplored realms that lie beyond. Zen uses a single-pointed concentration on koans, riddles nonsensical to ordinary thinking, to perplex the linear mind and break through into the *real* mind, which is as clear and cloudless and vast as this night sky is.

If time or at least its linearity is a construct—a way of identifying a feature of reality by a particular name, 'time'— and if we allowed our mind to drop it completely, will we still think of our lives as beginning at one point and ending at another? Or will we become aware of ourselves as blips in the mighty wave of life that is continuously being and becoming and dying out, and then moving towards a beginning again?

In this starlit darkness, notions of time found in old eastern wisdom traditions come to mind. In most of them time is cyclical, divided into epochs or yugas, each one coming to an end with some sort of doomsday scenario that wipes the slate clean for a new cycle to begin. The idea of samsaric existence can itself be seen as one way of delineating time. Also cyclical, samsara is the mechanism that extracts the toll of karma from created beings. All actions whether in word, thought or deed must be accounted for, and their consequences good and bad borne out to maintain the balance of the created world. The scope for such is usually unavailable in the span of one lifetime, for, ignorant of the heavy price it extorts, we continue to spin out new karma even while wrapping up the old and so must return to samsara until our entire karmic fund is exhausted.

The same wisdom traditions that talk of karmic bondage in repetitive cyclical existences also present the possibility of slipping the harness and opting *out* of the time/samsara continuum altogether, into moksha, liberation, and nirvana, a final extinguishment.

If there is a likelihood of escaping samsara, and thus a time-bound existence, one can conceive of timelessness too. Enlightened minds have spoken of how, for the mind unimpeded by constructs and contexts, the flow of life emerges as a timeless present where changes occur in the body and in the natural world, but not really in the all-encompassing quality of consciousness. The body obeys the laws of nature and moves towards decay and death, but the mind remains clear and cloudless. What happens to such awakened minds when the body falls away? Do they dissolve into nothingness, making good the ultimate escape? Do they choose the time and place of their next samsaric appearance in the manner of bodhisattvas? Or do they become refined into dimensionless beings, powered by purified consciousness alone, outside the realm governed by laws of nature and physics?

The last possibility appears in the form of a unique pantheon of immortals in Indian lore. They are not to be confused with deities and semi-divine creatures. Most immortals are said to begin their samsaric journeys as regular human beings, sometimes as animals and insects too if the scope of their legend accounts for an inner evolution spanning several lifetimes, as in the case of the Jataka tales that provide the Buddha with several births, each being significant for the learning attached to it. The individual gradually progresses to an enlightened, or at any rate heightened, state of consciousness. At this point, legends differ. The Buddha died a human death and has as of now not given any indication that he is looking over the state of affairs from on high. But there are others who are said to have become transmuted, through advanced yogic practices, into pools of awakened consciousness.

The immortals represent a spiritual fantasy that is rich in its aspirational implications. Those seeking inner growth would like to believe that the path is not flat and unending and is made of a variety of pinnacles of attainment, adequately exemplified by credible role models—the immortals. That they are also made to engage with 'deserving' seekers through interventions at crucial junctures in their spiritual growth provides a source of comfort to the seeker. God may not be in His heaven, but the immortal certainly is in his. We are being watched over and taken care of as we tread the path that is a razor's edge at times and a lonely battle with our own frustrating ignorance at others. When all seems lost, the slivers of light under the door indicate that this darkness is not irresolvable. Others have gone before, and they continue to look out for us and shine their wisdom upon us when the darkness is the greatest. They are gurus, but also something more. They are milestones on a lonely path, and custodians of the art of sacred seeking.

I glance up again at the night sky. The stars seem somewhat less *fixed* now than a few moments before. It is as if they know the koan they have pushed me into thinking of, and are now boiling with the excitement of what will happen next. They are my immortal gurus in this moment, nudging me to push the boundaries of my mind, urging an exploration into the range of possibilities that open up once the familiar is left behind.

For the longest while after lying back in bed, the starlight remains impressed upon the spot just behind my pupils. I think of how my journey into Dharamsala shifts character with each sunset; every sunrise brings something to begin upon anew. It is no coincidence that tonight I have become enchanted of the immortals, that my thoughts have turned to yogis and siddhas. They have begun to spring up in my mind like old, repressed memories ever since my visit to Bhagsu, where I promised myself an exploration into the hints of an ancient sacredness that are scattered everywhere, I only have to look. Since then, amid the swirling waves of Tibetan monastic maroon, there has appeared a thread the colour of a sadhu's ochre robes that will lead me into the old spirit of Dharamsala.

Is it a dream or has the night sky grown brighter, so that I am aware of its brilliance even from behind closed eyes?

The last half century has seen everything about Dharamsala change incomprehensibly—its map, its population, its landmarks, its entire character. Its old sanctified vestments must no longer fit, having become fragile with disuse, I think one stormy morning when incessant rain has precluded my stepping out. Perfect weather for some armchair sleuthing, and I sit on my bed piecing together a chart of the area's significant sacred sites. I have asked around and been unable to find a map of Dharamsala or McLeodganj since the old one is defunct and the new one is in the process of being prepared. While exploring the town, I rely on a handmade map that a Dharamsala veteran kindly drew for me in Delhi, and of course on instructions from Pema and Thondup and the kindness of strangers on the road. But what I am doing today requires more information, and I sorely miss the bird's-eye view that a map provides even the eye untrained in cartographical intricacies.

Names of places are good indicators of the feel of the place that has become impressed upon local psyche. Places that have been renamed by conquerors at times manage to remember their old names even when there is no choice but to accept the new ones. So while Dharamsala has remained Dharamsala, it has yielded up parts of itself to be renamed McLeodganj and Forsythganj. But it is not these newer names that interest me at this point.

I am looking keenly at the place names that are indicative of an ancient sacredness. From these, I am able to piece together a rough sacred geography of Dharamsala and its surrounding areas. As I suspected, there are several clues inherent in the lay of the land and one just needs to get it all together and make relevant linkages for the Indra's net of jewels to begin to materialize. The first clue is the most obvious—place names with a comprehensible and direct sacred implication. 'Dharamsala' itself; 'Dharamkot', an outpost of McLeodganj, denotes a similar meaning.

Then there is the valley of Sidhbari, where the Karmapa resides, which means 'home of the siddhas', and 'Sidhpur' nearby that stands for 'city of the siddhas'. Siddhas are advanced spiritual practitioners who have mastered the siddhis through various yogas of mind, body and spirit. Siddhi is a word which may stand for paranormal attainments like the ability to change form at will, mastery over the physical world and so on, but which also denotes refinements of the mind like the correct use of reasoning, careful study, generosity and detachment from suffering. Names like Sidhbari ('sidh' from siddha and 'bari' meaning home) and Sidhpur would logically establish these places as practice grounds for aspiring and accomplished siddhas.

Historically, the Himalayas have been intertwined with spiritual seeking in an intimate way. Their general impenetrability was considered ideal for the solitary practitioner looking to retreat from the hubbub of ashrams and gurukuls to spend time alone immersed in his practice. He would seek out a cave or crack in the side of a mountain, and spend days and nights in good weather and bad, sustained by fruit, mountain springs and the healthful air of the hills.

Solitude was accompanied by an experience of altitude whose inspiring connection with the spiritual ideals of ascendance and transcendence must occur immediately to the yogi. Immovable and grounded, clear and strong—the mind must become as these mountains are. An acquaintance who meditates regularly once told me while we were out walking in Dharamsala that he had looked out of his hotel window one morning, and had seen the mountains emerge out of a flurry of clouds. In that moment, it was as if he had been shown the quality of the unshaken mind—ever-present in the midst of clouds, storms, snow and fair weather too.

In Dharamsala, the Himalayas occur near and immediate.

They are right there, rising sheer and high in front of your nose as it were. If one walks higher into the surrounding areas, one finds secluded spots such as Triund, a ten-kilometre walk from McLeodganj, whose name I imagine refers to Shiva's trident, a comparison most likely prompted by odd geographical features. It is one of several spots around Dharamsala that are now also being used by Tibetan practitioners for their meditation retreats and which may have had old goat-paths used by yogis leading up to them. Triund has also become a popular hiking destination for tourists. There is another place which offers greater seclusion, which can be reached while walking from Dharamkot on a path that circles the mountain. After a couple of kilometres of walking on dry, slippery pine needles, one comes upon a mass of multicoloured prayer flags. They are markers for a cluster of stone huts that house monks withdrawn from the community and living out a period of time completely immersed in spiritual practice.

I walked that path made gentle by the tread of yogis past and present. It has no traffic, no people except the odd hill-woman gathering grass for her cattle, no sound except birdsong and insect chirp. It feels timeless and eternal, as if the mountains and the forests and the meditators were, and will be, always inhaling and exhaling into the still air, just like this. The following poem was sparked from that walk:

If you keep walking
down this narrow path
that winds around
the waist
of this mountain
guided by heaps
of ordinary stones

then
you will come
upon a space
where regular hill stones
have acquired
mani mantra characters
and a thousand prayer flags
surge out into the wind.
There, my friend,
if you strain your ears
into the silence
you will hear
the murmur of meditating monks
their mind moments rotating slow
their gentle breath
drawing in and out . . .
And if, my friend,
should you walk further
on and on
until you find a crag
from where you can see
the children's village
far, far below
and hear their sounds
of delight in play . . .
there, my friend,
if you strain your ears
you will hear
the tinkle of dakinis' ankle bells
on their delicate airborne feet . . .
Further still, will you go
my joyful traveller friend?
Then where

the ground exudes
pine scent,
under the sky
facing the sun
please do sit
for a quiet moment
and wonder . . .
how did I
melt away
and become
the wandering stream below
the vast horizon beyond?

This rain-drenched morning has yielded up many treasures.
It is also wearing away with the passage of the sun in the sky,
unseen though it is behind dark, plump rain clouds, and I
have much to do. I put aside the leaf from which I have gleaned
the poem, and return to my labours on Dharamsala's sacred
geography.

The other obvious indicators of such would be the old
temples of the region. The apparition of the sadhu's ochre
thread unspools into the territory that takes me back into the
noise and dust of religion. The yogis and siddhas represent
the path of sacred seeking, which is one I instinctively prioritize
over other facets of sacredness because it echoes my own
endeavours, because their stories and journeys *feel* true to me.
But one must cast one's glance over the entire field of
experience and take into account all that exists therein if one
truly means to get rid of fixed, absolutist perspectives. I cannot
allow barriers to spring up in my mind that will affix
benchmarks, sift Dharamsala's sacredness according to them,

and hand me only that which passes muster. It is the essence
one must look for, without getting derailed by the form in
which it comes encased. That which is available through the
emaciated yogi may also waft forth from the cramped sanctum
of a hill shrine, and it may also murmur in the mantras of
death and life on the banks of swift mountain rivers.

To identify the sacred in the Indian context is a mammoth
and mind-boggling task if only because of the sheer variety
of paths, doctrines, scriptures, faiths and divinities present. It
is so also because of the splintering of the *spiritual* from the
religious, where the former most often implies a personal
journey towards inner truth, and the latter denotes a following
en masse of established and institutionalized versions of that
truth. What makes things confusing is that many times the
one merges into the other, or the other becomes the one.
That which started out as a spiritual journey becomes ossified
into sects, orders and institutions that stifle the radical enquiry
that seeded them in the first place, and the religious at times
may retain a kernel of openness and direct experience of truth.
Neither can be boxed into this or that without examining with
the eye of wisdom and discretion. The sacred may lie hidden
anywhere like a pearl in an oyster—you don't know where it
is until you crack open the hard shell and come upon the
gleaming treasure hidden within.

It is all or nothing, I tell my judging mind sternly, and
follow the guiding vision of the thread of ochre as it encircles
the temples of Dharamsala. These too belong in the chart of
sacredness that my fingers are crafting. I have already touched
upon one of them, Bhagsu Nag. Compared to others in the
region, it is a temple of minor importance mainly because its
deity is of uncertain significance. In the divine hierarchy, snakes
even holy, kingly ones are of lesser significance than the
heavyweights—the Trinity of Brahma, Vishnu and Shiva and

their avatars, as well as the many manifestations of the Devi.

Going by this scheme of things, Dharamsala is Goddess territory. The land is overlaid by a matrix of old Devi temples that celebrate the Divine Feminine in her various wrathful, benign and wish-fulfilling aspects. This could be proof of the ascendancy of Tantra here in the past. Perhaps its core teachings and practices still exist in circles of secretive yogis. What are available to the common eye are rituals of worship that indicate a rootedness in Tantric sensibility, just as the leaves blown into the guesthouse balcony by the storm bespeak the trees from whose branches they were torn.

The reason behind this prognosis is the centrality of the Devi in Tantra. Tantra sees creation as the interplay of Shiva and Shakti. Shiva is pure, all-pervasive consciousness; Shakti is the primal energy that creates all beings and phenomena, and in whom we exist. Shiva is the male principle; Shakti is the feminine one. They are polar opposites in a constant state of union, the one sustaining the other, and the other nurturing the one. They are visualized as diametric opposites that fit perfectly in one another—cosmic consciousness embedded within the creative impulse. Together, they hold up creation.

The cult of worship of the Divine Feminine as Shakti, primal energy, sees the Goddess as worthy of individual adoration. One could say that the Goddess finally came into her own through the Shakti cult. She had been her own person in the pre-Aryan era when she held the position of prime divinity as the fecund, life-nurturing earth mother. With the establishment of Vedic society, the practice of religion acquired a masculine orientation. Of course the Devi did not disappear; she only became relegated to a consort role. She continued to flourish, however, in those parts of India that were not as strongly Vedicized such as the north-west, Bengal and many areas in the south. It is from these places that she resurfaced circa the fourth century CE, surging forth on a wave of Tantric mysticism that would eventually spawn Vajrayana in association with Buddhism.

The Devi's presence in and around Dharamsala takes form on my chart through her many old temples. Perhaps this was one of the places where she withdrew to survive the Vedic onslaught, and in whose caves and cremation grounds the esoteric practices of her worship were intuited and perfected. If we take Dharamsala as the centre point, we find Devi temples radiating out up to a distance of eighty to a hundred kilometres in all directions. The Kangra temple is a shakti-peeth—one of the fifty-one places around the country made sacred as body parts of the goddess Sati supposedly fell there. I cast my mind around this myth that is as fascinating as it is gruesome. It has an element of crazy love, intense love gone awry. Sati was Shiva's wife and daughter of a mighty king, Daksha. Her father did not think much of his dreadlocked, ash-smeared, cremation-ground-haunting ascetic of a son-in-law. So at a lavish religious ceremony he organized, he neglected to invite Shiva. When Sati questioned her father about this exclusion, he proceeded to insult Shiva and his strange ways. Unable to bear her beloved's humiliation, Sati jumped into the sacrificial fire.

The news reached Shiva who immediately arrived to claim Sati's body. Overcome with grief, he slung his beloved's corpse upon his shoulder and began roaming the earth. His immense sorrow broke through the inner balance that kept his formidable yogic energies in check. The energy that was released decimated whatever came in its path, perhaps like the bolts of thunder flashing across the Dharamsala sky outside my window right now.

Vishnu arose to fulfil his cosmic function as preserver of creation and let loose his spinning discus at Sati's corpse, hacking the body into fifty-one pieces. These fell to the ground over an area that covers almost the entire country. With time, temples sprang up wherever Sati's body parts had fallen, to venerate places sanctified by the energy of the Divine Feminine.

I close my eyes for a moment's rest. The thunder has now quietened into a steady downpour. The sky is tumultuous with rain-bearing clouds that shift shape constantly, merging and then pulling apart. Remembering the Devi legends has set off a babble of voices within me. Myths rise one by one from the murky pool of memory. A vision of the Goddess rises alongside, each myth casting a glow upon a different aspect of her. Here she is Mahishasurmardini—slayer of the demon Mahish—and now she is Durga astride a roaring lion, and now she is the fearsome old crone Kali dancing naked with a garland of human skulls around her neck, and then she is plotting to kill Raktabeej, the demon who proliferated anew as each drop of his blood touched the earth . . . And finally she is a little girl in a red skirt with gold edging, innocent of her powers as Divine Creatrix and Mother of the Universe, the pure form that lies at the heart of the slaying, avenging angel she becomes to maintain earthly balance, and which is worshipped twice every year in pre-pubescent girls during the festival of the nine sacred nights of the Devi, Navaratri.

I smile at the vision of the little girl who wants to ride a lion, and open my eyes to the sacred before me. My bed is littered with papers and guidebooks and the clanging bells of Devi temples in and around Dharamsala that include Chamunda Devi, Jwalamukhi and Chintpurni. These draw their spiritual significance from fascinating myths and stand as markers of the local population's sacred universe. Jwalamukhi, which is fifty-six kilometres from Dharamsala, pays homage to 'She of the flaming mouth'. The temple here is built above natural jets of combustible gas which escape from fissures in the ground and are worshipped in the sanctum. I think of the time when I had visited it. The temple is perched on a hillock, and an unending line of devotees stretched down the stairs into the lane leading up to the temple. My bare feet blistered on the hot tar of the road as I waited in queue. The press of bodies all around me was overwhelming and, after a point, I lost much of my enthusiasm.

When I finally reached the sanctum, I folded my hands before the flames spurting from the ground as the priest plastered the Devi's sindoor between my eyebrows. This was indeed the most singular darshan I had ever experienced. There was no image to direct one's thoughts and mould them in a particular way. Just holes in the sunken ground from where blue tongues of flame licked at the offerings of rice and sindoor and flower petals, even the tiredness I had brought with me. Watching the flames, bowing before them, I felt the truth that flows at the heart of all Indian wisdom traditions, whether non-dualistic, monistic, polytheistic or any other kind. The sacred is *everywhere*; it lies buried in everything as its essence, the being-ness that causes things to be. Here, we are asked to look into the heart of what is a natural phenomenon, look deep enough so that we identify its very *core*. There is sacredness *there*, which is further expressed in the forms, legends, visions that come from human imagination. If one can only look through form into the essence, then here is the sacred, in stone, in river, in mountain, in fire, in heat, and in noise and dust and religion's quagmire.

It is this deep seeing that I practise when I next call upon the Goddess in Dharamsala. The temple of Chamunda Devi is fifteen kilometres from McLeodganj and echoes the trend of old stone structures made tender and quiet by moss and the vagaries of weather, being replaced by shiny new facades and massive complexes crowded with shops selling ritual paraphernalia. Loudspeakers blare poorly sung bhajans, and huge gates and high boundary walls clearly define where the sacred ground ends and the profane world begins, quite unlike the old sensibility of hill temples that nestled in a quiet corner of the forest and were innocent of such demarcations. The Chamunda temple complex is loud and glossy, but I determinedly ignore all surface disturbances and walk towards the sanctum.

It is a busy day with devotees milling about the shrine. I am lucky because the moment I enter the sanctum, it empties of all except a priest. I orient myself towards the image, and find it a startlingly plain, rough boulder just like ones scattered along mountain springs. It is daubed with orange sindoor and two large eyes have been placed near the top end to give it a semblance of a human face. Just behind the Devi's shrine is a Shiva temple, which is really a deep fissure in the wall of a mountain cave. A stone hidden under a massive rocky outcrop is Shiva's lingam.

The sight of these two stones designated as the twin poles of creation is strangely moving, for it bespeaks of a simple, organic, earth-loving exuberance that flowed towards all things natural, where the greatest shrines and divinities were to be found in the abundant body of nature, along with the realization that what occurred thence could not be matched by the skills of human hands. There is an endearing, childlike innocence in taking a rock and spinning impressive stories about it and weaving a web of rituals to take care of it and venerate it. It strikes me that the deep seeing that reveals the sacred core of things requires a mind not hassled by appearances or overly concerned with a limited factual reality. It needs innocence and imagination, and a depth of vision unhampered by the myopia of worldliness and material realities. Do I still have the child's warmth that can glean the sacred from a stone?

Maybe, maybe not.

The storm has finally abated. It is past noon and the sun appears high in the sky once the dark clouds have fallen away, their rain and fury spent. The world looks fresh and newly born out of chaos. The leaves on the deodars are still shivering from the shock of the thunderbolts, and the moss on the sides of the path that passes under my window glistens green under a fragile mesh of raindrops. The terrain through Dharamsala's old by-lanes is now winding away from the temples and heading towards me. The follower is soon to become the followed, it appears. For memory has excavated more than myths. It has brought me the holy ghost of a family legend, which for the longest time made up my sole sense of the inner journey because it had happened so close to me, and of the sacred ground on which it unfolded—Dharamsala.

The stars from last night grow in my mind as I think of the yogi whose life I am about to wander into. They continue to hold their koan behind my eyes, challenging my perception of things and people. They hold up for me a standard of uncertainty, of not knowing and of thus *trying* to know, that I must keep in mind on all exploratory journeys. This one into Dharamsala's old sacredness must now continue in the realm beyond temples, through the footsteps of a homeless, wandering, searching yogi.

The spectral ochre thread has since returned from its peregrinations, and I imagine it now curled in the hollow of my hand. It has shown me what it could, and now I must cast my vision carefully along a different route.

12

A Yogi's Footsteps

Decades before I was born, a grand-uncle took to the life of an itinerant sadhu. He roamed the land, speaking to those who were interested of soul and the formless one reality, singing bhajans in his gentle, mellifluous voice as he walked through mountains and deserts, allowing his inner compass to pick his way. One day, the trusted compass led him to a small Himalayan town, and refused to go further.

It was the early 1950s and Dharamsala was yet to open its arms to Tibetan refugees, while its days of glory as a summer retreat for British colonial officials and their memsahibs had been left behind. It had fallen back into its comfortable centuries-old rhythm, of harsh winters and pleasant summers and torrential monsoons, inhaling and exhaling with the mountains and their moods, its ground reverberating with pilgrims' footfalls.

The sadhu was immediately invited into the hearts and homes of Dharamsala's residents and adopted as parent, patron saint and wise elder. He would still wander away from time to time, but now the inner compass always pointed Dharamsala-ward. On the odd occasion that he visited his family in Delhi, he would bring with him the whiff of Dharamsala. He had been elevated to a suprahuman pedestal in their minds long ago and Dharamsala became a wondrous place of spiritual mystique brought on by the magnetism and wisdom they felt in his presence.

A month after I was born, the sadhu came to Delhi and held me in his warmth. He was dead in a few days, consciously offering up his prana (life energy) in samadhi within Mother Ganga's watery womb. The bird had flown; there were no footprints to follow. Just a lingering aroma of a simple sannyasin who had lived and taught in a place called Dharamsala.

It is difficult to talk about footsteps in the context of yogis. Not because they have acquired the facility of flying or travelling astrally, but footsteps in the sense of a corporeal heritage that bears their name and reminds people of their presence long after they have departed from their earthly existences. This is so because most yogis are also sannyasins, divested of all relationships of blood and property, wandering from one place to another with their meagre belongings tied in a single piece of cloth. The places they halt at are mere rest-stops, dharamshalas on the grand pilgrimage of inner seeking. Of course there are yogis who lead a settled enough existence in their families and work, but even so their presence in their worldly lives is light and loose, holding nothing too close or too dear. The yogi's footprints are as ephemeral as the bird's in the sky; his ego-personality is dissolved sufficiently to not leave many karmic marks upon the framework of samsara. Texts of Advaita Vedanta such as the Ashtavakra Gita and the Yoga Vashisht talk of the true yogi as a jivan mukta—one who is free in this life itself, while living in samsara he is not bound by it.

How then does one calibrate a yogi's legacy, especially one who has worn the cloak of life and then cast it aside with not a tear or even a crease, practising and perfecting his self in private? And does his or her life have a larger meaning beyond the individual search and self-realization? It is easy to know those yogis who speak about themselves, or who allow others to question them, thus revealing their true natures. But what of the anonymous wanderer? Who is to know what gems of insight lie hidden underneath the frayed hem of his robes?

As a seeker and writer on seeking, my nose is particularly sensitive to the whiff of an untold story of an ordinary life made rich and unusual by the compulsions of inner striving and exploration. But long before I was sniffing out such tales in cloisters and caves, I was handed my grand-uncle's story that marked me for life. It spoke of a journey so powerful that it was seared upon my mind as a young child and stayed with me through repetitions and variations by elderly relatives over the years. This tale of a yogi who did everything from fomenting revolution to complete inner transformation, followed by years of possessionless wandering, became my earliest introduction to the endless possibilities of human life.

This yogi's story is not out in the public domain. He isn't known beyond a small circle comprising his family and ageing devotees who live in the villages of Dari and Dadh in Dharamsala. The reason for this anonymity is simple—he didn't choose to be known. Also, he didn't pluck objects out of air nor display healing powers and such that make for easy and instant popularity. His life followed a pattern that has been replicated over and over in seekers' lives through the ages. He was in all appearances a regular person who for the last three decades of his life chose to live as a sannyasin, rather than rise in his career, sire children and retire into an old age spent playing golf, gossiping with buddies and investing in stocks and bonds on the side.

Why then do I find this ordinary yogi so fascinating? I

won't deny that it is partly because he was my grand-uncle, the wayward elder brother of my stiff upper lip grandfather. In the spiritual journey, which is what being in Dharamsala is for me as much as it is an exploration of others' journeys, one must dip into one's own history and uncover the influences that inform one's sense of self.

But there is more to this than familial loyalty or clannish affection. In the matter of spiritual seeking, *each* journey is unique though it may seem to follow the broad template of many others. And ordinariness and lack of histrionics are often indicators of attainment, for the true yogi has traded up his ego-self for a larger, deeper way of being. Such lives are the hardest to find, for the drama of awakening has happened in their inner world while the outer shell has remained unruffled and undramatic to the casual eye.

There is something else about ordinariness that is of great value to seekers. It plucks the possibility of self-realization out of the realm of the divine and the godly and thus the unattainable, and places it right in our midst. The yogi of Dharamsala was alive within the scope of living memory. There are people around who remember him as a human being as much as a saint. Even if we may be inveigled by the distance of several centuries into believing that someone like the Buddha was born enlightened, that he had to do little or no work to actually get there, it would be difficult to harbour similar misconceptions about an individual who was alive recently.

Being in Dharamsala, walking its lanes and exploring its spirit, has given me a precious opportunity to examine this yogi's life from a different perspective. For the people who came to know him here in Dharamsala, he was a stranger who became a trusted confidante and adviser. Their memories of him will complete the story; they will be able to illuminate the side of him that lies in darkness for me. Perhaps then, I could try and define this yogi's legacy, discern the footsteps he left upon the earth and sky of Dharamsala?

It is a golden morning. The air is sparkling and smells crisp and clean. I have boarded the bus that will take me from lower Dharamsala to Dari, a nearby village. I have telephoned ahead, and made contact with a retired colonel whose family has been closely associated with Guru Maharajji, for that is how the yogi is known in these parts. The good colonel has given me precise directions on how to make the short but complex journey from McLeodganj.

I have much to ruminate upon as the bus steadily fills up with schoolchildren and adult commuters with all kinds of loads which they request one another to accommodate. I am secure in a window seat, and after a while gaze up at the clear sky, lost to the clamour around in trying to decipher the babble within. All the accounts I have heard of the yogi's early life rise in my memory as patches, severally coloured by the relatives who recounted them, and I feel the need to sew these into a quilt of coherence before I unearth new things about him. When the bus finally jerks into motion, I am deep into sorting out grand-uncle's early life.

Born in 1894 to a high administrative official of the princely state of Kashmir and his first wife, he was named Sukh Chain Nath by his parents who, one can deduce from the name, aspired for a happy and contented life for their firstborn. The child had a privileged upbringing, though he did display a contrarian sensibility from a young age. To his mother's exasperation, he would invite home ragged sadhus much like some young children bring in mongrels off the streets. As an adolescent, he insisted on going in his father's stead to oversee preparations for the yearly Amarnath Yatra, the pilgrimage to the ice lingam in a high-altitude cave in Kashmir.

One night, when the party was camped not far from the cave, a great storm arose. All tents were blown away and, as they ran about looking for shelter, people noticed the young boy sitting in deep meditation. Of that night, he would say, 'That was the first time I felt the tremendous vastness of the cosmos, its oneness. It was the night I *felt* Vasudev Sri Krishna.'

That may have been the first glimmer for the boy of a different view of reality, a hint that what appears on the surface may just be the tip of the iceberg. But the glimmer would fall faint in the years to come, overlaid by various things—his father's expectations, his attempts at carving out a career in Singapore first as a lawyer and then as a schoolteacher. In 1942 the teacher came in contact with an Indian revolutionary who was cobbling together a people's army in Singapore to conquer India back from colonial British rule. The teacher found his idealism echoed in the words of the revolutionary, Subhas Chandra Bose, and signed up with the ragtag group of people who were to be trained to be India's liberators.

It was a grand, mad plan, high on ambition and idealism and low on practicality. It failed to come anywhere near accomplishing its objective. The teacher was a member of an espionage team created to gather information for the Indian National Army (INA). In 1943 he and eight others, ironically disguised as sadhus, travelled to India aboard a Japanese submarine and were dropped off near Bombay. Within a month of their arrival, their operation was uncovered and the entire 'saint squad' was imprisoned. After a secret trial in 1945, they were put on death row.

One can only imagine the darkness this period held for Sukh Chain Nath. What did he have to show for his life that was about to end? His one great act of passion had come to naught; his happy days as a teacher in a seaside community had receded far away. His wife from a forcibly arranged match had died within a year of marriage as if from a broken heart. He may well have sighed into the bitter loneliness of his cell: 'Nothing.'

Perhaps it was then that he remembered the ineffable experience from childhood, when he had felt connected to a universal oneness. This could have been the moment of truth that turned him away from his misery and upon the inward path of the yogi. There was something to be done still, for which his solitary confinement provided the perfect setting.

As he prepared to negotiate the tempestuous waters of his mind, he recalled a book he had picked up in Singapore. At the time, he had been struck by the simplicity and self-assuredness, that could only come from actual knowing, with which the yogi profiled in the book spoke about thorny spiritual matters and queries related to the nature of reality, the self, of its relationship with Brahman—the all-pervasive essence of creation. Though that book, Paul Brunton's *A Search in Secret India* (1934), was lost in the subsequent upheavals in his life, its message seemed to ring forth from the walls of his cell now.

What proved to be of great use was the method of self-enquiry that the sage had evolved from his own experience. It was based on repeatedly asking oneself the question 'Who am I?' Doing this, said the sage, would lead us into realizing the spuriousness of the sense of self with which we normally live, and point us in the direction of who we *really* are. Like the seed in a fruit, our real 'I' lies hidden under a mass of false identifications with the body as self, the ego as self, one's personality as self, one's reactions and emotions as self. The sword of self-enquiry slices through all these and lays bare the core—the real 'I'.

The yogi-to-be had found his guru without moving an inch from his prison cell. He began earnestly practising the method of self-enquiry. He persevered in his practice and, when he fell asleep, a pair of eyes that held a thundering silence in their depths would illumine the cave of his mind. Even though he had never met him, the yogi knew they belonged to his guru, the sage of Mount Arunachala—Sri Ramana Maharshi.

As the yogi changed within, the world was changing rapidly around him. He was released in November 1946 when an interim government was formed in preparation for independence. With a broken body animated by a shining spirit, the yogi emerged from his three-year-long retreat radiating an intense luminosity. Sukh Chain Nath was now Seva Das, 'one who serves'. His life had changed forever.

The bus is now rolling over a gently swelling flatland with fields whose green glitters bright in the sun. My stop is not far now. There is just one more patch to sew on to the quilt of remembrance before I get off into the arms of the present. It is about the time when the yogi finally worked up the courage to visit his beloved Ramana Maharshi. His journey spanned the length of the country, from the mountains through the immense expanse of the northern plains, across many mighty rivers, and finally into the tropical womb of the south.

A linguistic stranger in the land of his guru, Seva Das boarded the train that would at last take him to his destination. As he waited for the train to start, a young boy pulled him by the hand and gestured towards another train stationed alongside. Seva Das was nonplussed. The boy again pointed to the adjoining train. Now if something similar were to happen to me on this bus, I would probably try very hard to ignore that person, assuming that he was mistaken or crazy. But the yogi was much grown in patience and decided to investigate the other train. To his surprise, he was on the wrong train and the train to which the boy pointed was the correct one! He looked around for the boy who, in the good old tradition of miracle-making, had vanished from the scene.

The yogi bowed in gratitude to the grace that had turned up to guide him and continued on his journey. When he got off at the station, he thought, 'How can I go to my guru empty-handed?' With his meagre resources, Seva Das bought a bunch of grapes that he touched to his forehead and put away in his bag. He then proceeded towards the Arunachala hill that was well known and its sage well loved, and he simply needed to utter his guru's name for fingers to point him in the correct direction. After a while, he sank under a tree's cool shade to catch his breath.

'Are you very tired?' a soft voice asked. Seva Das opened his eyes to see a man standing before him. He nodded. 'Then why don't you take out those grapes from your bag and eat them?' 'No, they are an offering for my guru,' he said. The man persisted gently, 'Have some, and you can offer him the rest. You will not be able to climb the rest of the way if you don't take some refreshment.' Seva Das felt the wisdom of his words and brought the grapes out. He turned to offer the kind man some, but he was gone, suddenly, like the boy in the train. For the second time that day, Seva Das felt greatly blessed.

At the ashram, there was a crowd of visitors to meet the Maharshi. He was seated on a low divan, his thin body naked except for a loincloth. Without speaking, he would place a hand on someone's head or look quietly at another. His actions bespoke of a balance that could not but be rooted in deep inner stillness. Seva Das hung back, watching. He saw the anxiety with which people crowded around the Maharshi, and the stillness that seemed to descend as he looked at them.

At long last, Seva Das stepped forward. Ramana's mouth betrayed a hint of mirth. 'So, you made it? And those grapes you've got for me, may I please have them now?' The guru's voice was low and gentle. Seva Das didn't even wonder how he knew about the grapes. For, he was standing at the edge of his being, peering into his essence, his own basic–true–real nature. It was a place he may have touched upon, but had remained on the edge, there yet not there. Now as he leaped over in one grand motion, deep, unbroken, primal silence washed all over him. The silence felt familiar. It was the Silence of his guru's eyes.

With some reluctance, I shake off the silence of Sri Ramana's eyes and return to the present. Climbing over bundles, I make my way to the front and yell over the din to the driver to stop at Dari. It turns out to be a village of one school, one big ground for melas and Ramlilas, and several charming, slate-roofed cottages set in gardens and arranged along narrow rural lanes. One such is the home of the good colonel and I find it quite easily.

We set off after a cup of tea. Our first stop is a temple, small and old and presided over by a goddess, being renovated in a 'modern' manner. This means that everything is being cemented, and slabs of marble will soon line the temple's insides and outsides. A marble statue of Seva Das has been established here, which fills me with a sense of irony. This yogi voluntarily gave up worldly life and its accoutrements that could have been his had he been so inclined, such as wealth, fame, maybe a political career as well. He found the resolution of his inner search in the understanding of reality and divinity as formless, featureless, silent, one. He was loath to allow people to become attached to his form rather than his message, and would sometimes leave in the middle of the night when he felt such a dependence growing. He lived among these people long enough. Do they not sense the paradox in deifying one who resisted all attempts at binding him to a place or an identity?

As I am introduced to the yogi's followers at the temple, my judging mind softens under the warm rays of their affection. After all, I think, we *are* a culture that deifies at the drop of a hat, mostly qualities of the heart, mind and spirit. I do not think anyone has ever been deified for brute force, or that anyone has been able to enforce their deification. Through the centuries, people have deified those who through some extraordinary act or achievement or even a life well lived have been able to inspire and bring others in touch with goodness, compassion, love and honesty—values that are important to us as individuals and as a society. Also deified are spiritual heroes, such as the jinas who are revered in Jainism because they have conquered their ego-selves, a task deemed much more difficult, and significant, than the conquest of lands and peoples.

The small, ageing circle has embarked upon a bhajan before Seva Das's image, and I think I understand what may prompt the idolization of a guru, how worshipping his or her idol may seem the appropriate expression of one's love and gratitude, though I cannot shake off the feeling that it misrepresents this particular yogi's teachings. But then, even the Buddha could not escape this compulsion for deification despite repeatedly insisting that he was only to be remembered as a teacher. His motivation behind this appeal was simple— once someone comes to be worshipped, he transits from the realm of reality into that of divinity. He is enshrined in a temple and his praises are sung by all those who come to worship at his altar. The ordinariness that I would celebrate in this yogi goes out the window once he has been templified. He becomes special, and thus removed from us, and his inner journey becomes the stuff of legends rather than actual inspiration to others to follow in his footsteps.

Their bhajan over, one of the elderly followers hands me a small booklet that is a compilation of the beloved bhajans of Seva Das. It says in Hindi on the cover: Shri Shri 108 [the numeral has been crossed out and 1008 written over it in ink] Shriyut Shri Paramahans Shri Swami Seva Das ji Maharaj: His Life and Favourite bhajans. Cross-eyed with counting all the Shris, I turn the pages and find most of the bhajans to be simple folk ones of the kind that extol the virtues of chanting Hari naam (God's names). This brings to mind a conundrum about Seva Das that has often perplexed me. While his own realization was informed by Advaita, the philosophy of non-duality, his interactions with people were infused with the spirit of bhakti, devotion to the divine.

At the first opportunity, I present this question to the followers. We are now in the yogi's hut, a tiny, whitewashed room in the front garden of a disciple's home. I try to ignore another idol of Seva Das in the low room, where we all sit down to chat. The colonel answers my question, 'You see, he initially did talk of Vedanta. But then realized it would appeal only to a few, whereas the bhakti marg can be easily understood and followed by simple people, especially householders. So he laid stress on doing everything with bhakti, and seeing God in everyone.'

The wife of the owner of the house pipes in, 'He would say there is no need to even sit and sing or chant. You can do this while doing your household chores or any other work.

The important ingredient is dhyana [concentration] on the Supreme in everyone and everything.' This made spiritual practice accessible for women like herself, she points out, who had much housework, with extended families and children to take care of in the absence of their army-men husbands. Women's dharma, stree dharma, has traditionally been defined as familial responsibility; Seva Das encouraged them to simultaneously follow another dharma—that of the inner self. 'He would use the phrase *hansiba kheliba dharo dhyan*, which comes from an old bhajan and which teaches us to hold awareness but lightly, happily, with playfulness.' Her poise and dignified demeanour indicate she has put this into practice, and I admire Seva Das's sensitivity to, and insight into, women's lives.

I look around at the elderly faces, most of whom are retired school teachers or army-men. As they get into the flow of reminiscing, their faces betray great emotion. A former army captain recalls in a voice shaking with feeling, 'Guru Maharaj once asked me, "Will you be sad if you had to leave your bungalow allotted by the army?" I said I won't, because I know it is not mine. Then he said, "Don't think of your house in the village as yours too. Give it to your children and just keep one room for yourself." I agreed. Then, he said, "Similarly, this body is also like a house in which the atman lives. Don't hesitate to give up this house when the time comes. Nurture your body, use it to perform karma, but don't become attached to it. The atman is and will remain forever free."'

In these words, I sense the perfume of the jivan mukta, the lotus that grows in the muck but remains pure of it, the yogi who is in the world but not *of* it. I now ask about Seva Das's techniques, how he got them to practise what he taught.

'There were several small ways in which he got us to realize something,' says one. 'One day, I came to his hut when he was meditating. There was a bowl of water before him in which was floating a beautiful red flower. When he opened his eyes and saw me, he pointed to the flower and said, "Concentrate on this flower. Can you think of anyone who can craft a flower like this? Keep this thought in your mind, and you will see the Divine through this flower."'

To really watch something so intensely, one needs to be matured in the art of dhyana, of keeping awareness, of watching oneself. I again turn to the gathering. 'Guru Maharaj stressed the importance of Dhyana Yoga. It was to be practised at brahma muhurta, the quiet window of time between 3.30 and 5.00 a.m. He would say that at this time the atmosphere is soundless and it is easy to connect with the essence of the universe.' The stillness of Dharamsala's early mornings comes to me, when not even a bird stirs, and I imagine the yogi waking up at that sacred hour. The speaker continues, 'He instructed us to try and refine the breath until it became so imperceptible as not to move a thread hanging right in front of the nose. One was to concentrate upon the point between the brows that was the place of complete shunya, emptiness.' The yogi must have sat in this very hut as he watched the stillness grow deeper, and the shunya slowly expand until it encompassed everything. There is a gap in the conversation, and an unwitting silence takes hold of me as my breathing becomes deep and slow.

'I feel his presence still,' whispers a man who has not spoken as yet. He straightens his back and continues, 'Guru Maharaj was no ordinary man but a siddha purush [realized being]. For example, he would walk in the lanes of this village and distribute money to the children. Now where did he get the money from? He had no source of income.' Implying that the money was pulled out of thin air. This is the energy of idolization, the mind that needs the reassurance of miracles and miracle-makers. I politely respond with what I have heard—Seva Das had written mathematics textbooks in Singapore and the publishers would regularly send him royalty. 'No, no,' he insists. 'There was no such thing.' I sense a fear of faith being demolished, and retreat tactfully.

The conversation now turns to the yogi's death. Relatives have called it 'suicide', though it was anything but. The motivation is not known, though I presume it to be the yogi taking upon himself the supreme choice of death—not to await its arrival but to embrace it in a fitting culmination to a rich life. While a suicide is prompted in most cases by despondency brought on by failure to see any potential in the future, the yogi's decision to die followed from having fulfilled to the utmost the potential of his life.

So the yogi bid farewell to his family of devotees and followers and proceeded to Hardwar to the banks of the Ganga. His beloved disciple, in whose house we currently are, intuited that something was up—in the way only those who have known each other for a long time can—and followed his guru to Hardwar. They rented rooms in a dharamshala near the river. On the morning of 23 April, the yogi arose as usual at the sacred hour. He had decided upon this day because it would end in a full moon night, long held to be the purveyor of auspiciousness with its dark-dispelling luminosity, an event sanctified by sages before him, like the Buddha whose birth, nirvana and death are all celebrated together on a full moon in May.

The yogi set off for the ghat, his steps as unwavering as his mind. The disciple too had awoken and followed him. Close to the ghat, the yogi turned around and asked him to bring something from his room. When the disciple returned, he found the ghat empty of his guru. He searched for a long time, and then dived into the river and enlisted others' help. There was no sign of the yogi or of his body.

It is said that the yogi entered the river and consciously offered up his prana, life force. The gathering of disciples is of the opinion that yogic techniques helped make the body so heavy that it sank to the bottom, embedded forever in the sacred river, instead of rising to the top like ordinary corpses. Or perhaps it satisfied the hunger of river animals, I think to myself. That would be an end to the atman's temporary home the kind yogi would have liked.

It is dark by the time I board the bus back to McLeodganj. My tired eyes notice with some delight that it is the night of the full moon whose contours are slowly forming in the darkening sky. The deer musk of the yogi's life lingers from the day gone by. Did I find what I came for? To an extent, some gaps in the story have been filled; the yogi's life is more fleshed out now. I will never be able to access the whole truth about him though, only as much as he allowed others to see. His life must remain a patchwork quilt for me, never a whole picture.

Did I find a way of quantifying his legacy, of teasing out his footsteps upon the soil of Dharamsala, of the world?

Perhaps. The yogi's impact on the lives of those who came to know him is undeniable in that he handed them the mirror with which to know their selves better. Through his love and seva, his belief in equality and justice and the value of unconditional kindness, Seva Das brought them closer to these qualities in themselves. As a saying from these parts goes, *sant karey apu samana*, the sage makes others as he is. He shares of his knowledge with the intent of bringing the other person to the same level of attainment as himself. There is no worldliness, no manipulation and no selfishness in his interactions. He just wants you to see what he has seen for himself. This is ultimately the only legacy of that homeless wanderer, and it lies in the practice and conduct of those whom he taught.

This day didn't end with Seva Das, though. It twisted at the tail end towards another bend in the spiritual path. The hospitable colonel had taken it upon himself to introduce me to the Chinmaya Mission at Tapovan, a few winding roads from Dari. The complex houses the founder Swami Chinmayananda's Samadhi, which displays a statue of the departed Vedanta exponent. His apartment in the complex has been preserved and therein hangs a nameplate proclaiming 'Chinmayananda'. There are huge halls for discourses and courses, dormitories to house participants who come to attend them, a well-stocked shop that sells books and tapes produced by the mission, and a huge temple where aarti is conducted twice daily. This last has statues of apsaras at the entrance and inside, a vault that houses a written japa to which 7844 people from twenty-four nations contributed three pages daily for 100 days. Counting Seva Das's 'Shris' is child's play compared to this one!

Everything here is landscaped, cemented, and shining with marble and granite. I cannot help think how sharply this contrasts with the yogi whose austere mud hut I was in a short while ago. This too is a path, a significant facet of contemporary spirituality, through which the ancient knowledge of Vedanta has come to be disseminated all over the world. As footsteps go, those of Swami Chinmayananda and his mission are mammoth ones. It has its own value for people who need institutionalized spirituality, who wish to study from organized curricula and scriptures and would rather attend courses and retreats than impromptu discussions and bhajans by lamplight.

The Chinmaya Mission is a good example of enlightened

institution-building of the kind that combines social work with spiritual work and, in Tapovan and elsewhere, local families have benefited from the charitable work initiated by it. Here, a vocational training centre trains local women in weaving and tailoring and the mission helps them sell their products so that they can become economically independent. Other initiatives include dispensaries that provide good quality medical aid for free.

If one takes into account the big institutions and anonymous yogis and the snake oil variety, all of which exist in their own way in Dharamsala, this place could be seen as a microcosm of present-day spirituality. In the global spiritual supermarket, Dharamsala is an alleyway with a vast array of choices—you can pick according to your tastes and budget and the values you hold precious. Thus, along with reputed organizations and well-regarded teachers, there are others that offer instant solutions for everything from bodily ailments to emotional turbulence.

The bus rolls into McLeodganj, and I disembark into the bustle and chatter of its bus stand. I am reminded yet again of the *one measure* of Yuan Wu that I have had occasion to remember often in this journey through Dharamsala's ancient sacredness, and now its new one as well. New Age or old, it all exists in the one field, the one earth, of spiritual seeking. Perhaps Dharamsala is not a spiritual supermarket as yet, but an untidy, noisy Indian bazaar with everything spread out and people wandering about and chatting with shopkeepers before shelling out their scanty funds for that which for them is of greatest utility. So that there are institutions and imposing structures and temples and monasteries keeping company with famous gurus and their celebrity disciples, wannabe gurus and teachers of various disciplines. And weaving through the crowd, unconcerned and undisturbed, intent upon his way, is the simple yogi who passes unheard and unsung, whose footsteps are quickly rubbed out from the sands of time.

13

Monks, Nuns and Institutions

Over the days in Dharamsala, faces start becoming familiar. People I visited the temple with in the morning are later hurrying to work as I stroll into a cafe for breakfast, the women's chubas swishing smartly over their high-heeled shoes. The old woman who spreads out her wares along the pavement in the bazaar walks by me on the Lingkhor, her grey hair hanging in braids studded with strings of jade, her right hand busy at a prayer wheel. The young mother with two little children hurries them along to school in the morning, and in the evening peers out from behind the desk at an 'antiques' shop. A tall, handsome, young man walks up the road from the temple at dusk, his arm around a pretty girl. He smiles at me and bobs his head and I recognize him as one of the courteous security officers at the Dalai Lama's residence. I smile back, pleased to see him happily coupled.

In Delhi I wouldn't dream of smiling at people on the street unless I knew them really well. In Dharamsala, it seems the most natural thing to do. My on-the-road behaviour, moulded by the compulsions of walking Delhi streets and commuting on its buses, has undergone a definite change here. In Delhi with its lewd remarks, enforced physical contact and loutish behaviour on roads and on public transport, I don a cactus-like disposition—no eye contact, arms held close and an expression that I hope conveys a proficiency in one or more martial arts.

What a contrast I find in Dharamsala. People do look and may even stare, but never in a way that makes you feel threatened or uncomfortable. When strangers smile or say 'Tashi Delek', one is moved by the good-natured greeting to respond. I find myself shedding my cacti thorns and easing into a new zone of comfort and ease. That I am on my own does not bother me beyond the first couple of days of arriving. I walk by myself all over the place, negotiate its highs and lows, and heck, even pick up conversations at random. The fear that binds me tight on Delhi roads uncoils and sets me free in Dharamsala's lanes.

It is owing to this new-found freedom that I am able to strike up some interesting conversations with people, such as a monk fresh from Lhasa. His face is familiar to me from the 'Mind and Life' conference. We would greet each other then during coffee breaks, and after the conference I had often run into him on the streets. Sometimes he reciprocated my greeting enthusiastically and sometimes, with a slightly puzzled expression. I do not think much of it until one day I see two monks with the same recognizable face strolling down the street. They are identical twins and the one from the conference knows me and the other does not, which explains his confusion. The three of us laugh at my misapprehension, and decide to go into a cafe for some ginger tea and a chat.

Sengye, the monk from Lhasa, is eager to tell his story. Both brothers were born in Lhasa but, unlike his twin, Sengye made the difficult decision to stay on. I was not to take this to mean he endorsed the Chinese occupation of Tibet, he says emphatically. At every opportunity he got, he would apprise tourists of the ground situation in Tibet. 'I felt I was doing my bit for Tibet, you know. I could counter government propaganda by speaking the truth. Of course I had to be very careful, for Lhasa is overrun with spies and you never know when you may be reported.'

Wishing to seek the Dalai Lama's blessings, Sengye decided to make a pilgrimage to Dharamsala. He obtained a visa for Nepal, sneaked past its porous border with India and headed towards Dharamsala. His brother came from his monastery in Karnataka to be with him. Sengye had thought he would stay in Dharamsala for a few days, catch up with his brother, try to get an audience with the Dalai Lama, visit some of the reconstituted monasteries, then return to Nepal and back home to Lhasa.

But even before he could reach Dharamsala, Sengye's plans went awry. From Nepal he telephoned a correspondent for an international radio service with whom he had secretly recorded a truth-telling interview in Lhasa. 'I told him I was now out of Tibet. He took it to mean that I had fled as a refugee and immediately broadcast the interview and identified me as well.' Whether it was a faulty phone connection or Sengye's inability to explain things clearly, his return home was jeopardized.

'Initially I thought I could go back even after the interview was broadcast. When I apprised the Dalai Lama of the situation, he checked with his office and advised me that it would be best if I didn't return. The danger is too great, and anything might happen if I return now.' Sengye is a reluctant refugee, thrown by this sudden storm on the all-accepting shores of Dharamsala. The place he expected to be a short stopover has turned out to be the setting for the drama that will decide the course of the rest of his life. 'I can't go back home,' he repeats with a frustration unique to refugees, those severed from their homes and homelands forever.

Sengye's brother soothes him with words that sound like

pigeons cooing. Though alike, they are different in striking ways. Sengye is gaunt and intense, his eyes like smouldering coals. His brother is gentler, even healthier, with a smile that transforms his entire face. Sengye's struggle with the hardships of living under repressive rule seems to have strained his smile and imparted a restless watchfulness to his eyes. His brother, who lives in monastic institutions that try to recreate the old way of life in exile, has thrived in comparison. He appears calm and thoughtful, quietly processing his brother's dilemma without agitating about it overmuch. His presence allays his brother's tension somewhat.

Sengye is haunted by the deprivations that have stunted his life, especially those related to his monastic training. In the absence of good teachers, he says, monkhood is of no value. Since the Dalai Lama's departure in 1959, Tibet has emptied of masters. Those that remain are severely restricted in their teaching and dharma activities. But I have heard that recently things are improving, and some destroyed monasteries have even been rebuilt. 'Cement and wood don't make a monastery,' Sengye retorts. 'What is Tsurphu monastery without the Karmapa? What is Ganden without the Dalai Lama? What are you without breath in your body? Dead.'

Sengye explains how Tibet has been destroyed. The streets of Lhasa are lined with monks who are destitute because their monasteries either no longer exist or cannot keep them any more. They have no livelihood and survive by begging. 'The destruction is all-pervasive—no aspect of our life or culture has remained untouched,' he says. People have been turned away from their traditional ways of life by new socio-economic systems controlled by the government. Sengye explains, 'Since many old livelihood options do not exist any more, government jobs have become the most coveted occupation among Tibetans. Families sometimes spend all their resources grooming their children for government jobs. Then, when the young people fail to qualify, it is as if their world has come to an end and many even commit suicide.'

This kind of frustrating unemployment was unheard of in old Tibet, where all family members could be accommodated in the traditional tasks of garnering livelihood. Besides, many would be sent to monasteries at a young age. 'That option is also fast receding unless the parents send their children to India. In any case, many parents prefer to send their children to India even if it means a long separation. Here they are assured that their child will grow up within the embrace of their culture, which in future they may be able to re-establish in Tibet.'

Sengye's memories are beginning to take their toll on him. He suddenly wants to leave. Our teacups are long empty, and he refuses my offer for another one. I am worried about Sengye's future but also feel—perhaps too optimistically—that he may now have a better chance of finding his bearings as a monk, and as a Tibetan. Dharamsala might be disturbingly unfamiliar for him at the moment, but soon he will be enfolded like other refugees in its swathe of institutions, established by the Dalai Lama and his advisers and officers to ensure the preservation of their culture and values in exile.

The Dalai Lama has often stressed upon the preservation of Tibetan culture, for culture is the spirit of a people which if irredeemably destroyed would render political freedom soulless. Apart from this role of preservation, Tibetan institutions-in-exile have also proved invaluable in providing psychological support to the refugee community. They, along with families and elders, have enabled the maintenance of its collective identity, keeping alive the spirit of old Tibet. Through the apprenticeship of the young, the institutions have ensured cultural continuity while infusing new blood into old traditions.

As the nodal point of the exiled community, Dharamsala became the natural choice for setting up many of these institutions. So that there is the Men Tsee Khang, which preserves the Tibetan medicine system, the Norbulingka Centre for Arts at Sidhbari, where young people are trained by masters in traditional plastic arts, the Tibetan Institute of Performing Arts, the Tibetan Children's Village, among others. Several non-governmental agencies are also active in Dharamsala and are concerned with welfare schemes and environmental conservation.

Another remarkable presence in Dharamsala is of the Tibetan government-in-exile. It has been responsible for what can be called a *middle path* approach to administration, education, health and other aspects of governance. It has formulated policies not only for the diaspora but also for Tibet. This government is democratically elected through universal adult franchise by the Tibetan diaspora. The Kashag, council of ministers, is led by a prime minister, who is now officially the head of the government, the Dalai Lama having relinquished his absolutist powers in 1990 when he called for the Kashag to be elected by the Assembly of Tibetan People's Deputies instead of being nominated by him. The Dalai Lama has indicated that Free Tibet, as and when it happens, will also be a democracy, thus drawing a curtain over the feudalism that defined Tibetan society until the twentieth-century Chinese invasion.

Whether it is the attitude of ahimsa or the eschewing of extremes in favour of the middle ground, the flavour of Tibetan democracy is essentially Buddhist. It is a purveyor of the dharma into modern-day institutions such as democratic government. For instance, in 1987 the Dalai Lama proposed a peace programme to China that asked for Tibet to be declared a 'zone of ahimsa', that is, it should be free of military presence and destructive weapons including nuclear bases. The ahimsa needed to be extended to the environment as well by ensuring that Tibet became a sanctuary for ecological preservation. This would benefit the entire continent, many of whose major rivers originate in Tibet. China has ignored this proposal, but its formulation is indicative of the kind of enlightened governance that can follow from engaging the principles of dharma in policy-making.

In an interview in early 2004 published in *Resurgence* magazine, the prime minister of the Tibetan government-in-exile, Samdhong Rinpoche, spoke to me about how non-violence formed the bedrock of his Dharamsala-based government. Whether it was their China policy, their concern for the environment or the stress on 'human duties', the government-in-exile works through an overarching framework informed of the simplest, and one of the most profound, injunctions of the Buddha towards ahimsa in thought and deed. Said Rinpoche, 'All are equal by potential and birthright. No one can survive at the cost of others . . . Living at the cost of others is not good living, not worthwhile living. So we have to realize responsibility towards the whole universe . . . While talking of human rights, we've completely forgotten human duties. Without duties, everyone will try to protect his or her own rights at the cost of others. Human duties have to be taught—how to care for other beings' rights and not violate them, directly or indirectly. If you really care for the rights of others as much as your own, there is no alternative but to act non-violently.'

Though these ideals have been around for centuries, in exile the Tibetans had opportunity to re-examine them and make them relevant in a new context. For instance, the inspiration to use ahimsa in political struggle came from Mahatma Gandhi. Samdhong Rinpoche mentioned, 'They

[Buddhists] thought total adherence to this [ahimsa] was possible in a spiritual life alone, and that a certain degree of violence is indispensable for managing state and society. Gandhi taught for the first time that even in managing a state, in a political movement, total non-violence is possible. For Buddhists this is an eye-opener.'

The shock of exile that catapulted Tibetan society into the twentieth, and now the twenty-first, century thus provided the impetus necessary for change. To rebuild what was destroyed, it also had to be imagined anew. The challenge of this process has been a creative one—how to make old knowledge relevant to the life of the community in exile, and ensure that the culture of old Tibet finds a way to take flight into the future on the twin wings of ambition and adaptability.

The Men Tsee Khang, also known as the Tibetan Medical and Astro Institute, is one of the oldest refugee institutions of Dharamsala, set up by the Tibetan government in 1961. Its complex now houses a college for Tibetan medicine and astrology, a department for Tibetan astrology based on the Kalachakra Tantra, a ten-bed hospital and a pharmaceutical department, where medicines are prepared from traditional ingredients.

There is also a rather intriguing museum, which I find empty of people on a weekday morning. My eye is immediately attracted to colourful display cases that line the room. These contain samples of minerals and plant extracts used to make medicines, and there are all kinds of precious gems, stones and metals, even gold. Given the ingredients, how do they manage to sell the medicines at such affordable prices, I wonder. To the poor, they are even given free of charge. Men Tsee Khang also provides for the education, housing and other needs of its employees and their children, and offers health care at no or nominal charge at its clinics in Dharamsala and in other parts of India and Nepal. I do not know how profitable this warm-hearted institution is financially. Perhaps it needs the support of donors from time to time. But it does have a huge capital in terms of values, and typifies the spirit of Dharamsala's institutions that give precedence to good karma over good business.

I climb down the stairs to the museum's basement, and walk into a veritable vault of huge thangkas with glowing, jewel colours. But they are not the regular Buddha or bodhisattva thangkas and the eye finds it difficult to take in their intricacies in one sweep. Crafted with infinite patience, these thangkas demand as much from the onlooker. They do not have a decorative purpose; rather, they detail cycles of illnesses, implements for surgery, diagnostic aids, astronomical charts, predictive wheels and so on. These thangkas are to the Tibetan doctor what sutras are to the monk—repositories of old wisdom that must be consulted from time to time to cross-check the validity of one's insights.

The system of Tibetan medicine is actually sourced to an eighth-century Bon priest, Bon being the pre-Buddhist religion of Tibet. But it also has a relation with the Buddha that resonates with his vision for his monastic sangha. Sangha and society, according to the Buddha, were to have a symbiotic relationship where society provided the monastics with their survival needs who in turn fulfilled society's need for spiritual guidance. The sangha was to be embedded within society as opposed to being a reclusive, and exclusive, community of spiritual practitioners.

Over time, some among the sangha became proficient in the art of healing. These monk-physicians practised a holistic medicine, which, unlike modern systems that reduce the body to the sum of its parts, viewed the human organism as a whole. They would look for the cure of sickness not only in the body but also in the mind. Their treatment was multidisciplinary in that it made use of traditional knowledge of herbs and minerals along with reading the person's astrological chart and pinpointing appropriate days in the lunar cycle when the treatment would be the most effective. Perhaps this emphasis on a holistic paradigm for medicine emerged from the Indian, and later Tibetan, tendency to not sever the body from the mind, and in the sangha, the healer from the spiritual guide.

Even today there are physicians in the Tibetan medical tradition who dispense not only medicine but wisdom as well, for whom the practice of medicine is in itself a spiritual path. Some days after my encounter with the bewitching medicine thangkas, I have the good fortune of meeting one such wise physician, for which I return to Men Tsee Khang.

In a large room filled with brilliant sunshine and herbal fragrances, the doctor ushers me on to a padded sofa. He is examining a little girl who is ill. The child coughs painfully and moans to her father, who speaks to her softly in French.

The doctor checks her pulse. Luckily, the prognosis is not so bad, if you do not consider going off fried foods and sweets calamitous, that is. 'Pancakes?' the child protests weakly to her dad, who shakes his head. 'Okay, but only a little bit,' the doctor says smilingly. The father–daughter duo leave to get the prescribed Tibetan medicines from the in-house dispensary and the good doctor comes and sits by my side, ready for a chat.

Dr Tsewang Tamdin is the deputy director of the Men Tsee Khang, and part of a team of doctors that attends to the Dalai Lama's health. I cannot help but ask him about this duty, though I am apprehensive of breaching some protocol or security restriction. 'Our aim is to keep him healthy,' says Dr Tamdin, not at all discomfited by the question. 'His health is important not only for the Tibetan people but for the whole world. He is a very special person in these times who is taking care of everybody. So it is important to keep him healthy. Our main job is to keep an eye on his condition. If there is any imbalance, we prescribe medicines to correct it.'

I know that the Dalai Lama has encouraged collaborative efforts between Tibetan and modern scientific knowledge systems. Dr Tamdin confirms 'research in Tibetan medicine using scientific methods and in cooperation with western science', and says that the Dalai Lama stresses 'the need for clinical study and initiating a collaboration not only to evaluate and authenticate this system but also to enable Tibetan medicine to reach a wider population'.

However, this collaboration has not been easy, mainly because there has been a 'degree of scepticism' towards Tibetan medicine from the western scientific community. Another, more crucial reason has been that the two systems have very different roots and it is difficult to find common ground.

'The basic cause of disease in Tibetan medicine is the mind,' says Dr Tamdin. 'We say that the mind is the key to health. Ignorance produces three mental poisons—desire, delusion and anger. From these are produced three energies—wind, bile and phlegm. Without these three energies, our body cannot exist.' Somewhat like vata, pitta, kapha, the three bodily energies according to Ayurveda whose imbalance is the cause of disease. What is also evident is the influence of Buddhism on the philosophy of Tibetan medicine. For in Buddhist thought, it is not any external evil that causes mischief but our own ignorance that obstructs the mind and leads to wrongful thoughts and actions. It is all in the mind—the cause of suffering, and also the remedy.

Dr Tamdin agrees. 'You cannot give any medicine to detoxify the mind; it can only be done through spiritual practice.' If ignorance equals disease, then what about self-realized yogis such as Ramana Maharshi and Sri Ramakrishna Paramahamsa who suffered from cancer towards the end of their lives?

Dr Tamdin says, 'We can say that since this person is enlightened, he comes to this universe in a human form for a specific reason. Then his mind and body are connected with the human energy. He is not suffering on the basis of his spirit, but on the energy level. When you take human birth, your body is made up of five elements—space, earth, air, fire and water. These have a certain time span and cannot exist beyond that. The body that is made of flesh and bones must diminish. Sometimes, however, the suffering of an enlightened person may be a lesson for common people. I also feel that in the mind of such people there will be no suffering. They are free of ignorance, delusions and mental poisons.'

In a universe governed by cause and effect, as held by Buddhism, karma must come into play while dealing with physical suffering? The doctor explains, 'A person may suffer due to many causes some of which may be unrelated to their environment, such as karma. Karma cannot be gleaned from X-rays or ultrasounds. Many diseases are related to your lifestyle, behaviour and food, but there is a link with karma also. For karma-related suffering, you need to acknowledge it and bear your suffering because you cannot get rid of it without purifying your karma.'

But does this not lead to a non-acceptance of responsibility because everything can be conveniently laid at the door of past bad karma? The good doctor is patient with me. 'It [karma] depends on individual choice. Follow the path the best way you can, then you have no bad karma. The present life and well-being depends on past karma. Future life will depend on how you live in the present. This connection is from the beginning, a long process.'

I look at his kindly face and wonder about his own journey. I ask what brought him to Tibetan medicine. 'My first intention to become a doctor is very special,' he says. 'When I was in school in Dalhousie, I got a skin allergy on my face. It was in the 1970s, and there were no good doctors to take care of us. The Central Relief Committee provided a few doctors. I was given oxygen peroxide to apply on my face. It is a very strong acid, and turned some of my hair yellow and grey. At another time, I suffered from dysentery. These experiences made me feel that perhaps there is another way to give treatment.'

So, is the practice of medicine a spiritual path for him? 'Yes, we believe that if you practise medicine as a physician, according to the Medicine Buddha, you can get enlightened if you practise sincerely without desiring fame or money; it is not necessary to be a monk. The main aim of medicine is to maintain health. It is a way to relieve suffering. In the training course, there is a component of spiritual teaching for doctors that details what quality of mind the doctor should have. How should he behave with patients at the level of mind and body? All those who come to this do it because they sincerely desire to serve others.'

Dr Tamdin is a healer in the old tradition of monk-physicians of the sangha, only he is not a monk. But he is certainly a knower of afflictions of body and mind and a solver of the conundrums of life and health. Has dealing with life outside the Tibetan plateau challenged the efficacy of Tibetan medicine? Can it heal with the same confidence in Dharamsala as it did in Tibet?

Dr Tamdin feels the system has handled all challenges very well. 'Allopathy qualifies diseases such as stress and diabetes as "lifestyle diseases" because they say these are caused by modern lifestyles. Tibetan medicine will say these are caused by internal energy changes. So these are not new to us, even AIDS or cancer. Overall, Tibetan medicines have a success ratio of seventy to eighty per cent.'

If this is indeed true, Tibetan medicine has the potential to become widely followed in the future. 'Now many people in the west are turning away from allopathy because the treatment is not always effective and the medicine has many side-effects— it helps in one way and causes problems in another. If Tibetan medicine doesn't help you, it will not cause side-effects. And it is very good in preventing deterioration of the condition.' Here, in Dharamsala, many foreign visitors turn towards Tibetan medicine in times of crises. 'Yes, but sometimes Tibetans are more interested in allopathy. Maybe they like the change or need fast relief. Most people in the Tibetan community do use Tibetan medicine as well as allopathy sometimes. But westerners who have already experienced the shortcomings of that system are more likely to become committed to Tibetan medicine.'

A line of patients has formed outside Dr Tamdin's door, and it is time for me to leave. At a counter that sells products manufactured at the Men Tsee Khang, I choose herbal formulations that I hope will heal my hair and skin choking under the onslaught of Delhi life, just as being here in Dharamsala has divested me of some of my city-bred thorns and cured me of physical, and perhaps mental, lethargy too.

In Dharamsala, because the usual framework of my life does not exist, my reality feels fluid and in constant flux. Maybe it has always been so, but has been masked by my identification with a particular identity. Here, there is none of the external edifice that labels me so and so. And the internal structuring, which one builds to hold oneself up as 'x' with 'y' job and 'z' ambitions, is also becoming altered piece by piece. Who knows where I'll be by the end of this journey?

One evening, as I sit near the window of a roadside cafe generally watching the flow of humanity, quite unafraid to look or smile back, a woman I'd met at the 'Mind and Life' conference walks by. We greet each other warmly and she invites me to visit the Dolma Ling nunnery at Sidhpur, where she is based. I promise to see her the following week.

The undulating flatness of Sidhpur, which is alongside Sidhbari, is a pleasant change from the hilly angularity of Dharamsala. It is replete with fields and streams, with the mountains rising into the horizon, unlike Dharamsala where you are *in* the mountains. Dolma Ling nunnery is in a rural part of Sidhpur amid lush, cultivated fields.

Its large, modern building comes as a surprise in the rustic setting. Some of its wings are still under construction. I wander through the unpainted rooms that smell of wood shavings and find a clutch of buildings that appear inhabited. I finally reach an office and ask for Dr Elizabeth Napper. The staff members ask me to wait and offer me tea and their brochures to browse through.

From these I gather that Dolma Ling is the headquarters of the Tibetan Nuns Project (TNP), started in 1987 to deal with the influx of nuns from Tibet. It seeks not only to help the nuns find their feet in a new environment but also to provide them with modern education in tandem with traditional education to 'allow them to function in the modern world'. TNP is engaged in creating a new curriculum that combines religious studies with English, maths, science, computers and so on. Further, it aims to prepare nuns for 'positions of leadership and moral authority'. To ensure these measures are implemented across the board, TNP has networked with nunneries from different branches of Tibetan Buddhism such as the Kagyu Tilokpur Nunnery, the Nyingma Shugsep Nunnery and the Gelug Geden Choeling Nunnery, all located around Dharamsala.

TNP's work reminds me of the ongoing debate about the status of women in Buddhism. Venerable Khandro Rinpoche, one of the few women teachers in Tibetan Buddhism, once told me that it is not Buddhism or the Buddha that discriminated against women, but the patriarchal structure of the societies in which Buddhism flourished. About the apparent gender bias in Buddhist scriptures, she said, 'One thing is clear—it [the bias] may be grammatical. The second thing is the author's own mindset and the third is the level at which that text is written. These things have to be understood in their context. To balance the biases, one could examine texts where the author is a woman. Yeshe Tsogyal [the eighth-century yogini, consort of Padmasambhava] said, "The best life to attain enlightenment is that of a woman." Such remarks can be looked at as opinions of masters, and the individual can decide which way to go. Are you going to be stuck in the pessimistic attitude of someone who lived in the sixteenth century, or are you going to take the essence of the teachings?'

TNP has clearly taken on the challenge of transporting Tibetan monasticism into the twenty-first century by empowering its women. Nuns are not traditionally trained in philosophy and dialectics. The degree of geshe is unavailable to them, though this is something the Dalai Lama has said he wishes to reform. In his keenness to improve the status of ordained women, he is a valuable ally for TNP's efforts.

TNP is an institution that preserves *and* destroys, which

has realized that everything old may not be worth preserving and everything new may not require stonewalling. After all, cultures are living things and benefit from breathing the air of their times. TNP seems determined to clear out the cobwebs, and open the windows wide enough to let in fresh air and sunlight on to closed traditions that have become musty.

A bright 'hello' brings me out of my reverie. Dr Napper is standing before me. On our tour of the nunnery, we walk through wide corridors flanked by classrooms, workrooms and open courtyards. From its appearance, this may be an ace school anywhere in the world but for the flashes of maroon through open doors. In one courtyard, young nuns are chanting prayers. 'We often get requests from the Tibetan community to chant for a particular person or a cause, since this was one of the main functions of the nuns in Tibet,' she explains. Time is allocated for this in such a way that their studies are not disturbed, since in this nunnery it is the latter that is the prime focus.

'One of our nuns has completed her education and has now joined us as a teacher. That is one of our aims, to enable nuns to receive higher education so that they can take on teaching roles. Come, I'll show you something.' Dr Napper steers me towards a courtyard where adolescent nuns are practising their debating skills, using the distinctive clapping gesture where one hand is raised to strike the other when a point is made. I have seen monks do this a million times, but never nuns. 'That is because they weren't trained in philosophical debate. The first debate for women ever was held in 1995 by the Tibetan government-in-exile's Department of Culture. From the second year, the TNP has organized it annually as it helps build the nuns' self-confidence tremendously.'

I look at the earnest faces of the young nuns. In measured

voices they put forth their point, and then a vigorous swing and a clap! Their backs erect, their faces flushed with the adrenaline rush, the young nuns fling away centuries of inequality with every flourish of their arms. I ask Dr Napper whether these young girls were also 'given' into monasticism by their families like so many monks. 'Interestingly, most of these girls have made an independent decision to lead a nun's life,' she says.

The rules are not the same for boys and girls. While it may be a matter of pride to have a monk in the family, it may not be so where women are concerned. That holds true for all traditional societies, I think, where the spiritual life with its accent on renunciation and detachment is not the way to go for women, who are encouraged to remain engaged in familial responsibilities. That these young nuns are here out of choice means they have already combated some displeasure from their families and many have also made the difficult journey out of Tibet, arriving exhausted and penniless in Dharamsala. Their individual destinies have converged here, under the shade of this fledgling institution that will hopefully hand them the most valuable tool with which to shape their spiritual lives—knowledge.

I come away as the afternoon wanes into what is called 'godhuli' in North Indian villages, literally 'cow dust time' at the cusp of evening and night, when dust raised by cattle returning home flings a warm haze over everything in sight. I have a short distance to go, for I am staying at the guesthouse of the Norbulingka Institute near the nunnery. Tomorrow, I will explore Norbulingka's aesthetic environs some more.

This night is given over to dreams of nuns with bright smiles spinning out their own destinies upon the loom of change.

Norbulingka was the summer palace of the Dalai Lama in Lhasa. The Norbulingka complex here in Dharamsala is beautifully designed with a ground plan based on the sacred geometrical proportions of the beloved bodhisattva of Tibet, Avalokiteshwara.

It is meticulously maintained, with plants and flowering trees and artificial streams that gurgle over smooth river bed stones in an aesthetic reminiscent of a Kyoto temple garden.

The Norbulingka Institute aims to protect the arts and literary traditions of Tibet. Perhaps this is why an atmosphere of beauty has been carefully cultivated here. The guesthouse and cafe use bedcovers, trays, furniture and decorations handcrafted by Norbulingka's artists. The temple here has a breathtaking bronze Buddha statue, the largest made in exile by Tibetan artists. And on display at Norbulingka's Losel Doll Museum are 160 dolls depicting the traditional vocations, dresses and customs of Tibet that are of great value since many of these costumes have now ceased to exist along with the lifestyles they were a part of.

Walking around Norbulingka, I discover one by one, like successive whorls of petals in a flower, sections for making sculpture, thangkas, appliqué needlework, tailoring and woodcarving. Wherever I peep in, young people are at work in spacious, sunlit rooms, often under the guidance of a master. The guild system of old Tibet, where the master craftsperson worked with several apprentices and under which huge art projects were accomplished, is replicated in Norbulingka. Most of the masters here were trained in Tibet, and are keen to pass on their knowledge into the guardianship of young hands. For the Tibetan arts are arts of apprenticeship, where new aspirants must learn from tradition before striking out on their own. Even when they become proficient, they must keep the tradition before them both as a guiding light and a standard of quality. Consequently the artist merges into the vast stream of tradition, instead of standing out as a unique medium of self-expression. In that sense in Tibetan art, as in Buddhism, there is no 'self'. Each generation acts as the anonymous wave that leaves the tradition on the shores of the next. To this process, Norbulingka is dedicated as preserver and facilitator.

How crucial, I realize, is this opportunity, this ground, these institutions, for safeguarding the intertwined traditions that together form Tibetan culture. Dharamsala's role as refuge is not only of the people, but also of their culture and aspirations. Upon its soil, the people's will to save their culture was able to bring together requisite funds, land, infrastructure, teachers, students. Another institution, the Tibetan Institute of the Performing Arts (TIPA), is doing for Tibet's performing arts what Norbulingka is doing for its plastic arts.

TIPA is on the road that meanders towards Dharamkot up from McLeodganj. Entering its grand gate, one is in a huge courtyard that has a permanent stage for performances at one end. On the other three sides are buildings that house classrooms, music and dance studios, and workshops for artisans. The day I visited TIPA, the deep sound of the Tibetan horn hovered in the air like the eagles soaring high above in the sky. In classrooms, young people were studying the history of Lhamo, Tibet's traditional opera based on stories that illustrate Buddhist values. In the workshops, young artists were being shown how to make masks that are integral to Tibetan performing arts.

A group of young people were bent over masks with their brushes, and an older artist who seemed to be their teacher was daubing black paint on to the snout of a papier mâché yak mask. Handing over his brush to an apprentice, he came over to chat. He was an artist, he said, and had come to TIPA as a monk to construct its grand entrance. Here, he fell in love with a singer and they got married. Over the years, he has helped develop TIPA's painting section. All TIPA members live on the premises, and collaborate on diverse efforts to build a repertoire of as many Tibetan performing traditions as possible. TIPA has a programme to identify children who show an inclination towards the performing arts and admit them for intensive training. It also trains teachers who then take the arts into the Tibetan schools in exile.

In these institutions, there is a commitment to the young, to the process of passing on, to the traditions of teaching and learning. Tibetan culture may be destroyed in Tibet, but it will live on in different parts of the world, wherever these young minds travel. Through them, it will make its journey into the future and, who knows, at some point, back to the source, to Tibet?

How do the young respond to this immense responsibility? For change often comes through the young who are impatient with tradition; it is they who carry the energy of revolution, the will to better the world. Perhaps because they have seen the suffering of their preceding generation, Tibetan youngsters are more responsive to the call of tradition. I decide to explore their world here in Dharamsala, to seek out their desires and listen to their dreams.

I think of little Tenzin at the guesthouse. He is a twenty-first-century child, growing up in a world that is fast changing into a monocultural entity held together by technology and the internet, and blown apart by politics of selfishness and ideologies of violence. He no longer has the protective insulation of old Tibet, and must pick his own way through the maze of options before him. Will he choose to remain in the fold of his culture, preserving and guarding it? Will he want to look for happiness in money and material fantasies? Or will he find a balance between the ancient and the modern, both of which are irrevocable aspects of his own self?

The choice will not be easy for little Tenzin.

14

Mothers and Mentors

Most mornings in Dharamsala, I am up at daybreak. The empty streets, returned to nature for the night, are quiet and peaceful. Pre-dawn mist evaporates on rooftops and on the rough bark of trees, leaving them wet with dew. The crisp, clean air feels like breath drawn from the lungs of mountains, untouched by the sighs and exhausts of humanity. Even the drains seem less smelly, and it is almost possible to ignore the garbage piled in uncleared dumps. The temporarily abandoned streets and structures of commerce are littered with dry leaves and withered flowers, nature's delicate debris, left there by the wood-fragranced wind that swept through the town at night. As the first tentative sunrays struggle out into the sky they warm the darkened, mossy mountainsides into a lighter, brighter shade of green. At this early morning hour, Dharamsala belongs to beauty alone.

By the time I return, the guesthouse's nightly blanket of serenity has been shot through and dispensed with by the morning rush hour. People need to get to jobs, somebody has overslept, and breakfast won't cook itself now, will it? I regularly bump into male inmates wearing nothing more than a towel around their waists, rushing to or from the common bathroom. I pretend to be lost in deep metaphysical thoughts to relieve some of their acute embarrassment. Later, when I stand under the shower that came attached with my room, I am grateful for the luxury of privacy, and it no longer matters that the geyser is perpetually broken and the cold water chills me to the marrow of my bones.

Because of the morning rush, little Tenzin's mother prefers to bathe him in the evenings. The common bathroom is adjacent to my room, and I am often party to their happy sounds of splashing around. Sometimes the mother sharply admonishes her son. Though I cannot understand what she is saying, from the tone of her voice it is obvious that little Tenzin is up to no good. And sometimes he will whimper, probably because the soap has gone into his eyes, or any one of the countless things that are likely to make kids fuss about bathing.

My return from morning walks coincides with little Tenzin's departure for school. This is his most sober incarnation on any given day. Thondup, his mother, has carefully creased his blue trousers, and his shoes are polished to perfection. His restless little hands are slapped away as he fiddles with the buttons on his well-ironed blue and white checked shirt. He is forbidden from getting distracted from the task at hand, which is getting to school as smartly turned out as his mother can manage. So no unnecessary activity and no sidling along the walls that will bleed their cheap powdery paint on to his uniform.

Pema and Thondup are in a 'walk pool', where parents take turns rounding up all the children of the neighbourhood and walking them to school, like car pools in cities but closer in spirit to shepherds herding flocks of sheep. Thondup returns from these trips with her arms laden with vegetables, her long, fine hair streaming behind her as she rushes homewards to cook her husband lunch to take with him to work. I run into her one day in the bazaar, and offer to carry some of her bags. She is grateful, and I marvel for the thousandth time at the strength packed into this petite woman. The bags are pretty heavy and, though I am double her size and tower half a foot above her, I do not think I could carry the weight she can up the incline from the market.

'Tenzin goes to TCV?' I ask her as we fall in step. To me the Tibetan Children's Village is synonymous with education for Tibetan children. This autonomous institution is something of a marvel, having risen through sheer necessity and the determination of its architects from a small nursery in the early 1960s to a mammoth organization that has over 14,000 children in its care in different parts of India today. Thondup nods. 'My husband and I are trying to make more money, so we can send Tenzin to a good boarding school,' she says, her eyes gleaming with dreams of unknown tomorrows clustered around her child of hope like so many bright suns. 'We are trying our best to give him a good future.'

This surprises me because I had assumed TCV was the perfect choice for Tibetan parents-in-exile, where their child is taught aspects of Tibetan culture as part of his or her education. I mention this to Thondup. 'No, there is no problem with TCV,' she says quickly. 'When we had nothing, at least our child was assured an education. Now things are different for us. If we could get him into a good school, his chances of making a career would be better, wouldn't it?' She turns her hope-filled eyes to me, and I cannot deny the truth in what she says. Still, I don't agree with her. TCV's curriculum is designed keeping in mind the needs of Tibetan refugee children, and the Dalai Lama himself has taken a keen interest in it from the beginning. Little Tenzin cannot hope to get that kind of education of mind and heart anywhere else.

I am reminded of what the Dalai Lama said at the 'Mind and Life' conference when the scientists presented to him the possible use of neuroscience for optimizing human potential.

They had two options—to provide access to everyone, or to identify the brightest and cultivate them as leaders of society. His Holiness was categorical in his opposition to the latter, saying that a 'tiered society could not be allowed to develop'. Then, he had said as an afterthought, 'But I understand your dilemma. Even among Tibetans, those who can afford it send their children to fancy schools. In this way, discrimination is becoming ingrained in our society.'

So I persist with Thondup. 'What about culture and values? Tenzin won't get that in a non-Tibetan school.' 'Well, he can get all that from his father and me,' says Thondup. 'What you say is more for children whose parents are in Tibet, or who are orphans.' In that moment, I feel Thondup has shown me the iron in her soul, the source of strength that powers her and urges her up every steep slope she encounters. At its core is a mother's resolve to protect and nurture her child and secure the finest future she can in the face of all odds. Thondup's resolve feels oddly familiar to me, and it takes just a moment to figure out why—it reminds me of my own mother.

I offload her bags outside her living quarters. As I open my door, I see her still standing outside hers, thoughtfully unlacing her shoes. Little Tenzin is on both our minds as we walk into our spaces and close the doors behind us.

Over the next few days, I often think of TCV. Though each Tibetan institution in exile is remarkable, TCV is for me the grand hero of them all. And not the least because it has taken care of one of the most pressing problems of the refugee community—the welfare of its children that are its most vulnerable, and valuable, constituent. Built brick by painful brick, the organization has established an impressive countrywide network that includes five children's villages, seven residential schools, four day schools, three day care centres, four vocational training centres and many outreach programmes. In Dharamsala alone, there is one full-fledged village (along the lines of SOS children's villages) in Dharamsala Cantonment, a residential school in lower Dharamsala and a day school in McLeodganj.

Like so many stories of the Tibetan diaspora, that of TCV too originated in Dharamsala. One tumultuous year had passed since the Dalai Lama's flight from Tibet. The refugees who followed him had to deal with the loss of homes and loved ones, a strange climate, and economic and social deprivation. The children suffered the most. There were many who were rendered orphan or destitute by the upheavals and in 1960 a group of fifty-one such children arrived in Dharamsala. They were unkempt and undernourished, and many were ill. His Holiness immediately proposed a centre to care for them, and his elder sister, Tsering Dolma Takla, volunteered to do so herself. Soon, word of this fledgling 'Nursery for Tibetan Refugee Children', as it was then known, spread through the community and children began arriving from areas where Tibetan refugees had been given employment in the building of roads in Himachal Pradesh, Sikkim, even Bhutan and Nepal.

Lekshey Tenpa, now a senior TCV official, recalls the trauma he saw when he first arrived in 1963. 'There were many children, some in distress, some completely lost and many on their bare little feet,' he says. So moved was he that, along with teaching Tibetan, he began repairing the children's shoes. In 1964 the founding director, Tsering Dolma Takla, passed away suddenly, and her younger sister, Jetsun Pema, took over. During this time, news of the struggling nursery reached international aid circles and funds began trickling in. Just as well, for the Mother, which is what the nursery had become to those in its care, had long outgrown its original facilities and functions and now needed to urgently expand and mature to accommodate an increasing number of children and their different needs. This happened in a way in 1972, when the nursery was admitted as a member of SOS Kinderdorf International and formally became the Tibetan Children's Village.

Since then, the Mother has grown from strength to strength, trying to keep up with the ever-increasing number of children that seek out her warm bosom year after year. The scope of her actions has also widened considerably and, as her children grow up and enter the world, she tries not to let go of their hands until they are able to take care of themselves.

The congruence between TCV and the ground it is based in, Dharamsala, goes beyond the obvious. They share a quality of spirit that is both special and significant. TCV is the enabler of transformation—healing little children of sadness and loneliness and recreating them as bright young citizens, just as Dharamsala recasts social and spiritual outcasts into seekers of truth and meaning. Both provide refuge to the dispossessed, and the gift of rest and rejuvenation to the world-weary, children though they may be in the case of TCV. Both try and show the path(s) forward, and are in themselves points where passers-through can transition from one phase of their lives into another, richer one.

The TCV at Dharamsala Cantonment is the mother of all TCVs, having descended from the initial Nursery for Tibetan Refugee Children. It is also the biggest branch, with some 1900 students and forty-five 'homes', where children live under the tutelage of 'home mothers'. It is known as 'Upper TCV' situated as it is in 'Upper Dharamsala'.

The entrance to Upper TCV is next to a pond named, somewhat audaciously, the Dal Lake, which is nowhere close in size and majesty to its famous namesake in Kashmir. It is early afternoon when I reach the Dal Lake on my way to TCV. A couple of years ago, TCV students had undertaken a project to excavate temple structures at the edge of this lake that were buried during the great earthquake of 1905. I had once seen them then, arriving here in groups after school and settling down to work cheerfully. In the earliest days, when the then-nursery had no playground, children would often be brought to the Dal Lake to play. For a while, I linger by the edge of this pond-lake in the mellow sunshine and dream of generations of Tibetan children laughing on its banks.

From the Dal Lake, the road winds gently upwards to TCV. On entering the complex, low buildings appear on both sides of the path. I assume them to be the children's homes. Outside most of them, washing hangs on clotheslines to dry. It is still school time, so the homes are quiet. A short way up, there is a large quadrangle with a playing field flanked by buildings— a veritable plateau. Was it designed this way to simulate a plateau experience for these children, exiled from the highest plateau in the world?

Right behind the school complex, the Dhauladhars rise almost vertically into the sky. Prayer flags astride whispering wind-horses flutter countless benedictions towards TCV from their perches all along this mountain. Paths curve around the mountain like a snake's coiled embrace, and I remember walking on one of them and looking down at children in this very playground from high above. Distance rendered everything miniature, and the children were moving dots, though their excited voices were carried to me through the still morning air, also by wind-horses?

I have to go to the main office to find Tsamchoe-la, a senior official who has been at TCV almost all her working life. I ask around until I find a kindly, and brisk, middle-aged woman in a large, airy room sitting behind a desk piled high with files and papers. Despite being very busy, Tsamchoe-la finds the time to speak with me. No, it will not be possible to visit classrooms because we do not allow that. But you can observe the nursery class and some of the homes, and please feel free to talk to whoever you wish to.

I begin with the nursery that has a trail of little shoes leading up to it. It is a cheerful room with wooden floors and wide windows through which sunlight streams in. The walls are full of artwork made with the delightful randomness of little children. The children are gathered in the middle of the room for what must be the highlight of their day—one whole hour of singing. They are quite young, maybe three to five years old, and are as yet not wearing the transgender blue trousers and checked shirt uniform of TCV. When I arrive at their door, they are singing a French song, much to my surprise. Two chuba-clad women teachers walk around the room, singing and holding up their hands to gesticulate the meaning of the song. The French nursery rhyme gladdens me as evidence of a looking beyond, that the fostering of a strong Tibetan identity does not preclude openness to the wider world. No longer confined to snowy highlands, this kind of internationalism is a precious attitude for the Tibetan diaspora to cultivate in their children.

The flow of songs has now turned to English, and rhymes familiar from my own childhood fill the air. Most of the children know the songs and the accompanying hand gestures. Though I am trying to remain as inconspicuous as possible, half-hidden behind the door, some children have seen me and get distracted. They giggle and become self-conscious. Soon, those with their backs to me catch on that something of interest has appeared behind them, and begin turning their heads surreptitiously to get in on the joke. This distraction lasts a few minutes until my novelty wears away.

Some children in this jovial group are not so happy. They are not apparent at first, but gradually catch my eye. There is one near the left window and a couple in the middle who do not know the songs. One child stands still in her place, a faraway look in her eyes, until one of the teachers notices her and tenderly begins moving her hands to the rhythm of the song. And here is one close to the door who looks like he is ready to leap out of the room any instant, a haunted look in his eyes. Could these be the new arrivals from Tibet, I wonder, children recently separated from their parents. The teachers are especially attentive to them, which seems to provide some consolation to these sad little ones with restless eyes and immobile faces.

The class comes to an end and the children are sent out in pairs. As they shuffle past me barefoot, a rash of giggles breaks out and some daring ones yell 'hello'. They get their shoes on, and the teachers bend down to help those who struggle with shoelaces and other such complicated matters. Soon they are on their way to the Tibetan singing class, and I wander out with them. The sad-eyed ones lag behind as if unsure of their place in the scheme of things. Until the kind teachers take their hands with motherly firmness, and lead them out into the sunlit courtyard.

'How can I help you?' a soft voice behind me asks. I am standing outside the office building, unsure which way to go. I would have happily tagged behind the little singers, but they were going to the classroom block, which is one place Tsamchoe-la has asked me not to go. The young woman who has appeared says she is the admissions officer of Upper TCV, and that Tsamchoe-la has told her to show me around. Grateful for the company, I ask the young woman if I could speak with her. 'Sure,' she smiles readily. 'Let's sit over there?' she says, pointing to the far end of the playground.

We find a comfortable spot on the low boundary wall. Ahead, the ground drops away and the valley spreads out below us, shimmering in the afternoon sun. The young woman's name is Tsering Tsamchoe—the second namesake for the day. She thinks I am looking for facts and figures about TCV, and rattles them off with practised ease: over 1900 students, forty-five homes, 240 teaching and non-teaching staff members, oh and that is excluding head office staff. 'I keep all the records here,' she says.

'And where did you study?' I ask her.

'Here, in this very school. Since 1985, when I was seven years old,' Tsamchoe says, a little impatiently, eager to give me more information about TCV. But I really want to know her story. 'Did you come from Tibet, or were you born in India?' For the briefest moment, Tsamchoe is sad-eyed like the little kids in the nursery class. Then the calm young woman takes over, and begins to state the story of her life in a series of factoids.

'I was born in Tibet. I am from Dhingri village in U–Tsang province. It is a rural area very far from Lhasa. My father brought me here in 1985, along with my little sister. I completed school in Upper TCV and then went to Delhi to do a two-year course in secretarial practice. In 2002 I got this job. I live here in the staff quarters. My sister has done her master's in commerce and has an accounting job in Norbulingka Institute at Sidhbari. We meet once in a while.'

Tsamchoe raises her eyes to me, as if to say, 'What else?'

Her neat summary of her life leaves out too much. The words indicate heartbreaking separation that continues till today, displacement, loneliness. The voice that utters these words is dispassionate, as if sterilizing them of all painful associations. I ask her about her work, leaving the more personal questions for later, if at all. 'Why did you return to TCV to work? You could have worked in Delhi too.'

'When I was in Delhi, I thought of working there,' she says. 'But Delhi is a hectic place and it is very different from here, from the environment I was used to. I had been here for twenty-one years. It was difficult to adapt in Delhi. I wanted to work here, in this area, in Dharamsala.' She giggles unexpectedly at this, perhaps at her own lack of courage? Then, a torrent ensues, and Tsamchoe seems to have got over her earlier hesitation to speak about herself.

'These days it is very difficult to get jobs in the Tibetan community,' she says. 'Many students are graduating and there are limited seats in the institutions and the government-in-exile. We have to sit for the entrance exams for recruitment. Because I was brought up in TCV, my first preference was to work here. I didn't even try elsewhere. After my course I did voluntary work for six months in TCV. Then I was made admissions officer and things have been fine since then.'

I cautiously broach the subject of her childhood journey out of Tibet. Why was she brought to Dharamsala? Her facial muscles tighten as if guarding against a spasm of pain. In her lilting, Tibetan-accented English, she says, 'I don't remember much as I was very young. We lived in a rural area where it was difficult to get an education. I think my parents thought we could get an education here in TCV. Also, we didn't have blessings from His Holiness the Dalai Lama.' Had her parents given her these reasons when she was sent here? Tsamchoe shakes her head. 'I never asked. I assume these could be the reasons we were sent here.'

'Did you see your parents again?' 'Only my father. He came in 1998 and then returned to our village. But we do talk to them on the phone sometimes,' she says, brightening at the thought of this one connection with her family. 'It is very expensive, but my sister and I save our money and when we have enough we call our parents.'

What is the news from home? 'My parents had more children after my sister and I came here. I have never seen them, but they are my brothers and sisters. I sometimes speak to them also. One of my younger brothers was being sent to school in our village. He was eager to study and was good at Tibetan and maths. They don't study English there. But the charges in the school were so high that my parents could not afford to continue his education, because my family is poor and relies on farming for income. Now, he is no longer studying.' I cannot help ask, 'Why don't you get him here?' Tsamchoe shakes her head and looks down. I leave it at that.

To change the topic, I ask Tsamchoe how many children there are in TCV whose parents are in Tibet. 'About 900 out of 1900,' she answers. As admissions officer, Tsamchoe must deal with all of them when they first arrive in Dharamsala. 'Yes, naturally. When they first arrive here, I suppose they go through what I did when I first came here.' I suddenly realize why she is so guarded. Her work must constantly rake at old scars. Every new arrival in TCV brought a new story of pain and loss, a new story, but also an old one in its retelling, again and again, through countless young lives constricted under the weight of loss. In such a situation, what dignity was there in recounting one's own sad story?

Tsamchoe is still speaking of the new arrivals. 'When we ask them about their parents' particulars, they just cry. Maybe they feel lonely. Sometimes there may be language problems because different dialects are spoken in the three provinces of Tibet—Amdo, Kham and U-Tsang. It is difficult to understand what some of the newcomers are saying. In the homes at TCV, there are thirty-five to forty students each and one home-mother. Slowly, the new ones mix with the others and learn the language. Then, they don't feel so lonely.'

Tsamchoe grows quiet. 'Was it easy for you to adjust?' I ask. 'Actually many of the children I grew up with were destitute or orphaned,' she says. 'So at that time, I didn't feel so bad because I at least had a family. Now I am working and can take care of my own needs. When I went to college, TCV gave me a scholarship but there were so many extra expenses, and there were no relatives or parents to support me. It was difficult to manage but I was able to do it. TCV helped me a lot, and that is why I am working here with full devotion and hope.'

Tsamchoe looks at the red-roofed buildings of TCV. The Mother that guided and protected her through the darkness of her childhood and into the shiny future her parents had imagined for their little girls. Tsamchoe is living her parents' dream. Perhaps she too is convinced the separation was a good thing—that the lonely little girl who grew up with an education and in freedom did far better than the boy on the farm who must remain uneducated because the government that rules his land speaks socialism but practises capitalist feudalism. Why must these children make such gut-wrenchingly hard choices? Why must the cost of education be family or vice versa?

Amid the boisterous racket of children let out to play, I am ushered into the director's office. It overlooks the playground where I sat with Tsamchoe a short while ago, and is now swarming with students who seem to be rushing about randomly without any apparent order lent by a sport or game. There were several questions that came bubbling up in my mind after the chat with Tsamchoe and, though normally wary of high officialdom, I ask Tsamchoe-la if it would be possible to speak with the director. True to the image of great efficiency she has acquired in my mind, not unlike a boon-granting goddess, Tsamchoe-la does not disappoint. In the shortest wait I have ever experienced between requesting an interview and being granted it, I am sitting face-to-face with Phuntsok Namgyal.

He is now in his thirtieth year with TCV, and has been director of Upper TCV for a year. The first thing I want to know is the reason for the flood of children from Tibet to Dharamsala. 'What are you giving these kids that they can't get in Tibet?'

'The situation in Tibet is pathetic,' says Phuntsok Namgyal. 'Though there are government-run schools, many parents can't afford to send their children to them. They are very expensive—they charge for every little thing, from stationery to food. The only "free" part is the tuition. Another reason is that the education system in the Chinese-run schools has an agenda to make Tibetan children similar to the Han Chinese. They deliberately ignore and belittle Tibetan culture, religion and language. Third, the exposure of children to a wider world, and expansion of knowledge, is limited in Tibet, where the Chinese government purposely bans external influences and restricts education to Chinese culture, language and so on.

'The facilities we provide at TCV are very good and the education is strongly based in Tibetan culture and language. Our emphasis is on helping these children grow up as true Tibetans, not only in body but in spirit as well. We take care of their spiritual and emotional development and not just teaching.'

The mention of 'spiritual development' catches my attention. I have noticed a gentleness in the students at TCV, the motto of which is 'Others before self'. This thought is the essence of Mahayana Buddhism, that one dedicates one's efforts on the spiritual path for the eradication of everyone else's suffering. I am curious to know if this is an actual strategy or more an expression of a deeply ingrained idea in Tibetan culture.

'First of all, we are fortunate to have our school here so close to the residence of His Holiness the Dalai Lama. There are periodic teachings and festivals that are organized at the main temple in Dharamsala and our children are an important part of these. There is a natural exposure to dharma-related activities. Also, we teach the basic tenets of Buddhism through activities and discussions. Occasionally dharma teachers come and give talks.'

I think of Thondup and her concern for little Tenzin, and ask about professional opportunities available to the children once they pass out of school. 'We encourage them to study up to the level that they can and then we want them to go back to Tibet and merge in the community and work within the society there. So if a child comes from Tibet, we readily admit him. For Tibetan children in India to get into TCV is very difficult. Wherever there is a Tibetan settlement in India, there is a Tibetan school for them, which is not TCV. Many of these schools are funded by the central Tibetan government, some are run with aid.'

He concedes that unemployment is growing within the Tibetan diaspora. 'We cannot absorb all the students who complete their studies and training. We try our best to accommodate them. Those whom we cannot, we encourage them to be entrepreneurial and work on their own, and also work in Indian community and industry.' But I have come across so many young people like Tsamchoe who are unable to break out of the protective womb of TCV and the community. So much so that at one point I used to wonder if this is because Tibetans are actually barred from working in mainstream jobs in India because of their refugee status. I now know that this is not the case.

My questions about jobs and survival have triggered a thought in the director's mind that he is eager to share. 'The aim of the education we provide is not only to earn bread and butter but to be self-reliant. If you don't get a job, that's not the end of the world. You have to be innovative and explore new opportunities. You have to be able to fend for yourself. We try and inculcate a mindset in our children to take responsibility for themselves and their actions from a very young age.'

The bright afternoon has diminished into a cool and cloudy evening. Thinking of TCV, I realize she is mentor as well as mother. She is a nurturer and moulder of character. Like the devis, TCV is many-armed in the multiplicity of her functions for her children's welfare. As if on cue, Tsamchoe-la materializes by my side and reveals to me the actual arms of the Devi—the many mothers of TCV.

TCV's home-mothers, or 'Ama-la' as they are known, are legendary. In the early years, many of the women who came to work as home-mothers had lost their children, some their entire families, and in the destitute children they found a way of dealing with their loss and channelling their love to those who most needed it. Says Ama Lhakpa, a veteran home-mother,

'It was the autumn of 1962 when I saw many orphaned and destitute children at the nursery. I just couldn't stop myself from becoming their mother! Later, when more children came, I was assigned home number 11 and since then, I have become Ama-la to hundreds of children.'

As Tsamchoe-la and I walk into the sturdily built 'home' buildings, I meet many home-mothers. Some are cooking, with children helping them. Others are directing the kids to clean up their rooms. 'These women and many who have now retired spend every day of their lives cooking, cleaning, washing, even in the cold winter months when it snows,' says Tsamchoe-la. And when they get off-days once a week, the Ama-las like to go into town and hang out with friends too. One day, I meet two home-mothers on their way into McLeodganj in the late morning, after having cooked a meal of rajma-chawal for their children and leaving older ones in charge of younger ones. They titter not unlike excited schoolgirls as they share their plans for the day—shopping in the bazaar, going to the temple, catching up with old friends.

Each home at TCV has two large dormitories with bunk beds, one for boys and one for girls, a large living room, bathrooms and kitchen. The rooms are tidy and I do not see clutter in any of the ones I visit. In the inner courtyards, older children are helping younger ones with the washing. Some homes have a trough outside, where the leftover food is kept for stray animals. One home bears the unlikely nameplate of Tintin Home. Tsamchoe-la explains, 'This home was made from the money donated by the wife of Herge, creator of the comic book hero Tintin, from the sale of his *Tintin in Tibet*. She wanted the home to be called Tintin Home. Isn't it beautiful?'

Of course it is. TCV belongs to beauty. In its arms, it lovingly holds the future of the Tibetan community. It epitomizes what kindness and careful nurture can achieve in the gravest circumstances, and offers a safeguard against cultural assimilation of young Tibetans with both the Han Chinese in Tibet and the Indians in India. That the dharma is part of the education ensures that the children of exile do not lose touch with their unique, deeply spiritualized culture.

In the forty-five years of its existence, generations of Tibetans have passed through TCV's portals and have gone on to hold positions at institutions of the community and the government-in-exile. Future generations may not be so lucky, though. They may not find any ready answers for problems of unemployment, deracination and unfulfilling career choices. Children sent from Tibet may find that the dream of their parents no longer lives in Dharamsala. For the problems are there and growing fast, and the Mother must once again innovate, as Phuntsok Namgyal suggested, and find new avenues for her children's growth.

As the lukewarm sun sputters and fades away behind the Dhauladhars, I pause for a few moments beside the playground. The huge crowd of children, maybe all 1900 of them, is fast thinning. In the gathering dark, they are giving the evening's play their all before heading homewards, to their Ama-la and study-time. The children are grimy, and their uniforms are frayed and stained with the activities of the day. They do not have much to play with, and yet seem to be having a lot of fun improvising games, throwing balls made of tightly rolled rubber bands and chasing one another around the field. A visitor's car becomes a plaything too, and messages that contain lots of hearts are scrawled on its dusty windshield.

It is indeed remarkable that in a playground full of more than a thousand kids, everybody is getting along with everybody else. There is a lack of aggression even among teenagers. Perhaps TCV *has* succeeded in instilling in them some of the spiritual values of their ancestors. Life may knock them into a different shape later, but for now they are good. Joined with their community in camaraderie, and armed with the ability to find happiness in rubber bands and dust.

Behind me, two adolescent girls have been chattering for some time. I turn around and they smile at me. They are fourteen years old and in the eighth standard. They have been writing letters to the kind lady in New Zealand who sponsors their education. What do they want to do when they grow up? Bright-eyed Rinchen Palzom says, 'I want to become a doctor. If Tibet gets freedom, I want to go there, especially the remote areas and help the poor people there. Otherwise, I would like to serve TCV.'

I am touched by her sincerity. In her, and in a sense in TCV, there is an actualization of what His Holiness says about the value of kindness: 'Right from the moment of our birth, we are under the care and kindness of our parents. Then, later on in life, when we are oppressed by sickness and become old, we are again dependent on the kindness of others. Since it is the case that at the beginning and end of our lives we are so dependent on others' kindness, how can it be that in the middle we neglect kindness towards others?'

Rinchen is eager to talk, while her companion saunters away. I ask her whether she would like to be a doctor of Tibetan medicine. 'No, of western medicine. I know it means a lot of hard study and struggle, but I am prepared to do it.' Dr Tamdin and the Men Tsee Khang rise before my mind's eye, and I wonder about this westward-ho mentality one sees increasingly among Tibetan youth. Modernity is equated with the west and, slowly but surely, success with money. In Dharamsala nothing could make for greater irony. For the evidence of dissatisfaction bred by materialism is right here before us, walking the streets in old jeans, seeking lamas, looking for the meaning of life in the words of the Dalai Lama and in the life of the Buddha. Surely young Tibetans cannot throw away their precious inheritance for the mirage of money, which so many young people from the west leave behind in frustration to come here?

Night is upon me by the time I reach home, or the guesthouse that is home. In the transit point that is Dharamsala, where there are no permanent homes but only provisional shelters, this one is mine. Just as TCV is the children's. And the Ama-las are shelters from the heart-sickening void left by absent mothers. And the dharma is from the storm winds of destructive emotions.

From the inner recesses of the guesthouse, I hear Thondup softly singing little Tenzin to sleep. I pull my shawl over my head and step out into the dark once more, this time to call my mother.

15

Young and Restless

The room across mine at the guesthouse is let out to a young American woman. One evening, as I step out on to the terrace to savour the blush cast by the fading sun on the Dhauladhars, I see her sitting by herself in a corner, her head buried in a fat book. Now, I can hardly bear to have a book around me without knowing which one it is, so inching closer in a way I think is barely noticeable, I peer at the book in her hand. It is one of the usual suspects that foreign travellers seem to zero in on to get a 'feel' of India—Vikram Seth's meandering saga of family, politics, love and marriage in India, *A Suitable Boy.* My curiosity sated, I am about to withdraw when the girl looks up and regards me with a wary eye. She is very young, probably around twenty. I say, 'Hello,' and introduce myself.

She is a student on a break from her university for a year, time she plans to spend in Dharamsala studying Tibetan language at the library. Why does she want to study what in her cultural context must be an obscure language? Her answer is moving in its intensity. 'Tibetan language is gravely endangered, and one way a language can survive is by finding new speakers. By learning Tibetan now and perhaps researching its rich literature, I can find ways of ensuring its preservation and continuance. I also wish to join the worldwide movement for Tibet's freedom and work to end the injustice of its occupation. As for being "obscure", Tibetan is as obscure for me as English may be for many Tibetans. It is a matter of perspective.'

Indeed it is. But why come to Dharamsala? Surely she could have found an opportunity to learn the language as well as participate in international pro-Tibet campaigns in the United States? 'Well, I didn't even consider that. Mainly because I so wanted to travel to Dharamsala and live among Tibetans, know first-hand what their issues are, and also look for volunteering activities. After all Dharamsala is the epicentre of the Tibetan world!'

Over the next few days, I find her often on the terrace, her novel having been exchanged for a notebook in which have appeared squiggles that I assume are preliminary Tibetan. And then, the American girl finds her 'suitable boy'. He is a long-haired Tibetan youth, also twentyish, with an unusual sense of fashion. I soon learn to recognize his shadow on my window curtains, his top hat peaking his lean frame and his ultra-loose jeans poised to drop off any moment. He works for an Indian garments wholesaler and, from his heated outpourings on the terrace, one realizes he finds the experience frustrating. Sometimes the wind blows in snatches of their conversation to my room. The boy is saying, 'Then, I told him, you pay me a salary but that doesn't mean I am your slave.' I imagine the girl says something comforting, and he replies in a quieter voice, 'It is hard to manage here in Dharamsala. There are few jobs, they don't pay well. Rent is high. Delhi is as bad . . . You slog and slog for what? A couple of thousand rupees? . . . Must go away . . .'

One night, I hear the young man serenading his lady love on the terrace with a full-throated rendition of a popular Bollywood film song: '*Tujhe dekha to yeh jaana sanam, pyaar hota hai deewana sanam, ab yahan se kahan jaayen hum, teri baahon mein mar jaayen hummm . . .'* The girl is giggling and wants to know what it means. The boy translates, in melody though not in rhyme: 'When I saw you my love, I understood what love is. Now where should I go, I want to die in your arms . . .'

Now I am well and truly hooked on to this Dharamsala love story. Apparently the song was in preparation for . . . a marriage proposal! I can hardly believe my ears when the Tibetan Romeo says to his American Juliet, 'Will you marry me?' I think Juliet cannot either, for she is silent for a long time. When she speaks, her voice is soft. 'Too soon . . . big decision . . . not sure . . . you must understand . . .' and so on.

I do not know how this story ends—whether the couple headed towards a new future in the United States, or whether the girl returned alone. After the proposal, I did not see the Romeo for many days. Then he began visiting again and their love story seemed to have received a fresh lease of life. I had decided by then that I should not be invading their privacy, and would resolutely occupy myself elsewhere whenever they were within earshot. By the time I left, the girl had begun uttering her first halting sentences in Tibetan, while her boyfriend patiently ironed out her inaccuracies of accent.

If I am to believe what can be called 'bazaar gossip', this is not the first such love story to have played out under the Dharamsala sky. Young Tibetans, as young Indians I suppose, are becoming enamoured of the west and, through the tourists and seekers who pour into Dharamsala, have an opportunity to become acquainted with western culture and people. At times this intermingling sparks romance, for as the nineteenth-century Urdu poet Mirza Ghalib says, 'This [love] is a fire that ignites spontaneously; once kindled, it cannot be quelled.' Sometimes, these couplings end with the westerner's stay and sometimes result in a move away for the Tibetan. Does this trend, for there have been enough such relationships for it to be called so, reflect a rift in the psyche of young Tibetans? Not that I am cynical about love and the possibility of finding it anywhere. Rather, my interest is in exploring the psycho-social underpinnings of these relationships without casting aspersions on their genuineness of feeling and motive.

To be Tibetan and young in Dharamsala means for most to have a world circumscribed by a lack of opportunities. As they grow up, the young Tibetans of Dharamsala may find themselves at a crossroads with three broad options. One is to stay where they are, in the community in Dharamsala, and find work in its various projects to safeguard Tibetan culture or in the government-in-exile. The other road heads towards bigger Indian cities and mainstream occupations like accounting, business management, fashion designing or journalism. The third is to leave Dharamsala and India for good, and emigrate to a prosperous society in the west, where at least one's material requirements are fulfilled.

The first option represents what one imagines would qualify as the honourable thing to do—help build the community and its institutions. It is more or less a career of seva, of dedication, where the work is its own reward. It is a choice many young Tibetans make, and I have met some bright young people who are giving of themselves wholeheartedly. Their work is their *calling*, and not just a way to earn a salary. Like the maths teacher at TCV who is trying to formulate linguistic terms that will help teach modern maths in the Tibetan language, or the young man at Men Tsee Khang who wants the old medicine system to begin researching new diseases, or the adolescent schoolgirl who wants to do nothing as keenly as help settle new refugees from Tibet.

The energy of youth is of newness and vigour, of revolution and rebellion. If not channelled consciously and constructively, it is an energy whose swelling tide wants to break the banks of tradition. I am yet to witness any overt disrespect towards their traditions among Tibetan youngsters; rather I have seen many more passionate displays of patriotism. Whenever there are protest marches or candlelight vigils, the young form the groundswell that carries the demonstrations through. But then, tradition and patriotism are two different things. Their obvious emotion for their homeland notwithstanding, there is an increasing tendency to withdraw from old ways of thinking and doing things. It is an estrangement that is an inevitable side-effect of a sustained break from the sights, sounds and situations of their motherland. For culture is very much a response of a community to its milieu, habitat, neighbours, livelihoods, divinities. In the absence of these stimuli, the culture may not die wholly, for it is indeed so much more, but it must *change* into something different from what it was in its old ground.

As children of exile, most of the younger generation has not seen Tibet. More immediate is the environment they grow up in, which is Tibetan only to an extent. Outside those boundaries of school and home, through friends, television, internet and other media, they are free to explore a whole new world and absorb its influences—something that readily reflects in their choice of clothes, music, films and so on.

Psychologically, the stress of balancing on two boats may cause a fragmentation of the self into this *or* that, an imbalance may occur when one is unsure of where exactly to place one's identity. This experience is common to diasporic communities everywhere, especially among second- and third-generation immigrants. For they are not quite what their parents were, and are not as yet completely assimilated in the land of their birth. For Tibetan youth, this issue is complicated by the fact that they are *not* immigrants but refugees, and assimilation rather than being desirable may actually endanger the community's identity and cohesiveness.

Some years ago, I was researching for a newspaper article on Delhi's Tibetans in Majnu ka Tilla, the colony one may call 'little Dharamsala' the same way one refers to Dharamsala as 'little Lhasa'. I spoke with a young shopkeeper who had recently graduated from Delhi University and asked him how he dealt with being Tibetan. 'There is nothing to it,' he said coolly. 'There is no difference between me and my Indian friends. We share the same tastes, the same ambitions and hopes, and like the same music and films. We have the same education. I may not speak Hindi at home, but neither do many of them. We even eat the same food, Tibetan food being reserved for special occasions. Actually, you may call me Indian or Tibetan, it doesn't matter.'

I remember how shocked I was then, for I expected all Tibetans to be passionately, well, Tibetan. But talking to that young businessman and others like him afforded an insight into those young Tibetans who are neither politically active nor feel particularly bound to their Tibetanness. They carry their exile lightly, almost as a given that they do not have to be particularly concerned about, and do not expect to be repatriated to Tibet any time soon. They prefer to swim with the tide and focus on immediate concerns, following the basic human instinct towards a better life. When this instinct points westwards, as it often does, young Tibetans seek sponsorship from western supporters of the Tibetan cause or from relatives already settled abroad. A few find themselves in love relationships that act like the wind beneath their wings, landing them in foreign lands.

And so it has come to pass that the Tibetan diaspora has spread to all corners of the world. Wherever they might be, Dharamsala continues to be the central bead in their malas, a crucial symbol of their sense of self, identity and their place in the world.

Exploring the ideas and ideals of Dharamsala's young, I get into imagining diverse futures for little Tenzin. He is monolingual at the moment, but is particularly skilled in getting his point across in non-verbal ways. He assumes warmth from all alike and has no doubts about his own place under the sun. He is unafraid of strangers, quickly forges friendships and does not hesitate to cheerfully invade people's rooms and lives until he is dragged off by his apologetic mother. Given the signs, I think he will make for an excellent politician or diplomat and win people around the world over to the Tibetan cause. Then I shrug the thought away and remind myself the future will be what it will be. I do hope little Tenzin will have the opportunity to make his own choice and that it will be one that is the most attuned to what he intuits his own potential to be.

To be able to do this, little Tenzin will need a measure of self-knowledge and clarity, especially if he were to make a choice out of the ordinary, which goes against the grain of what he is *expected* to be and do. What will help is an ability to find a balance between diverse pulls and pressures, between self and one's society, between priorities one sets for oneself and the vagaries of one's chosen profession. I know of young people in Dharamsala engaged in similar journeys, who have made unusual choices and are trying to explore the middle ground between their ancient culture and their modern selves.

One artist, Tenzin Jamyang, comes to mind. He is a sensitive young man who taught himself to paint because he was not accepted into the Delhi College of Art. On workdays he is a member of the Dalai Lama's security force, which is how he earns his living. At all other times, including his annual month-long leave, he paints the mountains, monasteries, rivers and landscapes of Dharamsala and other parts of Himachal Pradesh. Rather than paint deities in the highly formalized convention of Tibetan art, he opts to use art as a means of expressing his deeply meditative connection with nature. Moody mountains are his Buddhas, immovable and still and vast as the mind of the enlightened ones, and trees and rivers are his ever-dynamic, helpful bodhisattvas.

When asked about his community's response to his work, the artist Tenzin turns thoughtful. The first exhibition of his work was organized in Delhi because Dharamsala has no gallery, but more importantly because there is little interest in his art in the Tibetan community. I can see this lack of interest is hard on him, though he jokes about his mother's objection to having his paintings on her walls. 'She won't put up my art in our home!' he laughs. For most Tibetans, he says, the only artwork worth adorning their walls are thangkas. Are there any other young Tibetans who are breaking that mould? Or is he a lone wolf?

No, he says, there are a couple of other Tibetan contemporary artists in Dharamsala but its limited artistic environment makes them claustrophobic. There are no avenues to show art, and no way can a Tibetan artist make a decent living. Tenzin cites two artists, a young man and a woman who trained in the modern arts in the Chinese-run education system in Tibet. They left Lhasa and rode into Dharamsala astride the wind-horses of hope. For a while, they made art high on the ecstasy of freedom, the man especially, who found a new flowering in his creativity.

Then the limitations of Dharamsala began to close in on them. They found themselves in a community preoccupied with survival and its old traditions, and an environment indifferent to their aesthetic endeavours. They fondly remembered the cafes in Lhasa that would proudly display their art and even throw parties when a work was sold. 'Why not duplicate the same experiment in the cafes of Dharamsala?' I ask. 'People come here from all over the world and it's a good way for the artists to get exposure. They might even find buyers.'

'They tried,' says Tenzin shortly. 'It didn't work.' The young woman was so distressed that she could not paint and cut off a finger in frustration. I close my eyes and try to imagine what it must be like for her. The running out of all hope like grains of sand from a clenched fist. How will I feel if no one wants to read what I write, if no one is interested in my ideas, if no one finds any meaning in my words? Will I stop writing; will I cut off the finger that taps on the keyboard?

What happened to those two artists? 'She went back to Lhasa,' he says simply. 'The man is still around and is teaching art. But he too threatens to return to Lhasa. He says Dharamsala is destroying him.' Perhaps they found that they were better adjusted with the politics of oppression than the freedom that left them stranded in artistic wilderness. Who says it was ever easy to compose a creative life? What about you, I ask Tenzin. He smiles. He is fortunate to be in the service of the Dalai Lama, he says. And he will always keep painting, and exploring more, and hoping his art will find its own viewers if not in Dharamsala then in Delhi, and maybe some day in Paris too?

As its long-time resident, I think Tenzin the artist has a better idea of the inadequacies of Dharamsala and is able to keep a healthier attitude towards the place. He sees it for what it can at best be for motivated young Tibetans like himself— a childhood cradle that they must outgrow, a facilitator of new futures, the catalyst for their journeys into the world.

Dharamsala for him is not the end point; it is the beginning. It is where he stands upon the spur and spreads his wings and leaps into the great unknown.

I have not seen little Tenzin for a couple of days, not even in the corridor where he often rushes about imagining himself to be a valiant hero astride a spirited horse. His guitar has not strummed in the evening and the terrace remains empty, the romantic couple too having abandoned it. I am done scribbling in my notebook for the day and have wondered about him enough times to decide to check up on him. I find his father, Pema, walking in through the main door. 'He has a slight fever,' he says. 'Can I see him?' I ask, unsure whether I should intrude upon the family's private space, but am reassured by the warmth with which Pema invites me in.

Little Tenzin is lying on a couch, covered with a blanket. The sparkle in his eyes is momentarily dulled and he shifts restlessly when I ask him how he is. His mother tells me that his fever has come down a bit. The Tibetan doctor at the Delek Hospital at the end of the bazaar says it is flu, nothing to worry about. Little Tenzin regards me with a feverish eye while I chat with Thondup. Somehow I find it difficult to come to terms with the sight of him quelled by fever. I know it is a temporary physiological condition and that within no time little Tenzin will be as frisky as he is wont to be. But it is his listlessness that I find hard to watch, his spirits laid low by the heavy hand of sickness. I tousle his hair and tickle under his fever-warmed chin, actions that otherwise elicit a mass of giggles, but not today. I come away a short while later.

The stories recounted by the artist Tenzin, and in an odd way little Tenzin's fever, turn my thoughts towards those among

Dharamsala's young that succumb to a fever of another kind— of anger, dissatisfaction and hatred, who trade the gentleness of the middle ground for the unforgiving crags of extremism. This fever of the mind, they say, is brought on by what they perceive as the shifting policies of their leadership. They have been brought up with the knowledge of their country's cruel oppression under China, and wish to throw themselves into the heat of battle for a chance at freedom. Except, there is no battle. And in recent years, there has been no talk of freedom either. The Dalai Lama, trying to take the middle path in negotiations with China, has scaled down his demand from total freedom to that of autonomy. Something the hot-blooded, young bravehearts find difficult to swallow, as they do the injunction to a completely peaceful political struggle.

And so the rebels, powered by a seething rage, seek new avenues for action, to do something, anything, that will keep the issue alive. In this sense, theirs is a valuable energy, for it not only reminds the world of the grave injustice of the occupation of Tibet but it also fulfils the role reserved for dissent in a democracy. If the Tibetan leadership is indeed committed to democracy, as it seems to be, it will not stifle this opposition and questioning of its policies.

This indeed tastes like a fruit of exile, where some young, and not so young, Tibetans have found a voice to criticize and disagree. Like other traditional Asian societies, the Tibetan society also functions on a social hierarchy that accords the greatest respect to age and wisdom. I know from personal experience how difficult it can be to surmount this barrier when one wishes to object to unfairness or put forth a different point of view. Thus I recognize the place of courage from where the rebels operate, and how it must not be an easy choice for them to make, especially since it pits them against the policies of the universally revered Dalai Lama.

I know of one such braveheart who seems to have all the courage of the world compacted in his slight frame—the resident activist, writer and poet of Dharamsala, Tenzin Tsundue. Tenzin was born to refugee parents while they laboured on the construction of roads in Himachal Pradesh. He was educated in Dharamsala and, after graduating in English literature from Chennai, made an unauthorized foray into Tibet. So great was his hunger to see the homeland that existed only in his imagination till then, pieced together from others' memories, that he decided upon great personal risk to sneak through the border from Ladakh.

Clandestinely he explored Tibet until he was discovered by the police and imprisoned for three months in Lhasa. In jail he saw a different aspect of the suppressed reality of Tibet which impressed upon him that nothing but complete independence would end the tyranny of the Chinese establishment. 'My visit to Tibet was an eye-opener,' says Tenzin in an interview dated 26 March 2002 in the *Times of Tibet*. 'My hope lies with the Tibetans in Tibet, many of whom are languishing in jail. Their belief in their future is very strong. Their convictions are unyielding. Many of them have never seen or met the Dalai Lama but they are completely loyal to him and, above all, to the cause of a free and independent Tibet. They will never give up. *Rangzen* (freedom) is their birthright.'

Since his return, Tenzin has relentlessly worked for the cause, written articles in the Indian media and in Tibetan publications, and has tried to ignite the spark of rebellion in the minds of young Tibetans.

Tenzin Tsundue reminds me of the great revolutionaries of the Indian independence movement in the first half of the last century. Passionate young men who subsumed their lives in their struggle to overthrow British colonial rule, who went to their untimely deaths singing patriotic songs. It is the kind of bravura and sentimentality that raises goosebumps on my flesh, but one that I cannot completely connect with. Would I be able to exhibit even a fraction of the commitment that Tenzin or those revolutionaries of old had?

In January 2002 Tenzin Tsundue scaled the facade of the Oberoi Towers hotel in Mumbai to unfurl a Tibetan national flag and a banner that read 'Free Tibet'. China's premier at the time, Zhu Rongji, was inside the hotel addressing a conference of Indian businesspersons. His act of courage won Tenzin accolades from the press the world over and gave him a chance to speak about Tibet's cause.

Tenzin's words glow with the slow burn of a long-smouldering fire. He is not alone though, and represents a section of politically active Tibetan youth that are finding it more and more difficult to accede to their government's rollback on the issue of independence. 'The Tibetan Youth Congress, the biggest [Tibetan] NGO with 20,000 members in 77 chapters all over the world, has consistently made its goal of Independence clear to His Holiness,' writes Tenzin in an article titled 'No Compromise on Tibet' (*Tehelka*, 9 April 2005). 'There is, however, pressure from elders to conform to the line of the Dalai Lama and the Tibetan Government-in-Exile.'

This is not only a generational divide, but an ideological one as well. Young Tibetans like Tenzin are impatient with the Dalai Lama's attempts at reconciliation with the enemy, with even his refusal to cast the Chinese as such. As refugees since birth, they are eager for some action, some change, some results. As Tenzin says at the end of the interview with the *Times of Tibet*: 'I respect him [the Dalai Lama] very much and very deeply. But I do not agree with his stand on autonomy. I want complete independence for Tibet. I cannot even dream of living in peace with the enemy. He is compassionate. I am angry. I am restless. I am young. I live and dream only of a free Tibet.'

Long before Tenzin Tsundue joined the ranks of Dharamsala's dissenters, there were other voices of protest, others who were young before him and carried the flame of revolution. One such is Lhasang Tsering, now settled in the comparatively peaceful job of running one of Dharamsala's best bookshops, Bookworm. Like the young activist, Lhasang is a poet and lover of literature. His outspokenness is legendary among Tibetans as well as visitors to Dharamsala and, whenever I pass his bookshop, I see him deep in conversation with all kinds of people, talking about the cause that has consumed his life—a free Tibet.

As a young man, Lhasang traded up the opportunity to study medicine in the United States to join the armed Tibetan resistance then operating out of Nepal. When the resistance was disbanded, Lhasang returned to Dharamsala and, some time later, was elected president of the Tibetan Youth Congress. In this capacity, he publicly opposed the Dalai Lama's policy to seek autonomy for Tibet when it was first announced in 1988. Even after leaving the youth congress, he refused any job with the government and has steadily opposed its policies on the issue of autonomy versus freedom.

Bookworm is on the way to the bazaar from my guesthouse. I stop there one afternoon to buy some books. Lhasang is chatting with a dreadlocked young man, who I deduce to be Scandinavian. I discreetly walk around them and browse the well-stocked shelves. Lhasang is briefing the young man on the situation in Tibet, and why it is important to act soon. 'I am worried that Tibet might have huge deposits of minerals and petroleum since it used to be under the sea at one time. Once the mining starts in that region, its fragile ecosystem will be destroyed forever!' he says. I butt in with the Dalai Lama's 'zone of peace' idea, and how that could preserve the ecology of the area. Lhasang looks at me and I distinctly feel like a small child who knows nothing. 'What will preserve Tibet is freedom. Give Tibet back to Tibetans, and we will take care of it,' he says.

There is something about Lhasang's pure passion that connects with everyone, especially the young, and the dreadlocked Scandinavian who steps out of the shop with me exclaims, 'What sincerity and honesty! Sometimes I think we get too engrossed in our own selves. Meeting somebody like Mr Tsering helps dispel that preoccupation. I came to India to find myself. I have been to Rishikesh and Banaras, and then I came here to Dharamsala thinking I could maybe learn meditation. But after talking to Mr Tsering, I think I will stay on for some time and volunteer to help the Tibetans in some way.' I hope you'll still learn to meditate, I say, and he laughs and nods. He looks towards the sky; his spectacles catch the last ray of the setting sun and glint for a brief moment, one that is as ephemeral as youth itself. Then darkness descends rapidly around us.

In a way, the young Scandinavian and my neighbour at the guesthouse are also among Dharamsala's young. Every year, backpackers out to explore the world and young seekers looking to explore themselves make their way to Dharamsala. The restlessness that propels young Tibetans out of Dharamsala is precisely the energy that brings these young people to it. The Tibetans search for identity, balance, avenues for growth, which is part of the universal search for meaning that begins when the young person asks of herself, 'Why am I here? What should I do with my life? Who am I, really?' While the Tibetans may fly out to find the answers, others follow the gleam of Dharamsala across continents to land on its ground and begin their restless journeys within. The promise of Dharamsala for them is that of a bridge, the modern tirtha, where they will make the connection with their selves and find the mirror that will unveil the secrets of mind and reality, of truth and its true knowing.

I feel a pull at my kurta and find little Tenzin smiling up at me. As predicted, he has recovered rapidly and his cheeks are ruddy with laughter again, his legs are strong enough to run about. Watching him I think how childhood is also the absence of rigidity, of holding our experiences too close. It is an innocence we give up the moment we begin hardening into a particular personality with its peeves and particular ways of doing things.

I often think that we, the young people of today, live in a world of excesses, extreme views and rigid postures. Dharamsala is the perfect place to begin to let go of some of those certainties and inflexibilities. To survive in Dharamsala, one needs to be an acrobat of the mind. There is a manyness of options available for individual growth if only one has the mental suppleness to explore them. Once one has set upon a path, one needs to flow with it gracefully, neither dictating it nor overly manipulating it. Above all, one must have a lightness of touch, so thorns when they appear do not dig deep into our flesh but merely brush against us as we pass by.

Dharamsala is ideal for young seekers because of what one may call a secular openness towards spiritual seeking. Spirituality is not bound to any particular religion here, even though Tibetans seem to dominate the landscape. Tibetan teachers help maintain this openness with their penchant for pointing towards the truth, and prescribing a practice that can be as religious as the practitioner wishes, and as devoid of it too.

The spiritual streams of which Dharamsala is a confluence bend with the temperament of the seeker, and this affords a good opportunity to young people to form an acquaintance with a practice before entering its waters. For instance, at the library, one can get a feel of Buddhist philosophy without really committing oneself to a teacher or practice. Anyone who seeks direction is welcome and assured of equal access to teachings and practices.

Starting point for some, destination for others, refuge for all. Is that what Dharamsala really is, balancing many identities of its own, like earthen water pots atop a desert woman's head? How integrated is its world, how holistic and what fraction unwholesome? It shows us ways to find our reality, but what of its own truth, its own real, bred-in-the-bone nature? It is a caravanserai on countless journeys, but is that all it is?

There can be no dénouement to my journey, until I make a measure of peace with these questions that have followed me like hungry ghosts throughout. They have been answered in various ways, in this side-alley and that, in this loop of the journey and that. Each mini-journey within Dharamsala has tried to respond in a way to these questions, each beam of sunlight and starlight has been pulled together to cast some illumination on them. Will I be able to satisfy the numen of the place that has sat upon my shoulder throughout, before my time in Dharamsala runs out?

16

Dharamkot

There is another mini-journey I must make before I leave Dharamsala, to Dharamkot, a sister hamlet two kilometres up from the McLeodganj bus stand. I have skirted it in my forays and walks to explore what I am increasingly coming to think of as the jalebi-like shape of Dharamsala. Like that spiral of a sweet, Dharamsala too has a nucleus—McLeodganj, the knob in the jalebi's middle where the flour paste first makes contact with the sizzling oil, the point of beginning. Thereon, a spiral grows as the drip of flour steadily snakes outwards, the whorls twirling in oil, turning golden brown in its embrace. Dharamsala's twists and turns dance into one another as the jalebi's; its expansion into its surrounding villages and hamlets providing the interstices necessary to separate the whorls, to keep the spiral from collapsing into the centre. McLeodganj is spared an even worse overcrowding than it currently experiences because neighbours like Dharamkot share its burden of ever-increasing travellers.

Dharamkot initially appeared on my map as the marker of the bend in the road from where one arm leads into the Vipassana meditation centre and the other towards the Tushita Mahayana centre. I have been to both, but overlooked the village entirely because on casual observation it looks exactly like the kind of village I have seen over and over across the

Himalayas. A scattering of wood-and-mud homes across the mountainside, slate roofs glinting in the sun, narrow paths, patches of cultivated land. It had its obvious rural charm but I didn't feel the need to explore much. Until I heard the buzz around Dharamkot, that is.

It started one day as a friend, a student of Tibetan Buddhism, was telling me about the delight of a retreat spent in silence and meditation. He was saying something like, 'You can become so still, watching yourself, that you can locate the exact point when a thought arises,' when I was reminded of the Vipassana centre in Dharamkot, its huts surrounded by a quiet, deep forest, and said how much easier it must be for the meditators there to experience that kind of quiet. Creases appeared on his forehead.

'Silence?' he snorted. 'And what about the all-night rave parties in Dharamkot?'

Parties? In Dharamkot?

'Not any old parties, r-a-v-e parties. Meaning that basically, you get seriously stoned.'

Apparently, Dharamkot is a favourite haunt of the young backpacking crowd because the cost of living is cheaper than in McLeodganj. It is also quieter, does not have too many concrete buildings and you do not feel the press of people as keenly as in McLeodganj. The rumoured psychedelic underground possibly heightens its attraction in the eyes of some. Though Dharamkot may not be as advanced or famous (yet) as Rishikesh and other such places on the great Indian psychotropic trail, it definitely gets its share of those desperately seeking highs, and not only the mountainous kinds. Nor of the sort you may come upon occasionally on the meditation cushion.

To get a feel of things for myself, I set out one morning for Dharamkot. It has rained the previous night and the road is slick with wet mud. The torrential monsoons earlier in the year have washed away the tar in places, making for an uneven, slippery walking surface. I often turn my face skywards for signs of another downpour. I heard someone say that out of 365 days, it rains in Dharamsala for 265. The thought is not very cheery at the moment, for rain now will mean a river of muddy water swirling down the road. Just then, the sun appears and warms all misgivings out of my head.

As the road winds and wends, I pass young people in groups or alone, some coming from the direction of Dharamkot, others moving towards it. During my stay in Dharamsala, I have met several young people from around the world. Like the girl from Ukraine who wanted to know if she could meet the Dalai Lama. My neighbour at the guesthouse and her earnest attempts to preserve a language. The Scandinavian in the bookshop looking to find himself in the hullabaloo of India. Though they may not have been terribly focused on particular goals, and may even be quite confused, there was a curiosity, a seeking, that had brought them to Dharamsala.

Are the denizens of Dharamkot different? Who *are* these people, really?

'How will I know I have reached Dharamkot?' I had asked a Dharamsala veteran friend before setting out. 'Just look out for the signs in Hebrew. Once they start appearing, Dharamkot is not far.' Indeed, much before the lime-washed walls of the village, I see handwritten posters in Hebrew nailed to trees and stuck on electricity poles. I am familiar with the characters of the script from signs in shops in McLeodganj, and recognize the strong, angular letters of this, one of the oldest human languages of the world. In places along the path, it appears alongside the curved roundedness of the Tibetan script that seems to echo the curve of the land, the rolling of the hills. One is the language of revelation in the desert, the other, of dharma on the plateau. Here, in the munificent embrace of Dharamsala, they link arms as it were, without the pressures of realpolitik, compelled to be nothing other than expressions of being human.

Am I just an incurable romantic, who must resort to beatific thoughts of peace and love at every opportunity? Perhaps. But there is a reason these thoughts arise now. A large proportion of the travellers that come to Dharamkot are from Israel. I even hear on the grapevine that the figure may be as high as 90 per cent, though I have no way of verifying this.

I reach the turn from where I must head down into the village of Dharamkot. A cafe abuts the road, its veranda overhung with giant orange stars that glow at night, a common enough sight in India outside homes and in markets around Christmas time. Here in the cafe, the stars are meant to stir up festivity and make one feel Christmassy regardless of the time of year. 'The good times need never stop,' the artificial stars seem to whisper, their garish gaiety out of place on this calm morning that calls for quiet contemplation or a long walk along one of the forested paths around Dharamkot.

Under the unlit stars, huddles of visitors are sipping tea bleary-eyed, probably trying to shake off hangovers. Reminded of the psychotropic gossip, I am convinced that this cafe is *the* rave party point of this area. Psychedelic art adorns its walls, where green goblin-like creatures from *Lord of the Rings* (or is it Harry Potter?) frolic among foliage straight out of a sci-fi film set. Crates of cheap beer are stacked against the wall, and empty bottles are lined on the floor. Its disjoint with the natural beauty of its surroundings is so great that it almost seems to exist in an alternative zone of perpetual partying. Or has it been blown into this mountain-ringed valley by the kind of ferocious storm that interweaves dimensions, like the one that transplanted little Dorothy from boring old Kansas to exciting, miraculous Oz? Is Dharamkot Oz, then?

I am about to enter the cafe, but something holds me back. Is it the wariness I feel from the people at the tables, or my own wariness of them? Sounds of an argument make me turn to the other side of the road, where the owner of an internet-cafe-cum-phone-booth is trying to get a customer to pay up. I walk into this cafe instead and, on the spur of the moment, sit down at one of the computers to check my long-neglected email.

The scale of operations here is not what you would normally expect in rural Himachal Pradesh. Good quality computers are arranged along the walls. The address window of the internet browser opens to reveal international email websites, many of which end with '.il', the country suffix for Israel. I sign in and plunge into the social world I have left behind—editors, colleagues, acquaintances needing to know when I'll be 'back'. Their voices engulf me like a whirlwind, and I quickly shut the browser window before I am sucked into shooting off responses and explanations. Dharamkot swims back into focus. Who says procrastination is always a bad thing?

The argument seems to have subsided, though the cyber cafe owner looks a bit downcast. I compliment him on his state-of-the-art cyber cafe. 'This is just for a few months every year,' he responds, still under a cloud. 'And this year it has rained so much that fewer people have showed up in Dharamkot.' I ask him about the travellers. 'You must meet all of them. What are they like?'

'They are okay. Just don't want to spend too much,' he

says. His good humour clearly restored, he says he is grateful that they come. 'Otherwise, I would be shepherding sheep up and down the mountain like my father and grandfather,' he laughs. He is a young man probably in his thirties, his fair skin untanned, unlike most Gaddi men who are sunburnt from spending most of their lives outdoors. The original inhabitants of this area, they are traditionally semi-nomadic, which means they own homes and bits of land which they may farm, but get their basic subsistence from herds of sheep and goat that they move from one place to another according to the seasons. 'That was a hard life, especially in winters,' says the cyber cafe owner. 'My life now has its shortcomings and struggles, but at least I don't have to wander from place to place. What satisfaction is there in wandering?'

The erstwhile nomad's words echo in my ears as I find my way through Dharamkot. It is often assumed that those who wander are condemned to restlessness, and that certainty of identity and self are the markers of surety, confidence, success that all of us must strive towards. There is security in solidity, in strong foundations and structures, in finding your groove and being set in your way of life. In following tradition, in keeping within boundaries, within the womb of your society and its ways.

Wandering, on the other hand, is taken to be inconclusive, an indication of confusion and unknowing. Yet, isn't it through our wanderings that we chance upon insights and experiences that teach us in ways our regular lives wouldn't, and isn't our confusion often what provides the impetus to grow in a new direction? In transcending tradition that we come to know the real scope of our potential, in breaking boundaries that we catch a glimpse of our true nature?

It is only when Dorothy is uprooted from the familiar and blown into a strange new land that she encounters the people and circumstances that teach her the life-skills she needs to grow into a mature and compassionate adult. Though she must ultimately return to Kansas, she is not the same as when she left it. Her wanderings in Oz have changed her irrevocably, and she must deal with her old environment according to her new self. Only if she can bring the lessons of Oz into play in Kansas have her wanderings proved useful. Otherwise, she is just another tourist, a pleasure-tripper, and has failed the sacred purpose of wandering through the ages—gathering knowledge of self and the world.

Are there any such wanderers in Dharamkot?

The morning is getting along and I decide to check out Dharamkot's claim to food fame—a pizzeria that dishes out the best pizzas anywhere in the world, including Italy! Now that's something that needs to be seriously investigated. To get there, I must veer off the tarred road into the village lane that is broad enough for one person to pass through at a time. Open drains run alongside and low stone walls mark the boundaries of homes. Each home has a flagstone-paved courtyard, which usually harbours a cow or goat. On rooftops, ears of corn are spread out over old sacks, their golden yellow slowly maturing into a rich orange in the sun.

There are obvious signs of a boom in the local economy. Almost every home advertises rooms for hire. Extensions have been added to rural family dwellings to serve as guesthouses. As I stop to watch sturdy hill women harvesting corn, it is hard to imagine this as anything but a regular village. But only for a few seconds, until the next young person from halfway across the globe emerges from a low-hanging doorway.

With the sun climbing towards its high point in the sky, many people are heading towards the famous pizzeria. I walk through the courtyard of a home, up a few stairs, and then there is a boulder with an arrow pointing on and 'Pizzaria' misspelled in red paint. A few more steps and I've arrived.

The pizzeria is actually a village home converted into a kind of restaurant. There are tables and chairs in the front and back courtyards, and in a room in the middle for when it rains. The family lives on the upper floor. A wood-fired clay oven has been built into the wall to cook the pizzas. This place was apparently set up by an Italian in partnership with the Himachali family, and I assume the oven, cooking methods, recipes and ingredients were transferred by the former to the latter. The Italian has since departed, and the place is now managed by the twenty-something son of the family. It is he who steps up to me with a menu as I stand under a tree that arches into the back courtyard from the wilderness beyond.

'The oven is being heated now, so it will take some time for the pizzas. Why don't you have something to drink in the meantime?' the good-looking young man says, smiling pleasantly. I thank him and ask for a glass of lemon tea. Settling into a chair that wobbles on the uneven flagstones, I look around. A wall of rough stones marks the boundary and is low enough to afford a view of surrounding foliage. On the side, the Dhauladhars appear breathtakingly close. Nascent clouds are beginning to mass around their peaks, though the sun is out at the moment as it usually is in the mornings in Dharamsala, rain being more of an afternoon or evening occurrence.

From my perch near the wall, I can see mountain birds flit in the trees that still glisten with the wetness of last night's rain. Crickets chirp unceasingly, filling the still air with their echoing drone. It is peaceful as only mountains can be. Sitting here, one feels an intimacy with the cycle of life revolving around a still centre, everything exactly where it is supposed to be in the web of nature. I am thinking how different this sense of natural harmony is from the cafe on the road, when I hear voices and find the table across me occupied.

A young man and woman have come in and are laying out a deck of playing cards. They are chattering in a language I assume correctly to be Hebrew, and order ginger tea before turning to the cards. I watch them for some time until they reach a lull in the game. 'Who won?' I call out. The woman turns around and says, 'He did, he is much better than me!' We fall into an easy chatter about this and that. Yes, they are from Israel and, like most other young Israelis who travel to Dharamsala (and elsewhere in India), have recently completed their mandatory military service. 'How old are you?' I ask, my manners clearly forgotten in a rush of curiosity.

The young man is twenty-three, and another friend of his who joins us is twenty-nine. They look years older. Their faces are lined and haggard and their eyes seem to carry the burden of centuries, along with the telltale redness that psychotropic users often have. The young woman is a contrast. She is actually the youngest, just twenty-one, already a two-year army veteran.

She exudes friendliness and goodwill that were palpable even before she spoke the first word. A gentle aura surrounds her in this watery sunlight. Her skin is unlined and smooth like a young child's, and her voice is reminiscent of a low birdcall. So when she says, 'I used to train soldiers in the army,' I could be forgiven for staring at her disbelievingly.

'Here it is so beautiful. You get up in the morning, and look at the sky and the mountains. You walk around the village, down those little paths. Then you come here and eat something good. It is heaven!' She turns to me with eyes luminous with emotion. It is unbearable for her to think how she never found this kind of beauty before, never knew life could be as simple as a bed to sleep in at night, food when hungry, and a few cigarettes in between. Her eyes are the colour of sky on a clear Dharamsala morning, and slowly grow distant as she examines something within herself.

The young man, who has been watching her with unconcealed admiration, takes over when she falls silent. Yes, being in the army was extremely tough. The discipline was exhausting, and being constantly at war exacted its toll on emotional and mental well-being. The tension of it all shows through, in little things like the network of wrinkles that springs on his forehead whenever he talks about home, the way he cannot sit still without a cigarette in his hand. In what he says, though it is guarded and carefully casual, he displays an almost compulsive need to relax, chill out, take it easy, have fun, do nothing.

He has been on his post-army break for a year already, and has travelled across Asia. He has been to almost every part of India. And he is still not ready to return home to face the rest of his life, to face himself really. Here is a wanderer who is yet to have his fill of his wandering ways, I think. 'Dharamkot's a great place to be doing nothing,' he says with a short laugh. 'Actually, the reason why many young Israelis come to India is because it is a great place to unwind, to de-stress.'

The young woman, back from her reverie, agrees with him. 'It is so important for me to be here because it is so calming.' Then, looking at her companion, 'You know, there are nice places in Israel too, but what I find here is a change in pace. That is something more than being out of a conflict zone, though that's important too. All my life, I felt I was constantly running a race, competing with others, trying to be the best at everything I did. There was a need to prove myself, to make a success of my life. I think all of us feel this strain. And here, in

Dharamkot, there is nothing to do. You can actually be as quiet and still as these mountains.' She turns around and looks at clouds flow out from mountain peaks like vaporous rivers. 'This is what I want to take back with me, this peace, how it feels to be simple, to just be . . .'

And you? What will you take back from Oz? I turn to the young man with that question in my eyes. He surprises me with his answer. 'You know, in India for the first time I have begun to think about non-violence. I have started reading Gandhi's writings, and though it seems strange to me I am drawn to it. I think all the time, "What this man says, is it really possible?" Then, I know it is, because it has been done. Yes, it is strange.'

I nod in camaraderie, to let him know that I get how 'strange' it must be for someone who has grown up in what is effectively a war zone and has in all likelihood internalized a divisive view of humanity, to come upon the Mahatma and his unwavering ahimsa. It would be like looking at everything upside down, but also a validation of the stress this young man felt in situations of violence and hatred, and of the human urge for peace and lasting happiness he could not ignore. And which brought him and others to this place where they can 'do nothing', forget their pasts and the hollow feeling in their hearts, and try and begin anew.

But isn't this persistent need for peace also what leads to drugs? My question perhaps surprises the young man with its directness, and he looks away. The girl replies. 'Those of us who come here are of two kinds—those who are seeking fun, and they will do it with alcohol and drugs, and others who are looking for peace and will also explore meditation and yoga. I belong to the second category, though I do love beer and I smoke too much!' She giggles and the mood around us lifts, though the clouds are almost overhead by now and the sun has disappeared under their grey shadow.

The pizza arrives thankfully before the rain does. Digging into slices on which melted cheese sizzles over mushrooms and herbs, I decide this is certainly the best pizza *I've* ever had. Tables quickly fill up. A flavoursome aroma wafts around the courtyard, and all of us busily eat our way through our pizzas. Over dessert, which is a huge slice of cake soaked with melted chocolate and vanilla ice cream, the young woman turns to me once more.

'In Israel, people who have been to India regularly organize India-oriented festivals where they talk about their experiences, and there are discussions around specific subjects like culture, food and so on. That gets others interested and they also want to come here,' she says. This is an example of the golden chain I had imagined forming around places like Dharamsala, where travellers return with stories that inspire a new wave of visitors to make the journey. 'I have a younger sister and brother,' she continues. 'I know they will want to come here when they hear about it from me.'

Soon after, she and the young man leave. I too get up and hurry along the village paths. The fragrance of pizzas mingles with the fumes of dung that hang about the village. Corn has been cleared from rooftops in anticipation of rain, and courtyards hastily divested of washed clothes and rickety chairs. Cows low a trifle mournfully as they are led into their sheds.

The rave cafe is now wide awake and young people cluster purposefully in the covered part of its veranda. Loud music is playing, the kind called 'techno-trance' or something like that, and its thudding beats follow me like the wailing of hungry ghosts right until the end of the road when I turn away, on to the swirl in the jalebi that will take me back to McLeodganj.

It rains steadily through the evening, and I am confined to the guesthouse. Grey clouds have cloaked the entire hillside in a pall of mist. Little Tenzin and his family are out, and the guesthouse is dark and quiet. I think of the young Israelis from the pizzeria and wonder about their future. Like Dorothy, they have been changed by their wanderings. In the young man and the girl and perhaps others as well, seeds of peace have been sown. Who knows when these seeds will fructify? And it is possible that at some point, when enough young people have come to Dharamsala and learnt to be as still as the mountains, peace might finally stand a chance in that long-troubled region of the world?

Maybe then, that desert will once more ring with revelations and words of prophets? Maybe then, God will once more descend on earth and talk to a chosen one through a burning bush?

Maybe…

17

Nirvana

Sunrise in my window
endless horizon
mountain upon mountain
rising from the mist.
Above them
in the sky
the graded blush
spreads
purple, pink, orange, yellow.
And below,
yesterday's world
appears
birthed anew.
From mountainous wombs
emerge
trees, valleys, homes, prayer flags
worlds into worlds
worlds upon worlds
Will they die
again tonight?

As dawn lightens the night sky, Dharamsala gradually crystallizes before my eyes clouded over with sleep. It is that enchanted early morning hour when consciousness oscillates between dimensions and dreams, simultaneously awake and asleep. I flow in this manner, savouring the pleasure of formlessness in fluid space until, quite unexpectedly, I am accosted by the blind creator-seers of old. Homer and Teiresias materialize out of a veil of vapour and beckon me to follow their ethereal trail. They show me how to see without eyes of flesh and blood, cutting out the curse of limited perception, and turn instead to the third eye of wisdom. My mortal sight blurs and, with it, the trees, mountains and homes disappear into a spiralling sandstorm. A vision appears before the mind's eye where the sand has settled to form one huge, brightly coloured cosmic mandala that enfolds past, present and future. It is neither static nor inanimate as a painting, but is alive and bristling with lines and circles and shapes that incessantly form and re-form, snaking in and out of one another, aglow with the vitality of life.

What does this panoramic mandala show?

Through the wisps of early morning mist, I discern a pulsating node that is the point of my meditations—Dharamsala. Like a neuron, it has live filaments branching off on all sides. These are the pathways of journeys old and new, alive with knowledge that was brought in, the insights that were gained here, and that headed back out into the world. Even as I observe it, new lines appear on the mandala, criss-crossing each other, energizing old paths with new footprints. Pathways are drawn, rubbed out and redrawn by successive journeyers until everything is one chaotic jumble. As one is about to give up on the mess, new energies arrive and begin creating afresh from the chaos. And so it goes on—the unceasing activity and at the centre of it all a nucleus that spins inwards, deeper and deeper into . . . nothing.

I am drawn towards that black hole of a nucleus. Pathways

throb towards it, extricating themselves from knots and bonds, looping and surging forth only to be swallowed into the vortex. What is it, I wonder? Death? Or samsara? And how does it connect with the numen of Dharamsala, the genius of this place that now pushes me on towards the centre, goading me to know for myself what it is all really about? With some effort, I direct my dream-self to follow the paths to the nucleus. At the edge, there is nothing to hold on to. It is a place thick with discarded fears, with a premonition of the unknown, the last stop where you must leave *everything* before plunging into the mouth of the volcano. I dig my nails into the ground and peer into the abyss. It is a gash at the base of a mountain, deep and dark and womblike. Watching, I suddenly feel no fear, just quietness that swells until it fills the whole of me. This vortex is magical, wielder of the alchemy that transforms ignorance to knowledge, and questions into resolutions . . .

And then, the mandala begins unravelling. Its sand flies about until it compacts into a spiral and whirls away. I open my eyes. Sunlight streams into them and, for a second, I am blinded again. As sleep evaporates, I realize what day it is.

The sand has finally run out of the hourglass that began ticking the moment I set foot in Dharamsala.

Among the silent deodar and pine
crickets chirp constantly.
Do they know
that winter's almost upon us?

Do *we* know how impermanent our lives are? We are like the fruitfly that lives for a day and thinks that day will go on forever. And so we build elaborate castles of our personalities with our ideas, needs, desires, dislikes, with our true selves buried deep inside, and our shallow ego in charge. Until one day, the entire facade collapses before the inevitable winds of change. Then, a life has been wasted, truth is unrealized and reality has remained untasted.

The characteristic of Dharamsala most likely to strike you the moment you come to it is its position as a refuge. Here refugees of all sorts gather—political and spiritual; Tibetan and Indian and American and European and Asian; human and dog and monkey; rich and destitute; young and old. People who live here rarely call it home. With a name like 'Dharamsala', colloquial for cheap and ready accommodation for peripatetic pilgrims, can it harbour any fantasies of permanence?

Being in this universal refuge, in the midst of waves of refugees sharpens one's own refugee-ness to a point where one can use it to peel away illusions of set identities and identification with a personality that is really a castle in the air. If life is the grand journey, then all of us *are* passengers in transit, wherever we may otherwise be in terms of flourishing careers, successful relationships and the apparent solidity of our world. The shifting sands of reality ensure that nothing remains the same for long, and as intrinsic parts of this dynamic pattern of change, neither do we. We move from one state of mind and being to another, one circumstance to another, one stage of our lives to another and still want to believe in the illusion of a fixed identity. When in fact life is changing rapidly around us and *in* us every moment, and we are like travellers on a speeding train who feel that the countryside is dashing by them when it is actually they who are rushing headlong through it.

On the surface, we may have nothing in common with the Tibetan who braves rough terrain looking for freedom in an alien land. But if we look carefully at ourselves, we will become conscious of a tyranny that may not lay our body to waste but that preys on our minds. It is the oppression of unmet expectations, unfulfilled wants and an ever-diminishing enjoyment in creature comforts. That which was satisfying some time ago no longer does the trick, and we flit from one thing to another searching for the ever-elusive high.

In this manner we are held captive to a certain way of being based on a permanent self-identity for which we seek pleasure and avoid pain. It is when we become aware of this limited self-perception and wish to grow beyond it that we prepare to make the difficult journey from the prison of unknowing, over the peaks and gorges of our own minds towards true inner freedom, that we become refugees on the spiritual path. At such times, we *need* to come upon places that will be sanctuaries to our spirit, which will allow us to simply be, that will provide spiritual sustenance in the form of guidance, gurus, teachings and gentle encouragement.

Dharamsala offers precisely such a refuge to the spiritual seeker. Through its various wisdom traditions and teachers and opportunities to learn directly from them, together with a vibrant community of co-travellers, it functions as a valuable retreat and helps bring us out of the comfortable grooves of habit and personality that we have settled into. In this way, Dharamsala fulfils the role of a cloister. In Tibetan Buddhism, practitioners lay and initiate will proceed on retreats that may vary in time from a month to several years. The objective is to deepen in their practice by focusing the mind single-pointedly upon itself in a space made pristine by filtering out as many extraneous influences as possible. In the absence of external stimuli, the mind has no option but to turn within and confront itself. The retreat can be likened to a scientist's petridish—a safe and ideal, and sanitized, environment in which to conduct experiments on the self.

Every scientist is aware that if experiments and their findings are to acquire wider significance, they must be duplicable outside the laboratory. This is so in spiritual life as well, for ultimately, there is only so much time that can be spent in isolation. Even if one has become initiated into a monastic order, one will have to deal with the world at some level, at some point. The validity of insights garnered in retreat is in fact tested when we emerge from its protective confines. How we bring them to bear upon the inescapable strains that infect our lives is the actual indicator of growth.

Dharamsala is cloister *and* community, a retreat that is at once out of the world *and* bang in the middle of it. It is the former because one can live here in quiet seclusion and study with a teacher or work on honing one's practice. And it is the latter because, well, it *is* a bustling, populous town that is not sealed off from vices and wiles and tensions. In its outward character, Dharamsala is not a mythic paradise populated by perfected individuals. It is as perfect, and imperfect, as we are. In this, it imitates the nature of life. And perhaps this is why it is even more ideal than the petridish to practise in. What you learn in philosophy class or during meditation is immediately put to test as you are almost run over by a speeding motorcycle on your way back. Or as you negotiate a viable rent with greedy landlords, or get no water in your bathroom, or deal with shrinking finances. For the mind that is training itself, every moment here can be the challenge that pushes what you thought were your limits of endurance, concentration, compassion. Every such attempt is a step towards realizing that the potentiality of perfection is our true nature.

In this way, the value of practising in Dharamsala is that it can very well become our training ground for life outside the cloister, even as we are in it.

Living in Dharamsala can cause the shift that transforms

the refugee to a pilgrim. Though both refugees and pilgrims are travellers who have come away from homes and familiar milieus upon a quest for meaning, the difference lies in their states of being. The spiritual refugee is as yet new to the work of inner seeking and may feel lost and tired. She may also feel frustrated with the incongruities and imbalances in herself and her world and relationships, and, in many cases, dispossessed of the faith she grew up with because it has failed to answer her dilemmas. She is looking for an escape out of her present condition and has arrived here in the hope of finding some resolution.

The course of the pilgrim is less frenzied. It is a journey motivated by the urge to connect with a deep truth— through a deity, her self, her teacher—and is an occasion to exchange her mundane existence for one of transcendence, at least for the length of her travels. The pilgrim is on an adventure of the spirit, and is alive to every opportunity to know and learn. Her thoughts are concentrated upon her objective and her being is attuned to the sacredness she feels at every step that brings her closer to her destination—that is both the place and the quietude she seeks for herself.

In Dharamsala, many whom we call refugees because politically they are so actually come bearing the attitude of a pilgrim. Dharamsala is sacred to them because of the presence of the Dalai Lama, monasteries and temples that have been reconstituted here, scriptures that are in safekeeping and the culture and traditions of old Tibet that have been preserved and seeded afresh. When they set out on their hazardous journeys, it is with the knowledge that they are coming not to a wholly alien country but to the land that mothered significant aspects of their civilization. If for a moment they are able to overlook the unfortunate circumstances of their flight, they could well imagine themselves on a pilgrimage to the cradle of the dharma, a land made venerable by the footsteps of the Buddha. Many report fortifying themselves against the severity of their journeys with these thoughts. Thus when they arrive in Dharamsala, they are able to glean the good from a situation that is otherwise quite dismal, and face their new lives with some measure of equanimity.

A more gradual transformation awaits those that come to Dharamsala as restless refugees thirsty for spiritual direction and comfort. Many of us become recurring pilgrims, if only because we cannot pitch our tents here forever. There are lives to get back to and resources to be marshalled and relationships and jobs that require attention. And there is something about Dharamsala that does not encourage a settling down. Its severe limitations, namely absence of viable long-term housing, non-existent livelihood options, water shortages, among others, leave one with an impression that somehow one is adding to an already overburdened township, and so must move on so that others in need may also come in and the wheel of journeyers, and their journeys, keeps rotating.

In some ways, Dharamsala is a pot that makes available a safe space for seeds to sprout and young saplings to take root. As the plants mature, however, they must break through the confines of the pot that were once valuably protective but are now restrictive, and find their own earth to grow. This is how it is with Dharamsala's refugees and pilgrims. Dharamsala welcomes them, gives much-needed succour, provides direction to those that feel lost, triggers the seed of the spiritual in those floundering to find meaning in life, and embraces in silence those who come to intensify their inner practice. Eventually, they must all move on—seeker, pilgrim, refugee— carrying the understanding they found here, secure in the knowledge that they may return whenever they need a safe haven to rest their world-weariness and refresh the learning grown dim in the storms of the world.

In the end, Dharamsala must be transcended. The gentle
bonds of familiarity that grow over a period of time and keep
us attached to its form must be broken. For Dharamsala is
refuge, a harbour to the spirit. It is a starting point, a bridge, a
midway point, depending on where *you* are in your life
journey. It feels immediate, not eternal. A caravanserai rather
than home.

Autumn is flowing into winter as I pack my bags. Soon, all
that is now green and gold and brown will be covered with
snow. In the deodars outside my window, the crickets herald
the beauty of impermanence.

Orange clouds
flame
against silver mountains.
A sunbeam has
pierced
through the clouds'
translucent grey bodies
and from within
glows
like a thousand scattered jewels.
This one light,
the many clouds.

I am at the terrace, waiting for my invoice. I will pay now,
though my bus does not leave till a couple of hours. I think of
all the happy times spent on this wide terrace watching sunsets
and moody morning skies and little Tenzin at play. There is so
much sky here! It is vast and endless and stretches everywhere,
interrupted only by the peaks of the Dhauladhars. One part

of the sky hosts the sun, brightly golden this moment, while another has clouds creeping in from the direction of the mountains.

I see the clouds form, as a thick mist rises from the snow and shrouds the mountaintops. It slowly spreads outwards, and I can almost detect the molecules sticking together to form cloud entities that get bigger and bigger until they cover the whole of the eastern sky. Drops start falling thinly, but nothing obscures the sun. Its warmth has acquired just a hint of cool to show for the rain. There is no thunder or bolts of lightning as I have seen during some dramatic night storms here. Only a quiet, warm rain.

Dharamsala is this sky, an open field of happening that allows everything and everyone to coexist. Like the sky, it takes on the appearance of whatever phenomenon is occurring at the moment. For instance, when the Dalai Lama is giving teachings, the whole town swarms with all kinds of people, monks and nuns, Tibetan as well as western, seekers and casual onlookers. At that time, I imagine Dharamsala becomes as the Indian cities that hosted the great Buddhist councils of old, when the whole sangha would gather in one place and debate the dharma. Then, during the 'Mind and Life' conferences, a part of Dharamsala acquires the character of a modern university, with a vigorous exchange of ideas, new inferences and intellectual vitality, while presentations are made and observers, like students, take copious notes. And at the height of winter, though I have not been here but have heard so, the town empties of all but permanent residents and grows quiet and sleepy as if hibernating under snow.

At the level of the individual, Dharamsala is the mirror that echoes our own state of mind. You get what you are looking for. This is why it moults into different things for different people. For some, it is a dirty little hill town with uncleared waste and the stench of putrefaction in the air. As a renowned scholar of history asked me in Delhi, 'Dharamsala? What will you find there except the Dalai Lama and lots of garbage?' For others, it is a scenic enough tourist spot with some good 'scenery', an interesting bazaar and food places to indulge their holiday mood. For yet others, it is a place of pilgrimage, a bridge to the blessings of bodhisattvas. To those that seek knowledge, it offers teachers and scriptures, conveniently translated; to those who look for silence it provides meditation retreats. And if you are searching for romance and a little excitement, who knows what walks on mountain paths perfumed with pine with a co-traveller may lead to?

I wonder whether one can really have a vision expansive enough to take it all in, or the skill, for Dharamsala will not reveal itself unless one goes looking for it. To the uncurious visitor, it will modulate its accent and turn on the scenery, leaving him enthralled and entertained. One has to be sufficiently curious to scratch the surface, and silent, to hear its heart beat. Like the mountains surrounding it, Dharamsala exists layer upon layer—all is true *and* none is. Where your attention focuses, how aware you can be of the subtext and the undercurrents that thrum beneath the surface, will ultimately determine what Dharamsala will reveal to you.

I will give you an example. Every day at the Tsuglag Khang, I would see a tiny old woman in a muddy brown chuba doing her prostrations. I would always find her at the same spot in the ground floor courtyard. After finishing her prostrations to the Avalokiteshwara idol, she would turn around and face the Dalai Lama's home and do some more. What drew me to her were her quiet dignity and the calm determination with which she carried on with her labours.

One day, the old woman was in the midst of her prostrations

when a group of women appeared. They were Tibetan, but clearly foreign to their surroundings. The old woman saw them and noticing their confusion as to where to go next, interrupted herself to extend her arm out to the group to show the way to the main hall. She was right in front of them, and yet the women didn't notice her gesture. When they came around from their circumambulation of the ground floor, the old woman again observed their hesitation and pointed them on to the first floor. She was aware of them; they were not of her. They may have looked around with active eyes, taking in the idols and the monks and the prayer wheels, but they surely did not *see*.

Dharamsala, and perhaps life too, is like that old woman. It is all right in front of our noses, the greatest truths lie revealed in every moment. It is where we look and what we choose to become conscious of that determines what we learn and experience. Perhaps that is why a characteristic of the enlightened mind is 'choiceless awareness'—an all-encompassing openness where consciousness is not fractured and attention not parcelled out in fragments. It is an awareness of the whole, with complete absence of the judging that cuts and pastes before us the reality that we *want* to see, as opposed to what *is*.

Dharamsala is you. Marcel Proust said, 'Every reader is, when he reads, reading only about himself.' Every traveller is in the end only making travels and pilgrimages that bring her to her own self. In a delicious intertwining, every destination furthers one's knowledge of oneself; *and* everything we are able to garner from it reflects the colour of our mind in that particular moment. Dharamsala reveals to all something about themselves. It can be enabler, protector, healer, mentor, teacher, according to your needs. In this sense, is my Dharamsala different from yours?

Pema is here at last with my invoice. I pay my dues and thank him for all his help. 'I can now walk anywhere—uphill, downhill, no problem,' I say, unable to resist a parting shot. He laughs and says, 'Come again, next time?' I turn to go when all of a sudden, the terrace explodes with children. Little Tenzin has brought his friends home to play. Thondup follows carrying tea and barley flour-filled Tibetan cookies. She offers me some, but I decline, saying I need to start walking towards the bus. 'Then take some for the journey,' she says, and quickly wraps a few in tissue. I thank her for everything. In response, she shoves her way through the gaggle of kids and extricates her little one. I think she tells him to be a good boy and say 'goodbye' to me. Little Tenzin runs up to me. I tousle his hair and tickle his chin. He giggles and yells, 'Bye', and runs off to join his friends.

I watch the children for a few seconds. Their delight and energy is infectious, and I soon feel lighter about leaving than I have the whole day. There is something about the way children are passionately committed to this moment alone. What has happened has happened, what will be, who knows? Smiling, I pick up my stuff and wave to Pema and Thondup. Little Tenzin does not look away from his play. I wave to him in any case.

Through the cracked window
I watch
darkness come
to the deodars beyond.
The warmth melts
away from
their edges

and green turns to gold
and then grey
until nothing remains
except the crack
in the window
through which I look.

I have boarded the bus though it is yet to start. It is late evening, and the cracked window next to me is letting in some of the chill. Most passengers have stashed their luggage and are standing outside. A large group has come to see off a woman who is returning to her country after completing a course of study with her Tibetan teacher. All of them are wearing the ritual silk scarves of greeting and leave-taking, katas, around their necks. They are trying to cheer up the woman who is feeling low. One of them blows an imaginary bugle in her honour, another cracks a ribald joke. Until the woman is laughing at the ridiculousness of it all, and begins hugging her friends to bid them a happier farewell.

I run my fingers over the wooden beads of a rosary, enjoying their rounded smoothness upon my skin. In a moment of inspiration, I think that Dharamsala is a poem that refuses to arrange itself in metre, that runs on in garbage and goddess, through lama and wastrel, from scripture to doggerel. I am still mulling over the problem of point of view, and whether everyone finds a different Dharamsala. They do, but there are threads of commonality that run through everyone's experiences that are perennial in the understandings they touch upon, and act as the golden links that bind humanity together. So while it is true that I view according to my conditioning, I also am capable of experiencing away from these influences. It is the space common to all, the space of interconnection, of authentic, unrestricted knowing. I am certain all of us can taste it just as we are, imperfect and unenlightened. We may not be able to dwell in it forever. But we do certainly become aware of it in snatches, through a moment of unobstructed contact with beauty for instance, or with warmheartedness both our own and others', with nature at all times, with the unselfish and pure place in our selves, and perhaps with the numen of a place of special significance?

As the bus begins its descent, I am reminded of the sand mandala of my dream. Wasn't the nucleus the deepest truest part of me, of all of us? In my time in Dharamsala, as the dream indicated, I did *look* over the edge. But I haven't *flown* into it like all those seekers whose paths disappeared into that vortex of transformation and transcendence, where everything drops to reveal reality and one is scrubbed down to one's true nature. And now, the sand in the hourglass has run out on me. Perhaps there will be another time?

A cold wind whips around the bus. I trace the crack in the window and feel an intense, numbing cold on my finger. Winter is finally here.